P9-CMT-520

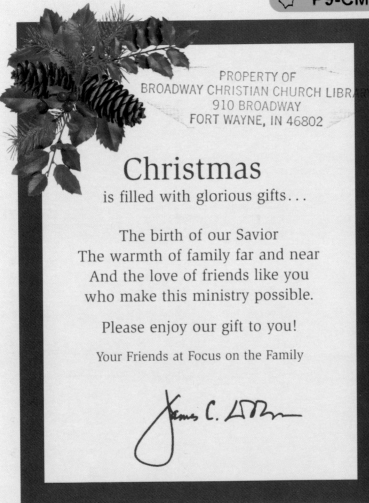

Christmas

is filled with glorious gifts...

The birth of our Savior
The warmth of family far and near
And the love of friends like you
who make this ministry possible.

Please enjoy our gift to you!

Your Friends at Focus on the Family

James C. Dobson

Stories
of the Heart
and Home

Dr. James Dobson

Stories
of the Heart
and Home

WORD PUBLISHING

NASHVILLE

A Thomas Nelson Company

Library of Congress Cataloging-in-Publication Data

Dobson, James C., 1936–
    Stories of the heart and home / James Dobson.
        p. cm.
    ISBN 0-8499-1659-3
    1. Christian life. I. Title.
    BV4501.2 .D594 2000
    242—dc21

                                                                00-043701
                                                                CIP

Printed in the United States of America

01 02 03 04 05 BVG 9 8 7 6 5 4 3

Contents

Introduction

One of my favorite stories comes from well-known Christian author Max Lucado. It deals with Chippie the Parakeet, who had had a very bad day. It all began when Chippie's owner decided to clean out his cage with a vacuum cleaner. She was halfway finished when the phone rang, so she turned around to answer it. Before she knew it, Chippie was gone. In a panic, she unsnapped the top of the vacuum and ripped open the bag. There was Chippie, covered in dirt and gasping for air. She carried him to the bathroom and rinsed him off under the sink, then realizing that Chippie was cold and wet, she reached for the hair dryer. Chippie never knew what hit him. His owner was asked a few days later how he was recovering. "Well," she said, "Chippie doesn't sing much anymore. He just sits and stares."

I always get a chuckle when I think of poor 'ol Chippie, but his story conveys an important lesson. There are times when we can be overwhelmed with life, whether it be running through an airport to catch a plane, only to arrive just as it pulls out onto the runway, or when guests are coming for dinner, and just as they arrive you see smoke curling out of the kitchen. I learned that the annoyances of life strike when you least expect them, and like Chippie, they always leave us dazed and disoriented.

I share Chippie's bad day with you in order to illustrate how a good (and often humorous) story can teach us a valuable life lesson as well. Over the years I have collected many such illustrations. Some have come just from observing what was going on in the world around me. Others evolved from

Shirley's and my days as parents, with two children and a dog scurrying around the Dobson household. Still others have come from colleagues who have shared their experiences with me over the years. There is one common denominator between all of these stories: each one has provided me with new insight into this fascinating thing that we call human nature.

My friends at Word Publishing have now compiled many of these experiences and illustrations into one volume entitled *Stories of the Heart and Home*. The stories you will read have been taken from my previous writings, such as *The Strong-Willed Child*, *Parenting Isn't for Cowards*, and *Life on the Edge*. They are presented to you as they were first written so you can you experience them just as my longtime readers have for over thirty years. As you read through these pages, you will experience the childhood of a young Jimmy Dobson, the son of James and Myrtle Dobson, his courtship and lifelong love affair with Shirley Deere, and life in the Dobson household both before and after children. Finally, we will examine together, through stories, our ultimate purpose in life: to give glory and honor to Jesus Christ in all we do.

So, pull up a chair, fix yourself a cup of hot chocolate, coffee, or tea, and relax. Feel free to have a good laugh or shed a tear. It is my hope that these timeless stories will be an encouragement to you, regardless of where you find yourself along life's long, winding road.

James Dobson
Colorado Springs, Colorado

CHAPTER ONE

Growing Up

A child between eighteen and thirty-six months of age is a sheer delight, but he can also be utterly maddening. He is inquisitive, short-tempered, demanding, cuddly, innocent, and dangerous. I find it fascinating to watch him run through his day, seeking opportunities to crush things, flush things, kill things, spill things, fall off things, eat horrible things—and think up ways to rattle his mother. Someone said it best: The Lord made Adam from the dust of the earth, but when the first toddler came along, He added electricity!

We parents know how quickly our children move from toddlerhood to childhood to young adulthood. In between are days of laughter and days of tears, lots of ordinary days where extraordinary things happen. It's all part of growing up.

~ Laughter: The Key to Survival ~

Laughter is the key to survival during the special stresses of the child-rearing years. If you can see the delightful side of your assignment, you can also deal with the difficult. Almost every day I hear from mothers who would agree. They use the ballast of humor to keep their boats in an upright position. They also share wonderful stories with me.

One of my favorites came from the mother of two small children. This is what she wrote:

Dear Dr. Dobson:

A few months ago, I was making several phone calls in the family room where my three-year-old daughter, Adrianne, and my five-month-old son, Nathan, were playing quietly. Nathan loves Adrianne, who has been learning how to mother him gently since the time of his birth.

I suddenly realized that the children were no longer in view. Panic-stricken, I quickly hung up the phone and went looking for the pieces. Down the hall and around the corner, I found the children playing cheerfully in Adrianne's bedroom.

Relieved and upset, I shouted, "Adrianne, you know you are not allowed to carry Nathan! He is too little and you could hurt him if he fell!"

Startled, she answered, "I didn't, Mommy."

Knowing he couldn't crawl, I suspiciously demanded, "Well, then, how did he get all the way into your room?"

Confident of my approval for her obedience, she said with a smile, "I rolled him!"

He is still alive, and they are still best friends.

Can't you imagine how this kid felt during his journey down the hall? I'll bet the walls and ceiling are still spinning past his eyes! He didn't complain, however, so I assume he enjoyed the experience.

Another parent told me that her three-year-old daughter had recently learned that Jesus comes to live in the hearts of those who invite Him. That is a very difficult concept for a young child to assimilate, and this little girl didn't quite grasp it. Shortly thereafter, she and her mother were riding in the car, and the three-year-old suddenly came over and put her ear to her mother's chest.

"What are you doing?" asked the mother.

"I'm listening to Jesus in your heart," replied the child. The woman permitted the little girl to listen for a few seconds, and then she asked, "Well, what did you hear?"

The child replied, "Sounds like He's making coffee to me."

Who else but a toddler would come up with such a unique and delightful observation? If you live or work around kids, you need only listen. They will punctuate your world with mirth. They will also keep you off balance much of the time. I learned that fact several years before I became a father. As part of my professional training at the University of Southern California, I was required to teach elementary school for two years. Those were among the most informative years of my life, as I quickly learned what kids are like. It was also an initiation by fire.

Some days were more difficult than others, like the morning a kid named Thomas suddenly became ill. He lost his breakfast (thirty-seven scrambled eggs) with no warning to his fellow students or to me. I can still recall a room full of panic-stricken sixth graders climbing over chairs and desks to escape Thomas's volcanic eruptions. They stood around the walls of the room, holding their throats and going, "Eeeeuuuuyuckk!" One of them was more vocal in his disgust than the others, prompting a fellow student to say, "I wouldn't talk, Norbert. You did it last year!"

It was quite a morning for a new teacher. The lunch bell saved me, and having lost my appetite, I went outside to supervise students on the playground. Since I had not grown up in California, I was interested in an apparatus called a tetherball. As I stood there watching two boys competing violently with each other, a cute little sixth-grade girl named Doris came and stood beside me. Presently she asked, "Would you like to play?"

"Sure," I said. It was a mistake.

Doris was twelve years old, and she was a tetherball freak! I was twenty-five years old, and I couldn't get the hang of the game. The tether would change the trajectory of the ball, and I kept swinging wildly at the air. My students gathered around, and I became very self-conscious about my performance. There I was, six-foot-two and a self-proclaimed jock, yet I was getting clobbered by this little girl. Then it happened.

Doris decided to go for broke. She spiked the ball with all her might and drove it straight up my nose. I never even saw it coming. The whole world began spinning and my nose was vibrating like a tuning fork. I really thought I was going to die. My eyes were streaming tears and my ears were humming like a beehive. Yet, what could I do? Twenty kids had seen Doris ring my bell, and I couldn't let them know how badly I was hurt. So I went on playing even though I couldn't see the ball. It's a wonder Doris didn't whack me again.

Thank goodness for the afternoon bell. I took my pulsating nose back to the classroom and resolved to accept no more challenges from seventy-five-pound girls. They're dangerous.

⤳ What Makes Them Do It? ⤳

I'll never forget the mother who had been cooped up with her toddler for several weeks. In a desperate effort to get out of the house, she decided to take her son to a Muppets movie . . . his first. As soon as they arrived in the theater, the mother discovered a minor technical problem. The child didn't weigh enough to keep the spring seat down. There was nothing left to do but hold this churning, squirming two-year-old on her lap throughout the movie.

It was a mistake. Sometime during the next two hours, they lost control of a large Pepsi and a king-size box of buttered popcorn! That gooey mixture flowed over the child onto the mother's lap and down her legs. She decided to sit it out since the movie was almost over. What she didn't know, unfortunately, was that she and her son were being systematically cemented together. When the movie was over, they stood up and the mother's wraparound skirt came unraveled. It stuck to the bottom of the toddler and followed him up the aisle! She stood there clutching her slip and thanking the Lord she had taken time to put one on!

Can't you see this mother desperately begging the child to drag her skirt back within reach? Parenthood can certainly be humiliating at times. It also seems specifically designed to irritate us. Tell me why it is that a toddler never throws up in the bathroom? Never! To do so would violate some great unwritten law in the universe. It is even more difficult to understand why he will gag violently at the sight of a perfectly wonderful breakfast of oatmeal, eggs, bacon, and orange juice . . . and then go out and drink the dog's water. I have no idea what makes him do that. I only know that it drives his mother crazy!

⤳ If I Hear a Peep Out of You . . . ! ⤳

Recently I received a letter from a mother who had just returned from a stressful vacation. For days, their two sons had whined and complained, insulting and fighting with each other. They kicked the back of their father's seat for hours at a time. Finally, his fuse burned down to the dry powder. He pulled the car over to the side of the road and jerked the boys outside. Judgment Day had arrived. After spanking them both, he shoved them back into the car and warned them to keep their mouths shut. "If I hear a peep from either of you for thirty minutes," he warned, "I'll give you some more of what you just had!" The boys got the message. They remained mute for thirty minutes, after which the older lad said, "Is it all right to talk now?"

The father said sternly, "Yes. What do you want to say?"

"Well," continued the boy, "when you spanked us back there, my shoe fell off. We left it in the road."

It was the only good pair of shoes the kid owned. This time Mom went berserk and flailed at the backseat like a crazy lady. So ended another great day of family togetherness.

⤳ We've All Been There ⤲

It does appear at times like life is intentionally designed to strip us of dignity and make us look ridiculous.

My friend Mike would certainly agree. When he was a university student, he had one of those unexpected little experiences that make a person feel stupid. He was on campus at lunchtime one day and decided to eat at an outdoor fast-food restaurant. Mike ordered a hamburger, some French fries, and a chocolate shake. He walked away carrying this food, in addition to his briefcase, some computer reports, and a couple of books. Unfortunately, every table was in use, and he had no place to set down all this stuff.

Mike stood there watching the students who were eating and talking at their tables. While he waited for someone to leave, the smell of his food got the best of him. He bent down to take a sip of the shake he was carrying. But instead of getting the straw into his mouth, he jammed it up his nose. The natural reaction would be to pull the shake down and move the head up. That is exactly what Mike did, which proved to be a mistake. The straw remained stuck in his nose and came out of the shake. And he had no hand available to remove it. There he stood in front of hundreds of his peers with a straw sticking out of his nose and chocolate shake dripping on his pants.

It was just a brief moment in time and an event that no one will remember except Mike. But he will never forget it. Why? Because it made him feel like a complete nerd. Have you ever been through anything like that?

I remember a high-school girl I'll call Mary Jane. She had secretly given her figure a little help by padding her bra with this and that. Then she made the mistake of going to the senior swim party—where the truth about Mary Jane bubbled to the surface. Everyone else thought it was funny. Mary Jane didn't laugh.

As painful as such circumstances can be, they are almost universal in human experience. We've all been there at one time or another.

∽ Dropping the Ball ∼

When I was in the third grade, I was playing right field in a hotly contested baseball game. How clearly I recall that black day. A kid came up to bat and hit a ball straight at me. It was a simple little pop fly—and all I had to do was catch it. But there in front of five million fans, most of them girls, I let the ball drop right through my outstretched fingers. In fact, it jammed my thumb on its way to the ground. I can still hear the pounding feet of four base runners heading for home plate. In frustration, I grabbed the ball and threw it to the umpire, who stepped aside and let it roll at least a city block. "Boooo!" yelled half the five million hostile fans. "Yeaaa!" shouted the other half.

I bled and died out there in right field that afternoon. It was a lonely funeral. I was the only mourner. But after careful thought in the days that followed, I gave up baseball and have seldom returned to it. I've run track, played basketball, and enjoyed four years of college tennis, but baseball bit the dust for me out there in right field. If you go to that playground today and scratch around in the northeast corner, you'll find the bones of a brilliant baseball career that died before it ever got started.

∽ Killer McKeechern ∼

Typically, power games are more physical for adolescent males than females. The bullies literally force their wills on those who are weaker. That is what I remember most clearly from my own high-school years. I had a number of fights during that era just to preserve my turf. There was one dude, however, whom I had no intention of tackling. His name was Killer McKeechern, and he was the terror of the town. It was generally believed that Killer would destroy anyone who crossed him. That theory was never tested, to my knowledge. No one dared. At least, not until I blundered along.

When I was fifteen years old and an impulsive sophomore, I nearly ended a long and happy manhood before it had a chance to get started. As I recall, a blizzard had blown through our state the night before, and a group of us gathered in front of the school to throw snowballs at passing cars. (Does that tell you something about our collective maturity at the time?) Just before the afternoon bell rang, I looked up the street and saw McKeechern chugging along in his "chopped" 1934 Chevy. It was a junk heap with a cardboard "window" on the driver's side. McKeechern had cut a 3" x 3" flap in the cardboard, which he lifted when turning left. You could see his evil eyes peering out just before he went around corners. When the flap was down, however, he was oblivious to things on the left side of the car. As luck would have it, that's where I was standing with a huge snowball in my hand—thinking very funny and terribly unwise thoughts.

If I could just go back to that day and counsel myself, I would say, "Don't do it, Jim! You could lose your sweet life right here. McKeechern will tear your tongue out if you hit him with that snowball. Just put it down and go quietly to your afternoon class. Please, son! If you lose, I lose!" Unfortunately, no such advice wafted to my ears that day, and I didn't have the sense to realize my danger. I heaved the snowball into the upper atmosphere with all my might. It came down just as McKeechern drove by and, unbelievably, went through the flap in his cardboard window. The missile obviously hit him squarely in the face, because his Chevy wobbled all over the road. It bounced over the curb and came to a stop just short of the Administration Building. Killer exploded from the front seat, ready to rip someone to shreds (me!). I'll never forget the sight. There was snow all over his face, and little jets of steam were curling from his head. My whole life passed in front of my eyes as I faded into the crowd. *So young!* I thought.

The only thing that saved me on this snowy day was McKeechern's inability to identify me. No one told him I had thrown the snowball, and believe me, I didn't volunteer. I escaped unscathed, although that brush with destiny must have damaged me emotionally. I still have recurring nightmares about the event thirty-five years later. In my dreams, the chimes ring, and I go to open the front door. There stands McKeechern with a shotgun. And he still has snow on his face. (If you read this story, Killer, I do hope we can be friends. We were only kids, you know? Right, Killer? Huh? Right! Howsa car?)

～ Trying to Buy Acceptance ～

Beverly lived in a neighborhood of older children who did not want her tagging along behind them. They could run faster, climb higher, and do everything better than she, and that fact had not escaped her notice.

One day, Bev came running into the house and shouted to her mother, "Lollipop, Mommy! I want lollipop."

Elaine went to the pantry and handed Bev a lollipop. But the child said urgently, "No, Mommy. I want lots of lollipops."

By this time the mother knew that something was up, so she decided to play along with her daughter. She handed her five or six lollipops and then watched at the window to see what she would do with them.

Beverly ran to a fence that bordered a field next to their house. Her friends were on the other side playing baseball. She stuck her arm through the fence and waved the lollipops at the children. But they didn't see her. They just went on with their game as though the little girl wasn't there. Then one of the kids looked over at her and saw that she was offering them something good. They all came running over and rudely snatched the lollipops out of her hand. Then without even thanking her, they went back to playing ball. Alas, little Beverly stood there alone, her gifts and her friends both gone.

Elaine fought back the tears as she watched her daughter standing sadly at the fence. The child had tried to buy acceptance, but it only brought her further rejection. How badly Beverly wanted the other kids to like her and include her in their games. What she learned that day, however, is that love can't be bought, and bribery usually brings only disrespect.

～ Awful Janet ～

Children often do great damage to one another by their cruelty and ridicule. Consider this note given to me by the mother of a fourth-grade girl, for example. It was written by one of her classmates for no apparent reason:

Awful Janet,

You the stinkest girl in this world. I hope you die but of course I suppose that's impossible. I've some ideals.

1. Play in the road
2. Cut your throad
3. Drink poison
4. Knife yourself

Please do some of this you big fat Girl. we all hate you. I'am praying Oh please lord let Janet die. Were in need of fresh air. Did you hear me lord cause if you didn' will all die with her here. See Janet, we're not all bad.

from Wanda Jackson

What is "Awful Janet" to think about a note like this? She may have the confidence to take it in stride. But if Wanda is popular and Janet is not, the stage is set for considerable pain. Notice that Wanda hit all the sensitive nerves. She insulted Janet's physical appearance and implied that all the other students think she stinks. Those two messages—"you're ugly" and "everyone hates you"—could scar a particularly sensitive child. He or she may remember it for a lifetime.

⟶ Courtroom of the Mind ⟵

Let's suppose you are an adolescent girl. You are sixteen years old, and your name is Helen Highschool. To be very honest, you are not exactly gorgeous. Your shoulders are rounded, and you have trouble remembering to close your mouth when you're thinking. (That seems to worry your folks a lot.) There are pimples distributed at random over your forehead and chin, and your oversized ears keep peeking out from under the hair that should hide them. You think often about these flaws and have wondered, with proper reverence, why God wasn't paying attention when you were being assembled.

You have never had a real date in your life, except for that disaster last February. Your mom's friend Mrs. Nosgood arranged a blind date that almost signaled the end of the world. You knew it was risky to accept, but you were too excited to think rationally. Charming Charlie arrived in high spirits expecting to meet the girl of his dreams. You were not what he had in mind. Do you remember the disappointment on his face when you shuffled into the living room? Remember how he told Mary Lou the next day that your braces stuck out farther than your chest? Remember him saying you had so much bridgework in your mouth that he'd have to pay a toll to kiss you? Horrible! But the night of your date he didn't say anything. He just sulked through the evening and brought you home two hours early. Mary Lou couldn't wait to tell you the following afternoon how much Charlie hated you, of course. You lashed back in anger. You caught him in the hall and told him he wasn't too bright for a boy with a head shaped like a light bulb. But the hurt went deep. You despised all males for at least six months and thought your hormones would never make a comeback.

When you arrived home from school that afternoon, you went straight to your room without speaking to the family. You closed the door and sat on the bed. You thought about the injustice of it all, letting your young mind play hopscotch over the many painful little memories that refused to fade. In fact, it seemed as though you were suddenly on trial to determine your acceptability to the human race.

The attorney for the prosecution stood before the jury and began presenting incriminating evidence as to your unworthiness. He recalled that fourth-grade Valentine's Day party when your beautiful cousin, Ann, got thirty-four cards and two boxes of candy, most of them from lovesick boys. You got three cards—two from girls and one from your uncle Albert in San Antonio. The jury shook their heads in sorrow. The attorney then described the day that sixth-grade boy shared his ice-cream cone with Betty Brigden but said he'd "catch the uglies" if you took a bite. You acted like you didn't hear him, but you went to the girl's rest room and cried until the recess was over.

"Ladies and gentlemen of the jury," said the attorney, "these are the unbiased opinions of Helen's own generation. The entire student body of Washington High School obviously agrees. They have no reason to lie. Their views represent truth itself. This homely girl simply does not deserve to be one of us! I urge you to find her guilty this day!"

Then the attorney for the defense arose. He was a frail little man who stuttered when he spoke. He presented a few witnesses on your behalf, including your mom and dad—and Uncle Albert, of course.

"Objection, Your Honor!" shouted the prosecutor. "These are members of her own family. They don't count. They're biased witnesses, and their opinions are untrustworthy."

"Objection sustained," quoted the judge. Your attorney, flustered and disconcerted, then mentioned how you kept your room clean, and he made a big deal about that A you got on a geography test last month. You saw the foreman of the jury suppress a yawn, and the others showed signs of complete boredom.

"A-a-a-and so, l-l-ladies and gentlemen of the j-j-jury, I ask y-y-you to find this y-y-young lady in-innocent of the charges."

The jury was gone for thirty-seven seconds before bringing in a verdict. You stood before them and recognized them all. There was last year's homecoming queen. There was the quarterback of the football team. There was the valedictorian of the senior class. There was the surgeon's handsome son. They all looked down at you with stern eyes, and suddenly shouted in one voice: "GUILTY AS CHARGED, YOUR HONOR!" The judge then read your sentence:

"Helen Highschool, a jury of your peers has found you to be unacceptable to the human race. You are hereby sentenced to a life of loneliness. You will probably fail in everything you do, and you'll go to your grave without a friend in the world. Marriage is out of the question, and there will never be a child in your home. You are a failure, Helen. You're a disappointment to your parents and must be considered excess baggage from this point forward. This case is hereby closed."

The dream faded, but the decision of the jury remained real. Your parents wondered why you were so irritable and mean during the weeks that followed. They never knew—and you didn't tell them—that you had been expelled from the world of the Beautiful People.

I wish I could talk to all the Helens and Bobs and Suzies and Jacks who have also been found unacceptable in the courtroom of the mind. They may never know that the trial was rigged—that every member of the jury has been charged with the same offense—that the judge himself was convicted more than thirty years ago. I wish I could tell each teenager that we have all stood before the bar of injustice, and few have been acquitted. Some of the adolescent convicts will be "pardoned" later in life, but a greater number will never escape the sentence of the judge! And the irony of it all is that we each conduct our own rigged trial. We serve as our own prosecutor, and the final sentence is imposed under our own inflexible supervision—with a little help from our "friends," of course.

∼ I'm Not Getting Old! ∼

Several months ago I was driving my car near our home with my son and daughter and my son's three-year-old friend, Kevin. As we turned a corner we drove past a very old man who was so bent and crippled that he could hardly walk. We talked about how the man must feel, and then I told the kids that they would someday grow old, too. That bit of news was particularly shocking to Kevin, and he refused to accept it.

"I'm not going to get old!" he said, as though insulted by my prediction.

"Yes, you are, Kevin," I said. "All of us will grow old if we live that long. It happens to everyone."

His eyes grew big, and he protested again, "But it won't happen to me!"

I again assured him that none could escape.

Kevin sat in silence for fifteen or twenty seconds, and then he said with a note of panic in his voice, "But! But! But I don't want to grow old. I want to stay fresh and good."

I said, "I know, Kevin! How well I know!"

The inability to stay "fresh and good" produced the tenth most common source of depression for the women who completed our questionnaire. Once again, the young age of the individuals surveyed certainly influenced the relatively low ranking of this item. I'm sure that it will move up on the scale in the next few years. There is something distressing about watching yourself disintegrate day by day, especially after it dawns on you that life itself is a fatal disease. None of us are going to get out of it alive!

I heard a story about three elderly people who were sitting in rocking chairs on the front porch of their rest home. One said to the others, "You know, I don't hear so well anymore, and I thought it would bother me more than it does. But there isn't much that I want to hear, anyway."

The second woman said, "Yes, I've found the same with my eyes.

Everything looks blurred and cloudy now, but I don't care. I saw just about everything that I wanted to see when I was younger."

The third lady thought for a moment and then said, "Well, I don't know about that. I sort of miss my mind. . . ."

⟶ Oh, My Papa ⟵

I'm sure there has always been friction between parents and children, but the nature of it has changed radically. The culture that once was supportive and respectful of parents has now become the worst enemy of the family. Let me illustrate.

The artistic creations produced by a society at a given time don't spring from a vacuum. They reflect the opinions and beliefs commonly held by its people. That being true, we can measure change in attitudes by looking at the evolution of music that has occurred in recent years. Let's go back to 1953 when the most popular song in the United States was sung by Eddie Fisher and was titled "Oh, My Papa." Here's a portion of the lyrics:

> Oh, my papa, to me he was so wonderful
> Oh, my papa, to me he was so good.
> No one could be so gentle and so lovable,
> Oh, my papa, he always understood.
> Gone are the days when he would take me on his knee
> And with a smile he'd change my tears to laughter.
>
> Oh, my papa, so funny and adorable,
> Always the clown, so funny in his way,
> Oh, my papa, to me he was so wonderful
> Deep in my heart I miss him so today,
> Oh, my papa. Oh, my papa.[1]

By the time I had reached college age, things were starting to change. The subject of conflict between parents and teenagers began to appear as a common theme in artistic creations. The movie *Rebel without a Cause* featured a screen idol named James Dean who seethed with anger at his "Old Man."

Marlon Brando starred in *The Wild One*, another movie with rebellion as its theme. Rock-'n'-roll music portrayed it, too.

Some early rock-'n'-roll lyrics mixed rebellious messages with humor, such as a number-one hit from 1958 called "Yakkety-Yak (Don't Talk Back)." But what began as musical humor turned decidedly bitter in the late 1960s. Everyone in those days was talking about the "generation gap" that had erupted between young people and their parents. Teenagers and college students vowed they'd never again trust anyone over thirty, and their anger toward parents began to percolate. The Doors released a song in 1968 entitled "The End," in which Jim Morrison fantasized about killing his father. It concludes with gunshots followed by horrible grunts and groans.

In 1984, Twisted Sister released "We're Not Gonna Take It," which referred to a father as a "disgusting slob" who was "worthless and weak." Then he was blasted out the window of a second-story apartment. This theme of killing parents showed up regularly in the decade that followed. A group called Suicidal Tendencies released a recording in 1983 called "I Saw Your Mommy." Here is an excerpt of the gory lyrics:

> I saw your mommy and your mommy's dead.
> I watched her as she bled,
> Chewed-off toes on her chopped-off feet.
> I took a picture because I thought it was neat.
>
> I saw your mommy, and your mommy's dead.
> I saw her lying in a pool of red:
> I think it's the greatest thing I'll ever see—
> Your dead mommy lying in front of me.[2]

For sheer banality, nothing yet produced can match "Momma's Gotta Die Tonight," by Ice-T and Body Count. The album sold five hundred thousand copies and featured its wretched lyrics on the CD jacket. Most of them are unfit to quote here, but they involved graphic descriptions of the rapper's mother being burned in her bed, then beaten to death with a baseball bat she had given him as a present, and finally the mutilation of the corpse into "little bitty pieces." What incredible violence! There was not a hint of guilt or remorse expressed by the rapper while telling us of this murder. In fact, he called his mother a "racist b____h," and laughed while chanting, "Burn, Mama, burn."

My point is that the most popular music of our culture went from the inspiration of "Oh, My Papa" to the horrors of "Momma's Gotta Die Tonight" in scarcely more than a generation. And we have to wonder, Where do we go from here?

∽ I Don't Need a Mother Anymore ∾

My parents handled me wisely in my late teen years, and it was rare for them to stumble into common parental mistakes. That is, however, exactly what happened when I was nineteen years old. We had been a very close-knit family, and it was difficult for my mother to shift gears when I graduated from high school.

During that summer, I traveled fifteen hundred miles from home and entered a college in California. I will never forget the exhilarating feeling of freedom that swept over me that fall. It was not that I wanted to do anything evil or forbidden. It was simply that I felt accountable for my own life and did not have to explain my actions to anyone. It was like a fresh, cool breeze on a spring morning. Young adults who have not been properly prepared for that moment sometimes go berserk, but I did not. I did, however, quickly become addicted to that freedom and was not about to give it up.

The following summer, I came home to visit my folks. Immediately, I found myself in conflict with my mom. She was not intentionally insulting. She simply responded as she had done a year earlier when I was still in high school. But by then, I had journeyed down the road toward independence. She was asking me what time I would be coming in at night and urging me to drive the car safely and advising me about what I ate. No offense was intended. My mother had just failed to notice that I had changed, and she needed to get with the new program.

Finally, there was a flurry of words between us, and I left the house in a huff. A friend came by to pick me up, and I talked about my feelings as we rode in the car. "Darn it, Bill!" I said. "I don't need a mother anymore."

Then a wave of guilt swept over me. It was as though I had said, "I don't love my mother anymore." I meant no such thing. What I was feeling was a desire to be friends with my parents instead of accepting their authority over me. Freedom was granted very quickly thereafter.

∽ Nobody Cares ∽

At one time I served on a high-school campus, and there I worked with many teenagers who were struggling with feelings of rejection.

One day I was walking across the grounds of the high school after the bell had rung. Most of the students were already back in class, but I saw a boy coming toward me in the main hall. I knew that his name was Ronny and that he was in his third year of high school. However, I didn't know him very well. Ronny was one of those many students who remain back in the crowd, never calling attention to themselves and never making friends with those around them. It's easy to forget they're alive because they never allow anybody to get acquainted with them.

When Ronny was about fifteen feet away from me, I saw that he was very upset about something. It was obvious that he was distressed, because his face revealed his inner turmoil. As he came a few feet closer, he saw that I was watching him intently. Our eyes locked for a moment, then he looked at the floor as he came closer.

When Ronny and I were parallel, he suddenly covered his face with both hands and turned toward the wall. His neck and ears turned red, and he began to sob and weep. He was not just crying—he seemed to explode with emotion. I put my arm around him and said, "Can I help you, Ronny? Do you feel like talking to me?" He nodded affirmatively, and I practically had to lead him into my office.

I offered Ronny a chair and closed the door, and I gave him a few minutes to get control of himself before asking him to speak. Then he began to talk to me.

He said, "I've been going to school in this district for eight years, but in all that time I've never managed to make one single friend! Not one. There's not a soul in this high school who cares whether I live or die. I walk to school by myself, and I walk home alone. I don't go to football games; I don't go to basketball games or any school activities because I'm embarrassed to sit there all by myself. I stand alone at snack time in the morning, and I eat lunch out in a quiet corner of the campus. Then I go back to class by myself. I don't get along with my dad, and my mother doesn't understand me, and I fight with my sister. And I have nobody! My phone never rings. I have no one to talk to. Nobody knows what I feel and nobody cares. Sometimes I think I just can't stand it anymore!"

I can't tell you how many students have expressed these same feelings to me. Ronny is one of many thousands of students who are overwhelmed by their own worthlessness, and sometimes this even takes away their desire to live.

⟋ A Boy Named Jeep Fenders ⟍

When I was nine years old, I attended a Sunday School class every week. One Sunday, a new boy named Fred visited our class. I didn't stop to think that Fred might be uncomfortable as a stranger in our group, because I knew everyone and had many friends there. He sat quietly looking down at the floor. During the morning class I noticed that Fred had very strange ears. They were shaped in a kind of half-circle. I remember thinking how much they looked like Jeep fenders. Have you ever seen the fenders on a Jeep, which go up and over the tires? Somehow I managed to see a resemblance to Fred's ears.

Then I did a very unkind thing. I told everyone that Fred had "Jeep-fender ears," and my friends thought that was terribly funny. They all laughed and began calling him "Jeep Fenders." Fred seemed to be accepting the joke pretty well. He sat with a little smile on his face (because he didn't know what to say), but it was hurting him deeply. Suddenly Fred stopped smiling. He exploded from his chair and hurried toward the door, crying. Then he ran out of the building and never came back to our church. I don't blame him. The way we acted was vicious, and I'm sure God was very displeased with me, especially.

However, the important thing to understand was how ignorant I was of Fred's feelings on that day. Believe it or not, I didn't really intend to hurt him. I had no idea that my joke made him feel terrible, and I was shocked when he ran from the classroom. I remember thinking about what I had done after he left, wishing I hadn't been so mean.

Why was I so cruel to Fred? It was because no one had ever told me that other people were as sensitive about being teased as I was. I thought I was the only one who didn't like to be laughed at. The teachers of my many Sunday School classes should have taught me to respect and protect the feelings of others. They should have helped me to be more Christlike.

⌐ Betrayed ⌐

Some of the most dramatic moments in my counseling experience have involved outright forgiveness by one spouse for the devastating wrongs of the other. I'll never forget the day Janelle walked into my office. She brought an air of depression and sadness with her as she sat head downward in a chair. Her husband, Lonny, had asked for my help after Janelle attempted suicide in the middle of the night. He had gotten up at 3:00 A.M. to go to the bathroom and found her in the process of taking her life. If he had not awakened, she would have been gone.

Lonny had no idea why Janelle attempted to kill herself or why she was so depressed. She wouldn't tell him. He knew she was dealing with something awesome, but he could not make her reveal it. Even after the suicide episode, she held everything inside, moping around the house in depression. Finally, she agreed to talk to me, and Lonny brought her to my office.

Lonny sat outside while Janelle and I talked. At first she threw a smoke screen around her emotions, but eventually the story broke. She was deeply involved in an affair with a business acquaintance, and the guilt was tearing her to pieces.

I said, "Janelle, you know that the only way you will ever settle this matter is to confess the affair to Lonny. You can't keep this enormous secret between you forever. It will be a barrier that will destroy what's left of your marriage. I think you should tell Lonny the truth and seek his help in ending the affair."

She looked at me sadly and said, "I know that's right, but I can't tell him! I've tried and I just can't do it!"

I said, "Do you want me to do it?"

Janelle nodded through the tears, and I said, "Go to the waiting room and ask Lonny to come in. You stay there, and I'll call for you in about an hour."

Lonny arrived with an anxious look on his face. He was worried about his wife, yet he had no idea what to expect. That was, I believe, one of the toughest assignments I've ever had—to tell a loving, faithful husband that he had been betrayed by his wife. As might be expected, the news hit him like a blow from a hammer. His anger and anguish were intertwined with compassion and remorse. We continued talking for a while, and then I invited Janelle back into my office.

These two wounded people sat in depression as I attempted to ease communication between them. But the atmosphere was extremely heavy. Finally, I prayed and asked them to leave and come back at 10:00 A.M. the next day.

Janelle and Lonny had a bad night. They didn't fight, but they were both so hurt and disturbed that they couldn't sleep. Nor could they talk to one another. They arrived back in my office the next morning in the same state in which they had left. I talked to them about forgiveness, about divine healing of memories, and about their present situation. I don't know how it happened even today, but a spirit of love began to permeate that office. We prayed together, and suddenly, Janelle and Lonny fell into each other's arms, weeping and asking for forgiveness and granting that forgiveness. It was an unbelievable moment of joy for all three of us, and it happened because a man who had been deceived and betrayed was willing to say, "I hold nothing against you!"

⟊ Horrible Hayley ⟊

Valentine's Day can be the most painful day of the year for an unpopular child, and many schools have either discontinued the exchanging of valentines or set rules that children cannot give selectively to some classmates and not others. Students do count the number of valentines they receive as a measure of social worth. At a class party for a group of fourth graders, the teacher announced that the class was going to play a game with boy-girl teams. That was her first mistake, since fourth graders have not yet experienced the happy hormones that draw the sexes together. The moment the teacher instructed the students to select a partner, all the boys immediately laughed and pointed at the homeliest and least respected girl in the room. She was overweight, had protruding teeth, and was too withdrawn even to look anyone in the eye.

"Don't put us with Hayley," they all said in mock terror. "Anybody but

Hayley! She'll give us a disease! Ugh! Spare us from Horrible Hayley." The mother waited for the teacher, a strong disciplinarian, to rush to the aid of the beleaguered little girl. But to her disappointment, nothing was said to the insulting boys. Instead, the teacher left Hayley to cope with the painful situation in solitude.

Ridicule by one's own sex is distressing, but rejection by the opposite sex is like taking a hatchet to the self-concept. What could the devastated child say in reply? How does an overweight fourth-grade girl defend herself against nine aggressive boys? What response could she make but to blush in mortification and slide foolishly into her chair? The child, whom God loves more than the possessions of the entire world, will never forget that moment or the teacher who abandoned her in this time of need.

Had I been the teacher of Hayley's class on that fateful Valentine's Day, those mocking, joking boys would have had a fight on their hands. Of course, it would have been better if the embarrassment could have been prevented by discussing the feelings of others from the first day of school. But if the conflict occurred as described, with Hayley's ego suddenly shredded for everyone to see, I would have thrown the full weight of my authority and respect on her side of the battle.

My spontaneous response would have carried this general theme: "Wait a minute! By what right do any of you boys say such mean, unkind things to Hayley? I want to know which of you is so perfect that the rest of us couldn't make fun of you in some way? I know you all very well. I know about your homes and your school records and some of your personal secrets. Would you like me to share them with the class, so we can all laugh at you the way you just did at Hayley? I could do it! I could make you want to crawl in a hole and disappear. But listen to me! You need not fear. I will never embarrass you in that way. Why not? Because it *hurts* to be laughed at by your friends. It hurts even more than a stubbed toe or a cut finger or a bee sting.

"I want to ask those of you who were having such a good time a few minutes ago: Have you ever had a group of children make fun of you in the same way? If you haven't, then brace yourself. Some day it will happen to you, too. Eventually you will say something foolish . . . and they'll point at you and laugh in your face. And when it happens, I want you to remember what happened today.

"Class, let's make sure that we learn something important from what took place here this afternoon. First, we will not be mean to each other in this

20

class. We will laugh together when things are funny, but we will not do it by making one person feel bad. Second, I will never intentionally embarrass anyone in this class. You can count on that. Each of you is a child of God. He molded you with His loving hands, and He has said that we all have equal worth as human beings. This means that Michael is neither better nor worse than Brian or Molly or Brent. Sometimes I think maybe you believe a few of you are more important than others. It isn't true. Every one of you is priceless to God, and each of you will live forever in eternity. That's how valuable you are. God loves each boy and girl in this room, and because of that, I love every one of you. He wants us to be kind to other people, and we're going to practice that kindness throughout the rest of the year."

When a strong, loving teacher comes to the aid of the least respected child in the class, as I've described, something dramatic occurs in the emotional climate of the room. Every child seems to utter an audible sigh of relief. The same thought is bouncing around in many heads: "If Hayley is safe from ridicule—even overweight Hayley—then I must be safe, too." By defending the least popular child, a teacher is demonstrating that there are no "pets." Everyone is respected by the teacher, and the teacher will fight for anyone who is treated unjustly.

～ Lonely Assassins ～

He began his life with all the classic handicaps and disadvantages. His mother was a powerfully built, dominant woman who found it difficult to love anyone. She had been married three times, and her second husband divorced her because she beat him up regularly. The father of the child I'm describing was her third husband; he died of a heart attack a few months before the child's birth. As a consequence, the mother had to work long hours from his earliest childhood.

She gave him no affection, no love, no discipline, and no training during those early years. She even forbade him to call her at work. Other children had little to do with him, so he was alone most of the time. He was absolutely rejected from his earliest childhood. He was ugly and poor and untrained and unlovable. When he was thirteen years old, a school psychologist commented that he probably didn't even know the meaning of the word *love*. During adolescence, the girls would have nothing to do with him, and he fought with the boys.

Despite a high IQ, he failed academically and finally dropped out during his third year of high school. He thought he might find acceptance in the Marine Corps; they reportedly build men, and he wanted to be one. But his problems went with him. The other marines laughed at him and ridiculed him. He fought back, resisted authority, and was court-martialed and thrown out of the Corps with a dishonorable discharge. So there he was—a young man in his early twenties—absolutely friendless and shipwrecked. He was scrawny and small in stature. He had an adolescent squeak in his voice. He was balding. He had no talent, no skill, and no sense of worthiness. He didn't even have a driver's license.

Once again he thought he could run from his problems, so he went to live in a foreign country. But he was rejected there, too. Nothing had changed. While there, he married a girl who herself had been an illegitimate child and brought her back to America with him. Soon, she began to develop the same contempt for him that everyone else displayed. She bore him two children, but he never enjoyed the status and respect that a father should have. His marriage continued to crumble. His wife demanded more and more things that he could not provide. Instead of being his ally against the bitter world, as he had hoped, she became his most vicious opponent. She could outfight him, and she learned to bully him. On one occasion, she locked him in the bathroom as punishment. Finally, she forced him to leave.

He tried to make it on his own, but he was terribly lonely. After days of solitude, he went home and literally begged her to take him back. He surrendered all pride. He crawled. He accepted humiliation. He came on her terms. Despite his meager salary, he brought her seventy-eight dollars as a gift, asking her to take it and spend it any way she wished. But she laughed at him. She belittled his feeble attempts to supply the family's needs. She ridiculed his failure. She made fun of his sexual impotence in front of a friend. At one point, he fell on his knees and wept bitterly, as the greater darkness of his private nightmare enveloped him.

Finally, in silence, he pleaded no more. No one wanted him. No one had ever wanted him. He was a most rejected man. His ego lay shattered in dust!

The next day he was a strangely different man. He arose, went to the garage, and took down a rifle he had hidden there. He carried it with him to his newly acquired job at a book-storage building. And from a window on the sixth floor of that building, shortly after noon, November 22, 1963, he sent two shells crashing into the head of President John Fitzgerald Kennedy.

Lee Harvey Oswald, the rejected, unlovable failure, killed the man who, more than any other, embodied all the success, beauty, wealth, and family affection he himself lacked. In firing that rifle, he utilized the *one* skill he had learned in his entire, miserable lifetime.

The Wounds of an Adolescent Heart

A sad little girl named Lily, an eighth grader, was referred to me for psychological counseling. She opened the door of my office and stood with eyes downcast. Underneath several layers of powder and makeup, her face was completely aglow with infected acne. Lily had done her best to bury the inflammation, but she had not been successful. She weighed about eighty-five pounds and was a physical wreck from head to toe. She sat down without raising her eyes to mine, lacking the confidence to face me. I didn't need to ask what was troubling her. Life had dealt her a devastating blow, and she was bitter, angry, broken, and deeply hurt. The teenager who reaches this point of despair can see no tomorrow. There is no hope. She can't think of anything else. The adolescent feels repulsive and disgusting and would like to crawl into a hole, but there is no place to hide. Running away won't help, nor will crying change anything. Too often suicide seems the best way out.

Lily gave me little time to work. The following morning she staggered into the school office and announced that she had ingested everything in the family medicine cabinet. We labored feverishly to retrieve the medication and finally succeeded on the way to the hospital. Lily survived physically, but her self-esteem and confidence had died years earlier. The scars on her sad face symbolized the wounds of her adolescent heart.

Trombone Serenades

I was working at Pacific State Hospital for the Mentally Retarded in Pomona, California, and every afternoon I heard a blaring trombone concert coming from a nearby hillside, something vaguely recognizable as John Philip Sousa marches. I had no idea who was responsible for the serenades. Then one day as I walked across the grounds of the hospital, a patient about seventeen years old ran up to me and said, "Hi. My name is James Walter Jackson [not his actual name]. I'm the fellow who plays the trombone. Now I need your help to get a message through to Santa Claus, because I've gotta have a new trombone. The one I have is all beat up, and I want a brand-new, silver Olds, with purple velvet lining in the case. Will you tell him that for me?"

I was a bit taken aback, but I volunteered to do what I could. That afternoon as I discussed James Walter Jackson with another staff member, he gave me a little background on the message to Santa. The year before, this patient had told several people that he would like Santa Claus to bring him a trombone. One of the hospital workers had an old instrument in the garage that had about seen its day, so on Christmas morning it was donated to James Walter Jackson with credit given to Santa.

James was delighted, of course, but he was a bit disappointed by all those bumps and dings. He figured he hadn't been specific enough in his prior message to Santa, so he would do better next time. He launched a yearlong campaign designed to let the North Pole know exactly what he had in mind. He stopped everyone he met on the street and told them precisely what to tell Santa.

Shortly after that, I saw James Walter Jackson for the last time. I was driving out of the hospital grounds when I noticed this amicable patient in the rearview mirror. He was running down the road behind my car, waving for me to stop. I pulled to the curb and let him catch up with me. He put his head in the window and said, panting, "Don't forget to tell him that I want the long-lasting kind!" I hope someone bought James Walter Jackson what he wanted so badly. His ability to compensate depended on it.

⟶ Season of the Empty Nest ⟵

A loving mother named Joan Mills expressed her feelings about her children in an article that initially appeared in a 1981 issue of *Reader's Digest*. It is called "Season of the Empty Nest," and I believe you will be touched by the warmth of these words.

Remember when the children built blanket tents to sleep in? And then scrambled by moonlight to their own beds, where they'd be safe from bears? And how proud and eager they were to be starting kindergarten? But only up to the minute they got there? And the time they packed cardboard suitcases in such a huff? "You won't see us again!" they hollered. Then they turned back at the end of the yard because they'd forgotten to go to the bathroom.

It's the same thing when they're 20 or 22, starting to make their own way in the grownup world. Bravado, pangs, false starts, and pratfalls. They're half in, half out. "Good-bye, good-bye! Don't worry, Mom!" They're back the first weekend to borrow the paint roller and a fuse and a broom. Prowling the attic, they seize the quilt the dog ate and the terrible old sofa cushions that smell like dead mice. "Just what I need!" they cheer, loading the car.

"Good-bye, good-bye!" implying forever. But they show up without notice at suppertimes, sighing soulfully to see the familiar laden plates. They go away again, further secured by four bags of groceries, the electric frying pan, and a cookbook.

They call home collect, but not as often as parents need to hear. And their news makes fast-graying hair stand on end:

". . . so he forgot to set the brake, and he says my car rolled three blocks backward down the hill before it was totaled!"

". . . simple case of last hired, first fired, no big deal. I sold the stereo, and . . ."

"Mom! Everybody in the city has them! There's this roach stuff you put under the sink. It's . . ."

I gripped the phone with both hands in those days, wishing I could bribe my children back with everything they'd ever wanted—drum lessons, a junk-food charge account, anything. I struggled with an unbecoming urge to tell them once more about hot breakfasts and crossing streets and dry socks on wet days.

"I'm so impressed by how you cope!" I said instead.

The children scatter, and parents draw together, remembering sweet-shaped infants heavy in their arms, patched jeans, chicken pox, the night the accident happened, the rituals of Christmases and proms. With wistful pride and a feeling for the comic, they watch over their progeny from an effortfully kept distance. It is the season of the empty nest.

Slowly, slowly, there are changes. Something wonderful seems to hover then, faintly heard, glimpsed in illumined moments. Visiting the children, the parents are almost sure of it.

A son spreads a towel on the table and efficiently irons a perfect crease into his best pants. (*Ironing board*, his mother thinks, adding to a mental shopping list.) "I'm taking you to a French restaurant for dinner," the young man announces. "I've made reservations."

"Am I properly dressed?" his mother asks, suddenly shy. He walks her through city streets within the aura of his assurance. His arm lies lightly around her shoulders.

Or a daughter offers her honored guest the only two chairs she has and settles into a harem heap of floor pillows. She has raised plants from cuttings, framed a wall full of prints herself, and spent three weekends refinishing the little dresser that glows in a square of sun.

Her parents regard her with astonished love. The room has been enchanted by her touch. "Everything's charming," they tell her honestly. "It's a real home."

Now? Is it now? Yes. The something wonderful descends. The generations smile at one another, as if exchanging congratulations. The children are no longer children. The parents are awed to discover adults.

It is wonderful, in ways my imagination had not begun to dream of. How could I have guessed—how could they?—that of my three, the shy one would pluck a dazzling array of competencies out of the air and turn up, chatting with total poise, on TV shows? That the one who turned his adolescence into World War III would find his role in arduous, sensitive human service? Or that the unbookish, antic one, torment of his teachers, would evolve into a scholar, tolerating a student's poverty and writing into the night?

I hadn't suspected that my own young adults would be so ebulliently funny one minute, and so tellingly introspective the next: so openhearted and unguarded. Or that growing up would inspire them to buy life insurance and three-piece suits and lend money to the siblings they'd once robbed of lollipops. Or that walking into their houses, I'd hear Mozart on the tape player and find books laid out for me to borrow.

Once, long ago, I waited nine months at a time to see who they would be, babes newly formed and wondrous. "Oh, look!" I said, and I fell in love. Now my children are wondrously new to me in a different way. I am in love again.

My daughter and I freely share the complex world of our inner selves, and all the other worlds we know. Touched, I notice how her rhythms and gestures are reminding of her grandmother's or mine. We are linked by unconscious mysteries and benignly watched by ghosts. I turn my head to gaze at her. She meets my look and smiles.

A son flies the width of the country for his one vacation in a whole long year. He follows me around the kitchen, tasting from the pots, handing down the dishes.

We brown in the sun. Read books in silent synchrony.

He jogs. I tend the flowers. We walk at the unfurled edge of great waves. We talk and talk, and later play cribbage past midnight. I'm utterly happy.

"But it's your vacation!" I remind him. "What shall we do that's special?"

"This," he says. "Exactly this."

When my children first ventured out and away, I felt they were in flight to outer space, following a curve of light and time to such unknowns that my heart would surely go faint with trying to follow. I thought this would be the end of parenting. Not what it is—the best part; the final, firmest bonding; the goal and the reward.[3]

CHAPTER TWO

Loving Discipline

The objective of discipline, as I see it, is to take the raw material with which our babies arrive on this earth, and then gradually mold it into mature, responsible, and God-fearing adults. It is a twenty-year process that will bring progress, setbacks, successes, and failures. When the child turns thirteen, you'll swear for a time that he's missed everything you thought you had taught: manners, kindness, grace, and style. But then, maturity begins to take over, and the little green shoots from former plantings start to emerge. It is one of the richest experiences in living to watch that progression from infancy to adulthood in the span of two dynamic decades.

~ Listen to the Expert ~

There were certain risks associated with my being a young father and simultaneously choosing to write and speak about the discipline of children. That placed enormous pressure on our imperfect family in those days. But God gave me good kids, and we handled the fishbowl experience rather well. There were a few tough moments, however, that proved to be quite embarrassing.

One of those nightmares occurred on a Sunday evening in 1974, when Danae was nine and Ryan nearly five. I was asked to speak on that occasion in a church service near our home. As it turned out, I made two big mistakes that night. First, I decided to speak on the discipline of children, and second, I brought my kids to the church with me. I should have known better.

After I had delivered my thought-provoking, witty, charming, and informative message that evening, I stood at the front of the sanctuary to talk to parents who sought more advice. Perhaps twenty-five mothers and fathers gathered around, each asking specific questions in turn. There I was, dispensing profound child-rearing wisdom like a vending machine, when suddenly we all heard a loud crash in the balcony. I looked up in horror to see Danae chasing Ryan over the seats, giggling and stumbling and running through the upper deck. It was one of the most embarrassing moments of my life. I could hardly go on telling the lady in front of me how to manage her children when mine were going crazy in the balcony; nor could I easily get my hands on them. I finally caught Shirley's eye and motioned for her to launch a seek-and-destroy mission on the second tier. Never again did I speak on that subject with our kids in tow.

I share that story to clarify the goal of proper child rearing. It is not to produce perfect kids. Even if you implement a flawless system of discipline at home, which no one in history has done, your children will be children. At times they will be silly, destructive, lazy, selfish, and—yes—disrespectful. Such is the nature of humanity. We as adults have the same problems. Furthermore, when it comes to kids, that's the way it *should* be. Boys and girls are like clocks; you have to let them run.

∼ Discipline Goes in the Toilet ∼

The young mother of a defiant three-year-old girl approached me in Kansas City recently to thank me for my books and tapes. She told me that a few months earlier her little daughter had become increasingly defiant and had managed to "buffalo" her frustrated mom and dad. They knew they were being manipulated but couldn't seem to regain control. Then one day they happened to see a copy of my first book, *Dare to Discipline*, on sale in a local bookstore. They bought the book and learned therein that it is appropriate to spank a child under certain well-defined circumstances. My recommendations made sense to these harassed parents, who promptly spanked their sassy daughter the next time she gave them reason to do so. But the little girl was just bright enough to figure out where they had picked up that new idea. When the mother awoke the next morning, she found her copy of *Dare to*

Discipline floating in the toilet! That darling little girl had done her best to send my writing to the sewer, where it belonged. I suppose that is the strongest editorial comment I've received on any of my literature!

This incident with the toddler was not an isolated case. Another child selected my book from an entire shelf of possibilities and threw it in the fireplace. I could easily become paranoid about these hostilities. Dr. Benjamin Spock is loved by millions of children who have grown up under his influence, but I am apparently resented by an entire generation of kids who would like to catch me in a blind alley on some cloudy night.

⁓ Two Toddlers ⁓

I remember boarding a commercial airliner a few years ago on a trip from Los Angeles to Toronto. No sooner had I become comfortable than a mother sat down two seats from me and promptly placed her three-year-old son between us. *Oh boy!* I thought. *I get to spend five hours strapped next to this little live wire.* I expected him to drive his mother and me crazy by the time we landed. If my son, Ryan, had been strapped in a chair at that age and given nothing to do, he would have dismantled the entire tail section of the plane by the time it landed. My father once said about Ryan, "If you allow that kid to become bored, you deserve what he will do to you."

To my surprise, the toddler next to me sat pleasantly for five long hours. He sang little songs. He played with the ashtray. For an hour or two he slept. But mostly, he engaged himself in thought. I kept expecting him to claw the air, but it never happened. His mother was not surprised. She acted as though all three-year-olds were able to sit for half a day with nothing interesting to do.

Contrast that uneventful episode with another flight I took a few months later. I boarded a plane, found my seat, and glanced to my left. Seated across from me this time was a well-dressed woman and a very ambitious two-year-old girl. Correction: The mother was seated, but her daughter was most definitely not. This little girl had no intention of sitting down—or slowing down. It was also obvious that the mother did not have control of the child, and indeed, Superman himself might have had difficulty harnessing her. The toddler shouted "No!" every few seconds as her mother tried to rein her in.

If Mom persisted, she would scream at the top of her lungs while kicking and lunging to escape. I looked at my watch and thought, *What is this poor woman going to do when she is required to buckle that kid in her seat?*

I could see that the mother was accustomed to losing these major confrontations with her daughter. Obviously, the child was used to winning. That arrangement might have achieved a tentative peace at home or in a restaurant, but this was different. They were faced with a situation on the plane where the mother couldn't give in. To have allowed the child to roam during takeoff would have been dangerous and impermissible under FAA regulations. Mom had to win—perhaps for the first time ever.

In a few minutes, the flight attendant came by and urged the mother to buckle the child down. Easy for her to say! I will never forget what occurred in the next few minutes. The two-year-old threw a tantrum that must have set some kind of international record for violence and expended energy. She was kicking, sobbing, screaming, and writhing for freedom! Twice she tore loose from her mom's arms and scurried toward the aisle. The mortified woman was literally begging her child to settle down and cooperate. Everyone in our section of the plane was embarrassed for the humiliated mother. Those of us within ten feet were also virtually deaf by that point.

Finally, the plane taxied down the runway and took off with the mother hanging on to this thrashing toddler with all her strength. Once we were airborne, she was able at last to release the little fireball. When the crisis was over, the mother covered her face with both hands and wept. I felt her pain, too.

Why didn't I help her? Because my advice would have offended the mother. The child desperately needed the security of strong parental leadership at that moment, but the woman had no idea how to provide it. A few sharp slaps on the legs would probably have taken some of the fire out of her. The affair could have ended with a sleeping child curled in her mother's loving arms. Instead, it set the stage for even more violent and costly confrontations in the years ahead.

It is interesting to speculate on how the mothers on these two airplanes probably felt about themselves and their very different toddlers. I would guess that the woman with the passive little boy was significantly overconfident. Raising kids for her was duck soup. "You tell 'em what to do and expect 'em to do it!" she could have said. Some mothers in her comfortable

32

situation hold unconcealed disdain for parents of rebellious children. They just can't understand why others find child rearing so difficult.

The mother of the second toddler, on the other hand, was almost certainly experiencing a great crisis of confidence. I could see it in her eyes. She wondered how she had managed to make such a mess of parenting in two short years! Somehow, she had taken a precious newborn baby and twisted her into a monster. But how did it happen? What did she do to cause such outrageous behavior? She may ask those questions for the rest of her life.

I wish she had known that at least part of the problem resided in the temperament of the child. It was her nature to grab for power, and the mother was making a serious mistake by granting it to her.

This is my point: Parents today are much too willing to blame themselves for everything their children (or adolescents) do.

∽ It's Hard to Let Go ∾

I'm convinced that mothers and fathers in North America are among the very best in the world. We care passionately about our kids and would do anything to meet their needs. But we are among the worst when it comes to letting go of our grown sons and daughters. In fact those two characteristics are linked. The same commitment that leads us to do so well when the children are small (dedication, love, concern, involvement) also causes us to hold on too tightly when they are growing up. I will admit to my own difficulties in this area. I understood the importance of turning loose before our kids were born. I wrote extensively on the subject when they were still young. I prepared a film series in which all the right principles were expressed. But when it came time to open my hand and let the birds fly, I struggled mightily!

Why? Well, fear played a role in my reluctance. We live in Los Angeles, where weird things are done by strange people every day of the year. For example, our daughter was held at gunpoint on the campus of the University of Southern California late one night. Her assailant admonished Danae not to move or make a noise. She figured her chances of survival were better by defying him right then than by cooperating. She fled. The man did not shoot at her, thank God. Who knows what he had in mind for her?

A few days later, my son was walking his bicycle across a busy road near our home when a man in a sports car came around the curve at high speed. Skid marks later showed he was traveling in excess of eighty miles per hour. Ryan saw that he was going to be hit, and he jumped over the handlebars and attempted to crawl to safety. The car was fishtailing wildly and careening toward our son. It came to a stop just inches from his head, and then the driver sped off without getting out. Perhaps he was on PCP or cocaine. Thousands of addicts live here in Los Angeles, and innocent people are victimized by them every day.

Such near misses make me want to gather my children around me and never let them experience risk again. Of course, that is impossible and would be unwise even if they submitted to it. Life itself is a risk, and parents must let their kids face reasonable jeopardy on their own. Nevertheless, when Danae or Ryan leave in the car, I'm still tempted to say, "Be sure to keep the shiny side up and the rubber side down!"

The Powerbroker

A child between eighteen and thirty-six months of age is a skilled power-broker. He or she loves to run things—and break things, squash things, flush things, and eat horrible things. Comedian Bill Cosby once said, "Give me two hundred active two-year-olds, and I could conquer the world." It's true. Toddlers, in their cute, charming way, can be terrors. They honestly believe the universe revolves around them, and they like it that way.

I remember a three-year-old who was sitting on the potty when a huge earthquake shook the city of Los Angeles. Dishes were crashing and furniture was skidding across the floor. The little boy hung on to his potty-chair and said to his mother, "What did I do, Mom?" It was a logical question from his point of view. If something important had happened, he must have been responsible for it.

No Peas for Me

Deeply ingrained in the human temperament is a self-will that rejects external authority. This spirit of rebellion manifests itself during the first year of life and dominates the personality during the second. The "terrible twos" can be summarized by this barbed question: "By what right do you or anyone else try to tell me what to do with my life!?" That same question will be bellowed during the adolescent years, along with sweet little comments such as, "I didn't ask to be born, you know!" Johnny Carson once said that if his teenager ever said that to him, he'd reply, "It's a good thing you didn't ask. I'd have said *no*."

My point is that human beings at all ages are inclined to test the limits of authority. At its most basic level, this resistance is an expression of mankind's spiritual rebellion against God. Anyone who doubts this stubborn nature need only observe the sheer power of a toddler's self-will. Have you ever seen an angry three-year-old hold his breath until he becomes unconscious? It happens. Consider the child whose mother wrote me the following note:

> My husband and I realized our two-year-old daughter was a strong-willed child the night she was introduced to green peas. Julie took one bite and then refused to swallow. But she also refused to spit out the peas, no matter what we tried to do. We attempted to pry open her jaws, then threatened to spank her. Finally, we pleaded with Julie to cooperate, but she wouldn't budge. There was nothing left to do but put her to bed. Twelve hours later she awoke bright and cheery with no peas in her mouth. We found them in a little pile down at the foot of her bed. Her father and I were very relieved that those green peas did not remain in her mouth all night long!

Could it be that a two-year-old girl is actually capable of outmaneuvering and outlasting the adults in her world? It certainly is. And if there is one blind spot in twentieth-century psychology, it is the failure to recognize this pugnacious human temperament and the importance of responding appropriately when willful defiance occurs.

But what is the appropriate action to take in moments of rebellion? I will permit a Certified Public Accountant, William Jarnagin, to answer that question. He wrote me the following letter, which speaks volumes about parent-child relationships.

Dear Dr. Dobson:

This is a note of thanks for your work in strengthening the American family. My wife and I have recently read four of your books, and we have profited very much from them.

35

Please permit me to relate a recent experience with our six-year-old son, David. Last Friday night, my wife, Becky, told him to pick up some orange peelings he had left on the carpet, which he knows is a "no-no." He failed to respond, and as a result received one slap on his behind, whereupon he began an obviously defiant temper tantrum.

Since I had observed the whole episode, I then called for my paddle and applied it appropriately, saw to it that he picked up and properly disposed of the orange peelings, and sent him straight to bed, since it was already past his bedtime. After a few minutes, when his emotions had had a chance to settle down, I went to his room and explained that God had instructed all parents who truly love their children to properly discipline them, etc., and that we truly love him and therefore would not permit such defiant behavior.

The next morning, after I had gone to work, David presented his mother with the following letter, together with a little stack of ten pennies:

From David and Deborah
To Mom and Dad

Ross Dr. 3d house
Sellmer, Tennasse
39718

Dear Mom and Dad

here is 10 Cints for
Pattelling me when I
really neded and that
gos for Deborah to
I love you

Love yur son David
and yur Doter Deborah

Oh, incidentally, Deborah is our one-year-old daughter whose adoption should be final sometime in June.

Keep up your good work and may God bless you.

Sincerely,
William H. Jarnagin

Mr. William Jarnagin understands the appropriate response of a father to a child's defiance. It is neither harsh nor insulting nor dangerous nor whimsical. Rather, it represents the firm but loving discipline that is required for the best interest of the child. How fortunate is the boy or girl whose father still comprehends that timeless concept.

The Brat Who Was Me

The mother and father of four-year-old Mark were concerned about his temper tantrums, especially since he habitually threw them when his parents least wanted him to misbehave. For example, when guests were visiting in their home, he would explode just before bedtime. The same outbursts occurred in restaurants, church services, and other public places.

Mark's parents were no strangers to discipline, and they tried every approach on their little rebel. They spanked him, stood him in the corner, sent him to bed early, and shamed and scolded him. Nothing worked. The temper tantrums continued regularly.

Then one evening Mark's parents were both reading the newspaper in their living room. They had said something that angered their son, and he fell on the floor in a rage. He screamed and whacked his head on the carpet, kicking and flailing his small arms. They were totally exasperated at that point and didn't know what to do, so they did nothing. They continued reading the paper in stony silence, which was the last thing the little tornado expected. He got up, looked at his father, and fell down for Act Two. Again his parents made no response. By this time, they were glancing at one another knowingly and watching junior with curiosity. Again, Mark's tantrum stopped abruptly. He approached his mother, shook her arm, then collapsed for Act Three. They continued ignoring him. His response? This child felt so silly flapping and crying on the floor that he never threw another tantrum.

Now it can be told: The illustration cited above was included in the first edition of *Dare to Discipline*, back in 1970. It is time now to reveal that Mark was not the real name of that child. It was Jim. Alas, *I* was the brat in the story. And I can tell you, it's no fun staging a performance if the crowd won't come!

It is clear that the reinforcement for my tantrums was parental manipulation. Through violent behavior, I had gotten those big, powerful adults upset and distraught. I must have loved it. With most children, tantrums are a form of challenging behavior that can be eliminated by one or more appropriate spankings. For a few like me, however, something else was going on. Like a pyromaniac, I enjoyed seeing how much commotion I could precipitate. That, in itself, was my reward.

⟋ Calling Robert's Bluff ⟍

In the absence of parental leadership, some children become extremely obnoxious and defiant, especially in public places. Perhaps the best example was a ten-year-old boy named Robert, who was a patient of my good friend Dr. William Slonecker. Dr. Slonecker and his pediatric staff dreaded the days when Robert was scheduled for an office visit. He literally attacked the clinic, grabbing instruments and files and telephones. His passive mother could do little more than shake her head in bewilderment.

During one physical examination, Dr. Slonecker observed severe cavities in Robert's teeth and knew that the boy must be referred to a local dentist. But who would be given the honor? A referral like Robert could mean the end of a professional friendship. Dr. Slonecker eventually decided to send him to an older dentist who reportedly understood children. The confrontation that followed now stands as one of the classic moments in the history of human conflict.

Robert arrived in the dental office, prepared for battle.

"Get in the chair, young man," said the doctor.

"No chance!" replied the boy.

"Son, I told you to climb onto the chair, and that's what I intend for you to do," said the dentist.

Robert stared at his opponent for a moment and then replied, "If you make me get in that chair, I will take off all my clothes."

The dentist calmly said, "Son, take 'em off."

The boy forthwith removed his shirt, undershirt, shoes and socks, and then looked up in defiance.

"All right, son," said the dentist. "Now get on the chair."

"You didn't hear me," sputtered Robert. "I said if you make me get on that chair, I will take off *all* my clothes."

"Son, take 'em off," replied the man.

Robert proceeded to remove his pants and shorts, finally standing totally naked before the dentist and his assistant.

"Now, son, get in the chair," said the doctor.

Robert did as he was told and sat cooperatively through the entire procedure. When the cavities were drilled and filled, he was instructed to step down from the chair.

"Give me my clothes now," said the boy.

"I'm sorry," replied the dentist. "Tell your mother that we're going to keep your clothes tonight. She can pick them up tomorrow."

Can you comprehend the shock Robert's mother received when the door to the waiting room opened, and there stood her pink son, as naked as the day he was born? The room was filled with patients, but Robert and his mom walked past them and into the hall. They went down a public elevator and into the parking lot, ignoring the snickers of onlookers.

The next day, Robert's mother returned to retrieve his clothes and asked to have a word with the dentist. However, she did not come to protest. These were her sentiments: "You don't know how much I appreciate what happened here yesterday. You see, Robert has been blackmailing me about his clothes for years. Whenever we are in a public place, such as a grocery store, he makes unreasonable demands of me. If I don't immediately buy him what he wants, he threatens to take off all his clothes. You are the first person who has called his bluff, Doctor, and the impact on Robert has been incredible!"

⤚ Magic Chalk ⤙

Several years after Danae was born, Shirley decided to substitute teach a few days a week to help us support my expenses in USC graduate school. The first thing she noticed when she went back to teaching was that it was much harder to control a class as a substitute than as a full-time teacher.

"Oh boy!" shouted the kids when they saw her coming. "We'll have fun today!"

Shirley and I sat down and discussed the struggles she was having with the children (grades two through five) she encountered each day. "Loving them isn't enough," she said. "I need some leverage to keep them in order."

We put our heads together and came up with a concept we called "Magic Chalk." This is how it worked. Shirley would get to the classroom early and draw a simple skull and crossbones on the left side of the chalkboard. Underneath were the words *POISON LIST*.

Beside the scary drawing she taped a single piece of paper. Then Shirley opened the doors and invited the students to come in. She did not, however, mention the skull as she pleasantly greeted her wide-eyed students. Within minutes, someone raised a hand to ask what everyone wanted to know: "What's that picture there on the board?"

"Oh yes," said Mrs. Dobson. "I meant to tell you about the Poison List."

"First," she said, "let me describe our class rules today." She told them they would need to raise their hands before talking, to stay in their seats until given permission to leave, and to ask for help if they needed paper or to sharpen a pencil, etc.

"Now, if you forget and break one of the rules, you will be asked to write your name on the board to the left of the poison symbol. Nothing will happen if you do. *But*, if you get your name on the board and then get two more marks by it—then—(she said with ominous overtones) . . . *then* your name goes on the Poison List." Shirley never quite told them what would happen to those unfortunate troops who made the big, bad list, but it *sounded* terrible. She hinted that it involved the principal, but she never explained how.

Then Shirley quickly walked over to her desk, where a brand-new piece of chalk sat in a cup on the edge of her desk.

"Does anyone know what this is?" she asked cheerfully.

"That's a piece of chalk," several said at once.

"Not so!" replied Mrs. Dobson. "It may look like ordinary chalk, but it is much more important than that. This is *Magic Chalk*. Believe it or not, this little white stick has the ability to hear. It has tiny little ears right there on the side. It can also see you. Tiny eyes appear right there on the end." (She had drawn them in.) "The Magic Chalk is going to sit here on the edge of my desk, watching you and listening to what you say. It is looking for someone in particular. The Magic Chalk is hoping to see a boy or girl who is working very hard and being very quiet. And if it finds a student like that, it will suddenly appear on that person's desk.

"If you are the one chosen by the Magic Chalk, you do not have to ask what to do. Just pick it up, walk to the board, and write your name over at the right side. Then for everyone chosen by the last class in the afternoon, you get a special treat." (Are you ready for this?) "You will be permitted to leave school three minutes early at the end of the day!"

Big deal? You bet it was. The three-minute factor was not so important in itself, but enjoying the status of being chosen by the Chalk, writing your name on the board for the entire world to see, and then walking out of class when others had to stay—it was a treasure. There was also the thrill of having the chalk show up on one's desk, while others were working on for the same goal.

The system worked like a charm because the kids loved it. In nearly two years of application every time Shirley was in the classroom, she usually managed to include most boys' and girls' names on the Magic Chalk list. But in all that time, she never once got a child's name on the Poison List.

⟳ Bedtime Battle ⟲

One of the earliest contests between parent and child begins at eighteen months and one day of age, give or take a few hours. At precisely that time, a toddler who has gone to bed without complaining since he was born will suddenly say, "I'm not getting back in that crib again for as long as I live." That is the opening salvo in what may be a five-year battle. It happens so quickly and unexpectedly that parents may be fooled by it. They will check for teething problems, a low-grade fever, or some other discomfort. "Why now?" they ask. I don't know. It just suddenly occurs to toddlers that they don't want to go to bed anymore, and they will fight it tooth and nail.

Although the tactics change a bit, bedtime will continue to be a battlefield for years to come. Any creative six-year-old can delay going to bed for at least forty-five minutes by an energetic and well-conceived system of stalling devices. By the time his mother gets his pajamas on, brings him six glasses of water, takes him to the bathroom twice, helps him say his prayers, and then scolds him for wandering out of his bedroom a time or two, she is thoroughly exhausted. It happens night after night.

A college friend of mine named Jim found himself going through this bedtime exercise every evening with his five-year-old son, Paulie. Jim recognized the tactics as a game and decided he didn't want to play anymore. He sat down with his son that evening and said, "Now, Paulie, things are going to be different tonight. I'm going to get you dressed for bed; you can have a drink of water and then we'll pray together. When that is done, I'm walking out the door, and I don't intend to come back. Don't call me again. I don't want to hear a peep from you until morning. Do you understand?"

Paulie said, "Yes, Daddy."

When the chores were completed, final hugs were exchanged and the lights were turned out. Jim told his son good night and left the room. Sweet silence prevailed in the house. But not for long. In about five minutes, Paulie called his father and asked for another drink of water.

"No way, Paulie," said his dad. "Don't you remember what I said? Now go to sleep."

After several minutes, Paulie appealed again for a glass of water. Jim was more irritated this time. He spoke sharply and advised his son to forget it. But the boy would not be put off. He waited for a few minutes and then reopened the case. Every time Paulie called his dad, Jim became more irritated. Finally, he said, "If you ask for water one more time I'm going to come in there and spank you!"

That quieted the boy for about five minutes, and then he said, "Daddy, when you come in here to spank me, would you bring me a glass of water please?"

The kid got the water. He did not get the spanking.

One of the ways of enticing children (perhaps ages four to eight) to go to bed is by the use of fantasy. For example, I told my son and daughter about "Mrs. White's Party" when they were little. Mrs. White was an imaginary lady who threw the most fantastic celebrations in the middle of the night. She ran an amusement park that made Disneyland boring by comparison. Whatever was of interest to the children was worked into her repertoire—dogs, cats, sweets of all varieties, water slides, cartoons, thrilling rides, and anything else that excited Danae's and Ryan's imaginations. Of course, the only way they could go to Mrs. White's Party was to be asleep. No one who was awake would ever get an invitation. It was fun to watch our son and daughter jump into bed and concentrate to go to sleep. Though it never happened, I wish I could have generated such interest that they would have actually dreamed about Mrs. White. Usually, the matter was forgotten the next morning.

By hook or crook, fantasy or reality, you must win the great bedtime battle. The health of your child (and maybe your own) is at stake.

⟶ You Can't Make Me ⟵

The Dobson household consists of a mother and father, a boy and a girl, one hamster, one parakeet, one lonely goldfish, and two hopelessly neurotic cats. We all live together in relative harmony with a minimum of conflict and strife. But there is another member of our "family" who is less congenial and cooperative. He is a stubborn twelve-pound dachshund named Sigmund Freud (Siggie), who honestly believes he owns the place. All dachshunds tend to be somewhat independent, I'm told, but Siggie is a confirmed revolutionary. He's not vicious or mean; he just wants to run things—and the two of us have been engaged in a power struggle for the past twelve years.

Siggie is not only stubborn, but he doesn't pull his own weight in the family. He won't bring in the newspaper on cold mornings, he refuses to "chase a ball" for the children, he doesn't keep the gophers out of the garden, and he can't do any of the usual tricks that most cultured dogs perform. Alas, Siggie has refused to participate in any of the self-improvement programs I have initiated on his behalf. He is content just to trot through life, watering and sniffing and stopping to smell the roses.

Furthermore, Sigmund is not even a good watchdog. This suspicion was confirmed the night we were visited by a prowler who had entered our backyard at 3:00 A.M. I suddenly awoke from a deep sleep, got out of bed, and felt my way through the house without turning on the lights. I knew someone was on the patio, and Siggie knew it, too, because the coward was crouched behind me! After listening to the thumping of my heart for a few minutes, I reached out to take hold of the rear doorknob. At that moment, the backyard gate quietly opened and closed. Someone had been standing three feet from me, and that "someone" was now tinkering in my garage. Siggie and I held a little conversation in the darkness and decided that he should be the one to investigate the disturbance. I opened the back door and told my dog to "attack!" But Siggie just *had* one! He stood there throbbing and shaking so badly that I couldn't even push him out the back door. In the noise and confusion that ensued, the intruder escaped (which pleased both dog *and* man).

Please don't misunderstand me; Siggie is a member of our family, and we love him dearly. And despite his anarchistic nature, I have finally taught him to obey a few simple commands. However, we had some classic battles before he reluctantly yielded to my authority. The greatest confrontation occurred a few years ago when I had been in Miami for a three-day conference. I returned to observe that Siggie had become boss of the house while I was gone. But I didn't realize until later that evening just how strongly he felt about his new position as Captain.

At eleven o'clock that night, I told Siggie to go get into his bed, which is a permanent enclosure in the family room. For six years I had given him that order at the end of each day, and for six years Siggie had obeyed. On that occasion, however, he refused to budge. You see, he was in the bathroom, seated comfortably on the furry lid of the toilet seat. That is his favorite spot in the house, because it allows him to bask in the warmth of a nearby electric heater. Incidentally, Siggie had to learn the hard way that it is extremely important that the lid be *down* before he leaves the ground. I'll never forget the night he learned that lesson. He came thundering in from the cold, sailed through the air—and nearly drowned before I could get him out.

When I told Sigmund to leave his warm seat and go to bed, he flattened his ears and slowly turned his head toward me. He deliberately braced himself by placing one paw on the edge of the furry lid then hunched his shoulders, raised his lips to reveal the molars on both sides, and uttered his most threatening growl. That was Siggie's way of saying, "Get lost!"

I had seen this defiant mood before and knew there was only one way to deal with it. The *only* way to make Siggie obey is to threaten him with destruction. Nothing else works. I turned and went to my closet and got a small belt to help me "reason" with Mr. Freud. My wife, who was watching this drama unfold, tells me that as soon as I left the room, Siggie jumped from his perch and looked down the hall to see where I had gone. Then he got behind her and growled.

When I returned, I held up the belt and again told my angry dog to go get into his bed. He stood his ground so I gave him a firm swat across the rear end, and he tried to bite the belt. I hit him again and he tried to bite *me*. What developed next is impossible to describe. That tiny dog and I had the most vicious fight ever staged between man and beast. I fought him up one wall and down the other, with both of us scratching and clawing and growling and swinging the belt. I am embarrassed by the memory of the entire scene. Inch by inch I moved him toward the family room and his bed. As a final desperate maneuver, Siggie jumped up on the couch and backed into the corner for one last snarling stand. I eventually got him to bed, but only because I outweighed him 190 pounds to 12!

The following night I expected another siege of combat at Siggie's bedtime. To my surprise, however, he accepted my command without debate or complaint, and simply trotted toward the family room in perfect submission. In fact, that fight occurred more than four years ago, and from that time to this, Siggie has never made another "go for broke" stand.

It is clear to me now that Siggie was saying in his canine way, "I don't think you're tough enough to make me obey." Perhaps I seem to be humanizing the behavior of a dog, but I think not. Veterinarians will confirm that some breeds of dogs, notably dachshunds and shepherds, will not accept the leadership of their masters until human authority has stood the test of fire and proved itself worthy.

There is an important moral to my story that is highly relevant to the world of children. *Just as surely as a dog will occasionally challenge the authority of his leaders, a little child is inclined to do the same thing, only more so.* This is no minor observation, for it represents a characteristic of human nature that is rarely recognized (or admitted) by the "experts" who write books on the subject of discipline. I have yet to find a text for parents or teachers that acknowledges the struggle—the exhausting confrontation of wills—that most parents and teachers experience regularly with their children. Adult leadership is rarely accepted unchallenged by the next generation; it must be "tested" and found worthy of allegiance by the youngsters who are asked to yield and submit to its direction.

Today, Siggie is twelve years old and no longer has the fire of youthful exuberance. In fact, he has developed a progressive "heart leak" and will probably not live more than one more year. So he takes life easy these days, yawning and stretching and going back to sleep in the sun. (We have nicknamed him "Hal" because of his constant halitosis in these declining years.)

It is difficult to explain how a worthless old hound could be so loved by his family, but we're all going to miss little Siggie. (Dog lovers will understand our sentiment, but others will think it foolish.) He is a year older than our eldest child and has been her pal throughout childhood. So we have begun to prepare both children for his inevitable demise.

One day last month, the moment of crisis came without warning. I was brushing my teeth in the early morning when I heard Siggie's sharp cry. He can scream like a baby, and my wife rushed to his assistance.

"Jim, come quickly!" she said. "Siggie is having a heart attack!"

I joined her in the family room with toothbrush still in my hand. Siggie was lying just outside his bed, and he appeared to be in great pain. He was hunched down on his paws and his eyes were unfocused and glassy. I bent down and petted him gently and agreed that he was probably experiencing heart failure. I was not sure what to do for a dog in the midst of a coronary thrombosis, since the local paramedics are rather sensitive about offering their services to animals. I picked him up and laid him carefully on his bed, and he rolled on one side and remained completely motionless. His feet were held rigidly together, and it did, indeed, look as though the end had come.

I returned to my study to telephone the veterinarian, but Shirley again called me. She had taken a closer look at the immobile dog and discovered the nature of his problem. (Are you ready for this?) There are little claws or toenails on the sides of a dog's legs, and Siggie had somehow managed to get them hooked! This is why he couldn't move, and why he experienced pain when he tried to walk. There is not another dog anywhere in the world that could handcuff (pawcuff?) himself, but with Siggie, anything can happen. Shirley unhooked his toenails, and the senile dog celebrated his release by acting like a puppy again.

When I am an old man and I think back on the joys of parenthood—the Christmas seasons and the camping trips and the high-pitched voices of two bubbly children in our home—I will remember a stubborn little dachshund named Sigmund Freud who played such an important role throughout those happy days.

CHAPTER THREE

Raising Children

Throughout the Scriptures, it is quite clear that raising children was viewed as a wonderful blessing from God—a welcome, joyful experience. And today, it remains one of the greatest privileges in living to bring a baby into the world . . . a vulnerable little human being who looks to us for all his needs. What a wonderful opportunity it is to teach these little ones to love God with all their hearts and to serve their fellowman throughout their lives. There is no higher calling than that!

Our sons and daughters grow so quickly, and then the days at home together become a distant memory. That's why we have to make the most of every moment as we are raising children.

～ Museum of Memories ～

I was walking toward my car outside a shopping center a few weeks ago when I heard a loud and impassioned howl.

"Auggghh!" groaned the masculine voice.

I spotted a man about fifty feet away who was in great distress (and for a very good reason). His fingers were caught in the jamb of a car door that had obviously been slammed unexpectedly. Then the rest of the story unfolded. Crouching in the front seat was an impish little three-year-old boy who had apparently decided to "close the door on Dad."

The father was pointing frantically at his fingers with his free hand and saying, "Oh! Oh! Open the door, Chuckie! They're caught . . . hurry . . . Chuckie . . . please . . . open . . . OPEN!"

Chuckie finally got the message and unlocked the door, releasing Dad's blue fingers. The father then hopped and jumped around the aisle of the parking lot, alternately kissing and caressing his battered hand. Chuckie sat unmoved in the front seat of their car, waiting for Pop to settle down.

I know this incident was painful to the man who experienced it, but I must admit that it struck me funny. I suppose his plight symbolized the enormous cost of parenthood. And yes, Virginia, it is expensive to raise boys and girls today. Parents give the best they have to their children, who often respond by "slamming the door on their fingers"—especially during the unappreciative adolescent years. Perhaps that is why someone quipped, "Insanity is an inherited disease. You get it from your kids."

But there are other things that we get from our kids, including love and meaning and purpose and an opportunity to give. They also help us maintain our sense of humor, which is essential to emotional stability in these stressful days. I'm reminded of Anne Ortlund's eleven-year-old son Nels, whom she described in her book *Disciplines of a Beautiful Woman*. She had taken this rambunctious boy to their pediatrician for a routine physical examination. Before seeing the doctor, however, the nurse weighed and measured the child and attempted to obtain a medical history.

"Tell me, Mrs. Ortlund," said the nurse, "how is he sleeping?"

Nels answered on his own behalf, "I sleep very well." The nurse wrote that down.

"How's his appetite, Mrs. Ortlund?"

"I eat everything," said Nels. She wrote that down.

"Mrs. Ortlund, how are his bowels?"

The boy responded, "A, E, I, O, and U."

A family is literally a "museum of memories" to those who have been blessed by the presence of children. Although my kids are now grown, I can recall ten thousand episodes that are carefully preserved in my mind. The "videotapes" of their early years are among my most valued possessions: Even now, I see a six-year-old girl coming home from school. Her hair is disheveled, and one sock is down around her ankle. It is obvious that she's been spinning upside down on the playground bars. She asks for a glass of milk and sits down at the kitchen table, unaware of the tenderness and love that I feel for her at that moment. Then she runs out to play.

Another "tape" begins to roll. I see a four-year-old boy with a Band-Aid on his knee and breadcrumbs on his face. He approaches my chair and asks to sit on my lap.

"Sorry," I said. "Only one boy in the world can climb on me when he chooses."

"Whoizzat?" he replies.

"Oh, you wouldn't know him. He's a kid named Ryan."

"But my name is Ryan!"

"Yes, but the boy I'm talking about has blond hair and blue eyes."

"Don't you see my blond hair? And my eyes are blue."

"Yes, but many kids have those. The only boy who can get on my lap is my son . . . my only son . . . whom I love."

"Hey, that's me! I'm your son. My name is Ryan! And I'm coming up!"

That little game was played for seven years, and it still has meaning.

But I can hear my readers saying, "You're just a sentimentalist."

"You bet I am!" I reply. I'm not ashamed to admit that *people* matter to me, and I'm most vulnerable to those people within my own family. I've enjoyed every stage in the lives of our two kids and wished that they (and we) could remain young forever.

Not only have Shirley and I enjoyed the developmental years, but Danae and Ryan have apparently shared that appreciation. Our daughter, especially, has loved every aspect of childhood and has been most reluctant to leave it. Her phonograph records and her stuffed animals and her bedroom have been prized possessions since toddlerhood. Likewise, she sat on Santa's lap for four years after she knew he was a phony. But, alas, she turned thirteen years old and began hearing a new set of drums. About a year later, she went through her toys and records, stacking them neatly and leaving them in front of Ryan's bedroom door. On the top was a note that Shirley brought to me with tears in her eyes. I read:

Dear Ryan:
    These are yours now.
    Take good care of them like I have.

Love,
Danae

That brief message signaled the closing of the door called "childhood." And once it shut, no power on earth could open it again. That's why the toddler and elementary-school years should be seen as fleeting opportunities.

⟳ **Black Sunday** ⟲

Shirley and I experience the same frustrations and pressures that others face. Our behavior is not always exemplary, nor is that of our children. And our household can become very hectic at times.

Perhaps I can best illustrate by describing the day we now refer to as "Black Sunday." For some reason, the Sabbath can be the most frustrating day of the week for us, especially during the morning hours. I've found that other parents also experience tensions during the "get 'em ready for church" routine. But Black Sunday was especially chaotic. We began that day by getting up too late, meaning everyone had to rush to get to church on time. That produced emotional pressure, especially for Shirley and me. Then there was the matter of the spilt milk at breakfast, and the black shoe polish on the floor. And, of course, Ryan got dressed first, enabling him to slip out the back door and get himself dirty from head to toe. It was necessary to take him down to the skin and start over with clean clothes once more. Instead of handling these irritants as they arose, we began criticizing one another and hurling accusations back and forth. At least one spanking was delivered, as I recall, and another three or four were promised. Yes, it was a day to be remembered (or forgotten). Finally, four harried people managed to stumble into church, ready for a great spiritual blessing, no doubt. There's not a pastor in the world who could have moved us on that morning.

I felt guilty throughout the day for the strident tone of our home on that Black Sunday. Sure, our children shared the blame, but they were merely responding to our disorganization. Shirley and I had overslept, and that's where the conflict originated.

After the evening service, I called the family together around the kitchen table. I began by describing the kind of day we had had and asked each person to forgive me for my part in it. Furthermore, I said that I thought we should give each member of the family an opportunity to say whatever he or she was feeling inside.

Ryan was given the first shot, and he fired it at his mother.

"You've been a real grouch today, Mom!" he said with feeling. "You've blamed me for everything I've done all day long."

Shirley then explained why she had been unhappy with her son, trying not to be defensive about his charges.

Danae then poured out her hostilities and frustrations. Finally, Shirley and I had an opportunity to explain the tensions that had caused our over-reaction.

It was a valuable time of ventilation and honesty that drew us together once more. We then had prayer as a family and asked the Lord to help us live and work together in love and harmony.

⟶ The Terrible Twos ⟵

Perhaps the most frustrating aspect of the "terrible twos" is the tendency of kids to spill things, destroy things, eat horrible things, fall off things, flush things, kill things, and get into things. They also have a knack for doing embarrassing things, like sneezing on a nearby man at a lunch counter. During these toddler years, any unexplained silence of more than thirty seconds can throw an adult into a sudden state of panic. What mother has not had the thrill of opening the bedroom door, only to find Tony Tornado covered with lipstick from the top of his pink head to the carpet on which he stands? On the wall is his own artistic creation with a red handprint in the center, and throughout the room is the aroma of Chanel No. 5 with which he has anointed his baby brother. Wouldn't it be interesting to hold a national convention sometime, bringing together all the mothers who have experienced that exact trauma?

When my daughter was two years of age, she was fascinated the first time she watched me shave in the morning. She stood captivated as I soaped my face and began using the razor. That should have been my first clue that something was up. The following morning, Shirley came into the bathroom to find our dachshund, Siggie, sitting in his favorite spot on the furry lid of the toilet seat. Danae had covered his head with lather and was systematically shaving the hair from his shiny skull! Shirley screamed, "Danae!" which sent Siggie and his barber scurrying for safety. It was a strange sight to see the frightened dog with nothing but ears sticking up on the top of his bald head.

When Ryan was the same age, he had an incredible ability to make messes. He could turn it over or spill it faster than any kid I've ever seen, especially at mealtime. (Once while eating a peanut butter sandwich he thrust his hand through the bottom side. When his fingers emerged at the top they were covered with peanut butter, and Ryan didn't recognize them. The poor lad nearly bit off his index finger.) Because of his destructive inclination, Ryan heard the word *mess* used repeatedly by his parents. It became one of the most important words in his vocabulary. One evening while taking a shower I left the door ajar and got some water on the floor. And as you might expect, Ryan came thumping around the corner and stepped in it. He looked up at me and said in the gruffest voice he could manage, "Whuss all this mess in hyere?"

⤙ Rivals for Love ⤚

My son arrived on the scene when his sister was five years old. She had been the only granddaughter on either side of the family and had received all the adult attention that can be heaped upon a child. Suddenly, her secure kingdom was invaded by a cute little fellow who captured and held center stage. All of the relatives cuddled, cooed, rocked, bounced, and hugged baby Ryan, while Danae watched suspiciously from the wings. As we drove home from Grandmother's house on a Sunday afternoon, about a week after Ryan's arrival, my daughter suddenly said, "Daddy, you know I'm just talking. You know I don't mean to be bad or anything. But sometimes I wish little Ryan wasn't here."

She had given us a valuable clue to her feelings in that brief sentence, and we immediately seized the opportunity she had provided. We moved her into the front seat of the car so we could discuss what she had said. We told her we understood how she felt and assured her of our love. We also explained that a baby is completely helpless and will die if people don't take care of him—feed, clothe, change, and love him. We reminded her that she was taken care of that way when she was a baby. Ryan would soon grow up, too. We were also careful in the months that followed to minimize the threat to her place in our hearts. By giving careful attention to her feelings and security, the relationship with her brother developed into a lasting friendship and love.

⟶ Sometimes the Best Answer Is "No" ⟵

My father had suffered a massive heart attack, which placed his future in jeopardy. As he contemplated his own passing, he became even more fascinated with life. Everything in God's creation interested him, from science to the arts. He even developed a personal knowledge of and friendship with the birds that gathered around his house. He named them all and had many eating out of his hand. That is what led to . . . the starling incident.

For some reason, a mother bird abandoned her four baby starlings before they were able to fend for themselves. That precipitated an intense effort in the Dobson household to save the starlings by all means possible. Admittedly, they belonged to a despised, disease-ridden species, but my father was a sucker for *anything* in real need. Thus, a rescue effort was launched. A couple of weeks later, I received the following letter from my mother, describing what had happened to their feathered little friends.

Dear Family:

If I could write like you, Jim, I'd make the last eleven days come alive as your dad and I lived them in a bird world. As you know, the four surviving starlings, Eenie, Meenie, Minie, and Moe, were evicted from their "under the shingle" nest, and we adopted them. Their feathers were down like fuzz, and their bodies seemed to consist of legs, wings, and mouths. They chirped constantly to be fed, after which their cries settled into a lovely lullaby. They outgrew their first cozy nest, and your dad transferred them to a larger box from which they could not escape. So the only exposure they had to the outside world was the 2' x 3' area above their heads. They seemed to know this opening was where the action was, so they huddled together with their heads turned upward, tweet-tweeting their little tunes. When your dad peered over the top with our dog, Benji, all four birds would open their yellow beaks—chirping, "Worms! Worms!"

As the foursome grew, they sat on a tree limb where your dad placed them. Sometimes jumping to the ground, they followed him around the yard, cuddling his shoes and not letting him get more than a few inches away. Their jerky movements made it impossible to keep pace.

From the beginning, we were unsure what we should feed them. Your dad gave them soft bread and milk—dipping it with tweezers into their wide-open beaks . . . along with worms, grain, and a few drops of water from an eyedropper. However, on the ninth morning, Jimmy found Moe dead. What to do? The tenth afternoon Meenie died. The eleventh night he looked down at the two remaining birds. Even while he looked at them, Minie gave a long "chirp," lay down, stretched out his legs, and died. That left Eenie, the strongest of the birds . . . the one with the most vitality and personality. This morning, however, his vocalizations were desperate and weaker. He only lived until noon. As Jimmy bent over the box nest, Eenie recognized his presence, reached toward him and gave one last "cheep," and was gone.

How sad we both were—that we somehow had failed the helpless creatures who tried so hard to live and fly in the beautiful sky. Your father's love for those insignificant birds and his sadness over their loss reveal the soul of the man I married and have lived with for forty-three years. Does anybody wonder why I love this man?

Your mother

The man who was so loved by my mother was not long for this world. He died a month later while sitting at the dinner table. His last act before falling into her arms was to express a prayer of blessing on the meal he would not live to eat.

And the starlings? The best explanation for their failure to thrive is that my dad overfed them. He was fooled by their constant plea for food. In an effort to satisfy their need, my father actually killed the birds he sought so desperately to save.

Does the point come through? We parents, too, in our great love for our children, can do irreparable harm by yielding to their pleas for more and more things. There are times when the very best reply we can offer is . . . no.

⤳ Sleeping in the Dark ⤳

I once consulted with a mother who was very concerned about her three-year-old daughter's fear of the dark. Despite the use of a night-light and leaving the bedroom door open, little Marla was afraid to stay in her room alone. She insisted that her mother sit with her until she went to sleep each evening, which was extremely time-consuming and inconvenient. If Marla happened to awaken in the night, she would call for help. It was apparent that she was genuinely frightened.

Fears such as these are not innate; they have been learned. If parents truly realized this, they would be more careful about what they say and how they act. The fact is, youngsters are amazingly perceptive and often adopt the behaviors and concerns they see in adults. Even good-natured teasing can produce problems for a child. If a youngster walks into a dark room and is pounced upon from behind the door, he quickly learns that the dark is not always empty!

In Marla's case, it was unclear where she learned to fear the dark, but I believe her mother inadvertently magnified the problem. In her concern for her daughter, she conveyed anxiety, and Marla began to think her own fears must be justified. "Even Mother is worried about it," she undoubtedly reasoned. Marla became so frightened that she could not walk through a dimly lit room without an escort. It was at this point she was referred to me.

Since it is usually unfruitful to try to talk children out of their fears, I suggested that the mother *show* Marla there was nothing to be afraid of. That would help the child perceive her mother as being confident and unthreatened. So she bought a bag of candy (okay, okay . . . I would use pieces of the popular rolled-up fruit today) and placed her chair just outside Marla's bedroom door. Marla was then offered a piece of candy if she would spend a few seconds in her bedroom with the light on and the door shut. This first step was not very threatening, and Marla enjoyed the game. It was repeated several times, and then she was asked to walk several feet into the darkened room while her mother, clearly visible in the hall, counted to ten. This was also easy, and Marla continued playing along for the bits of candy.

On subsequent trips, the door was shut a few inches more and the lights were lowered. Finally, Marla had the courage to enter the dark room and shut the door while her mother counted to three—then five—then eight.

The time in the dark was gradually lengthened, and instead of producing fear, it produced candy—ultimate pleasure to a small child. She also heard her mother talking confidently and quietly and knew she could come out whenever she wished. Through these means, courage was reinforced and fear extinguished.

∽ Waiting for Mr. Walker to Explode ∽

When I was a child, I once spent the night with a rambunctious friend who seemed to know every move his parents were going to make. Earl was like a military general who had deciphered the enemy code, permitting him to outmaneuver his opponents at every turn. After we were tucked into our own twin beds that night, he gave me an astounding description of his father's temper.

Earl said, "When my dad gets very angry, he uses some really bad words that will amaze you." (He listed three or four startling examples from past experience.)

I replied, "I don't believe it!"

Mr. Walker was a very tall, reserved man who seemed to have it all together. I just couldn't conceive of his saying the words Earl had quoted.

"Want me to prove it to you?" said Earl mischievously. "All we have to do is keep on laughing and talking instead of going to sleep. My dad will come and tell us to be quiet over and over, and he'll get madder and madder every time he has to settle us down. Then you'll hear his cuss words. Just wait and see."

I was a bit dubious about this plan, but I did want to see the dignified Mr. Walker at his profane best. So Earl and I kept his poor father running back and forth like a yo-yo for over an hour. And as predicted, he became more intense and hostile each time he returned to our bedroom. I was getting very nervous and would have called off the demonstration, but Earl had been through it all before. He kept telling me, "It won't be long now."

Finally, about midnight, it happened. Mr. Walker's patience expired. He came thundering down the hall toward our room, shaking the entire house as his feet pounded the floor. He burst through the bedroom door and leaped on Earl's bed, flailing at the boy who was safely buried beneath three or four layers of blankets. Then from his lips came a stream of words that had seldom reached my tender ears. I was shocked, but Earl was delighted.

Even while his father was whacking the covers with his hand and screaming his profanity, Earl rose up and shouted to me, "Didja hear 'em? Huh? Didn't I tell ya? I tolja he would say it!" It's a wonder Mr. Walker didn't kill his son at that moment!

I lay awake that night thinking about the episode and made up my mind *never* to let a child manipulate me like that when I grew up. Don't you see how important disciplinary techniques are to a child's respect for his parents? When a forty-five-pound bundle of trouble can deliberately reduce his powerful mother or father to a trembling, snarling mass of frustrations, then something changes in their relationship. Something precious is lost. The child develops an attitude of contempt that is certain to erupt during the stormy adolescent years to come. I sincerely wish every adult understood that simple characteristic of human nature.

∽ Checkpoints ∽

Our daughter, Danae, was compulsive about her room. She would not leave for school each day unless her bed was made perfectly and everything was in its proper place. This was not something we taught her; she has always been very meticulous about her possessions. (I should add that her brother, Ryan, does not have that problem.) Danae could easily finish these tasks on time if she were motivated to do so, but she was never in a particular hurry. Therefore, my wife began to fall into the habit of warning, threatening, pushing, goading, and ultimately becoming angry as the clock moved toward the deadline.

Shirley and I discussed the problem and agreed that there had to be a better method of getting through the morning. I subsequently created a system that we called "Checkpoints." It worked like this. Danae was instructed to be out of bed and standing erect before 6:30 each morning. It was her responsibility to set her own clock radio and get herself out of bed. If she succeeded in getting up on time (even one minute later was considered a missed item), she immediately went to the kitchen where a chart was taped to the refrigerator door. She then circled "yes" or "no," with regard to the first checkpoint for that date. It couldn't be more simple. She either did or did not get up by 6:30.

The second checkpoint occurred forty minutes later, at 7:10. By that time, she was required to have her room straightened to her own satisfaction, be dressed and have her teeth brushed, hair combed, etc., and be ready to begin practicing the piano. Forty minutes was ample time for these tasks, which could actually be done in ten or fifteen minutes if she wanted to hurry. Thus, the only way she could miss the second checkpoint was to ignore it deliberately.

Now, what meaning did the checkpoints have? Did failure to meet them bring anger and wrath and gnashing of teeth? Of course not. The consequences were straightforward and fair. If Danae missed one checkpoint, she was required to go to bed thirty minutes earlier than usual that evening. If she missed two, she hit the "lily whites" an hour before her assigned hour. She was permitted to read during that time in bed, but she could not watch television or talk on the telephone. This procedure took all the morning pressure off Shirley and placed it on our daughter's shoulders, where it belonged. There were occasions when my wife got up just in time to fix breakfast, only to find Danae sitting soberly at the piano, clothed and in her right mind.

∽ The Late Bloomer ∼

Donald is five years old and will soon go to kindergarten. He is an immature little fellow who is still his mama's baby in many ways. Compared to his friends, Donald's language is childish, and he lacks physical coordination. He cries three or four times a day, and other children take advantage of his innocence. A developmental psychologist or a pediatrician would verify that Donald is neither physically ill nor mentally retarded; he is merely progressing on a slower physiological timetable than most children his age.

Nevertheless, Donald's fifth birthday has arrived, and everyone knows that five-year-olds go to kindergarten. He is looking forward to school, but deep inside he is rather tense about this new challenge. He knows his mother is anxious for him to do well in school, although he doesn't really know why. His father has told him he will be a "failure" if he doesn't get a good education.

He's not certain what a failure is, but he sure doesn't want to be one. Mom and Dad are expecting something outstanding from him, and he hopes he won't disappoint them. His sister Pamela is in the second grade now; she is doing well. She can read and print her letters, and she knows the names of every day in the week. Donald hopes he will learn those things, too.

Kindergarten proves to be tranquil for Donald. He rides the tricycle and pulls the wagon and plays with the toy clock. He prefers to play alone for long periods of time, provided his teacher, Miss Moss, is nearby. It is clear to Miss Moss that Donald is immature and unready for the first grade, and she talks to his parents about the possibility of delaying him for a year.

"Flunk kindergarten?" says his father. "How can the kid flunk kindergarten? How can anybody flunk kindergarten?"

Miss Moss tries to explain that Donald has not failed kindergarten; he merely needs another year to develop before entering the first grade. The suggestion sends his father into a glandular upheaval.

"The kid is six years old; he should be learning to read and write. What good is it doing him to drag around that dumb wagon and ride on a stupid tricycle? Get the kid in the first grade!"

Miss Moss and her principal reluctantly comply. The following September, Donald clutches his Mickey Mouse lunchpail and walks on wobbly legs to the first grade. From day one he has academic trouble, and reading seems to be his biggest source of difficulty. His new teacher, Miss Fudge, introduces the alphabet to her class, and Donald realizes that most of his friends have already learned it. He has a little catching up to do. But too quickly Miss Fudge begins teaching something new. She wants the class to learn the sounds each letter represents, and soon he is even further behind.

Before long, the class begins to read stories about interesting things. Some children can zing right along, but Donald is still working on the alphabet. Miss Fudge divides the class into three reading groups according to their initial skill. She wants to conceal the fact that one group is doing more poorly than the others, so she gives them the camouflage names of "Lions," "Tigers," and "Giraffes." Miss Fudge's motive is noble, but she fools no one. It takes students about two minutes to realize that the Giraffes are all stupid! Donald begins to worry about his lack of progress, and the gnawing thought looms that there may be something drastically wrong with him.

During the first parent-teacher conference in October, Miss Fudge tells Donald's parents about his problems in school. She describes his immaturity and his inability to concentrate or sit still in the classroom. He's out of his seat most of the day.

"Nonsense," says his father. "What the kid needs is a little drill." He insists that Donald bring home his books, allowing father and son to sit down for an extended academic exercise. But everything Donald does irritates his father. His childish mind wanders, and he forgets the things he was told five minutes before. As his father's tension mounts, Donald's productivity descends. At one point, Donald's father crashes his hand down on the table and bellows, "Would you just pay attention and quit being so STUPID!" The child will never forget that knifing assessment.

Whereas Donald struggled vainly to learn during his early days in school, by November he has become disinterested and unmotivated. He looks out the window. He draws and doodles with his pencil. He whispers and plays. Since he can't read, he can neither spell, write, nor do his social studies. He is uninvolved and bored, not knowing what is going on most of the time. He feels weird and inadequate.

"Please stand, Donald, and read the next paragraph," says his teacher. He stands and shifts his weight from foot to foot as he struggles to identify the first word. The girls snicker, and he hears one of the boys say, "What a dummy!" The problem began as a developmental lag but has now become an emotional time bomb and a growing hatred for school.

The tragedy is that Donald need not have suffered the humiliation of academic failure. One more year of growing and maturing would have prepared him to cope with the educational responsibilities that are now destroying him. A child's age is the *worst* possible criterion on which to determine the beginning of his school career. Six-year-old children vary tremendously in their degree of maturity. Some are precocious and wise, while others are mere babies like Donald. Furthermore, the development of boys tends to be about six months behind the girls at this age. As can be seen, a slow-maturing boy who turns six right before school starts is miles behind most of his peers. This immaturity has profound social and intellectual implications.

Beauty and the Baby

When my daughter was fifteen months of age, her physical features seemingly appealed to adults. Her mother dressed her attractively. Considerable warmth and affection were shown to Danae wherever she went. People would hold her in their arms, tease her, and give her candy. The attention she received is typically given to any child who is thought to be cute or attractive. It is neither sought nor earned; it is given spontaneously by the adult world. However, three months after her first birthday, Danae rearranged her features for the worse.

I had driven home from the hospital at the end of a workday and was met by my wife in the driveway. She was holding our little girl in her arms, and they were both splattered with blood. My wife quickly told me the painful details: Danae was learning to run, and her mother was playfully chasing her through the house. Suddenly the little toddler darted to the left, losing her balance. She fell into the sharp edge of a table in the living room, catching her front tooth squarely as she went down. The tooth had been driven completely into her gums, appearing to be knocked out. The inside of her lip was slashed, and she looked terrible.

My daughter's permanent tooth was not due for six years, but it could also be damaged. Fortunately, however, that baby tooth refused to die. It gradually returned to its proper place, and the wound healed with no long-term damage. In fact, that same incisor made three more unscheduled trips into the gums before giving up the ghost four years later. It demonstrated uncanny courage in hanging on, despite the whacks and bumps it absorbed. By the time it finally turned loose, Danae considered her toothlessness to be a valuable status symbol in the neighborhood. At the time of the first accident, however, the situation appeared very discouraging.

Danae's head-on collision with the table temporarily distorted the shape of her mouth. Since the cut was on the inner part of her lip, she appeared to have been born that way. All the babyish appeal was now gone. The next evening I took her with me to a store, where I noted that people were responding differently to her. They would look at her and then turn away. Instead of the warmth, love, and tenderness previously offered to her, rejection and coolness were unconsciously demonstrated. People were not trying to be mean; they simply did not find her attractive any longer. I was irritated by the reaction because it revealed the injustice in our value system. How unfair, it seemed, to reward a child for something that had not been earned or to destroy another child for circumstances beyond control. Yet a child who is attractively arranged usually profits from the moment of birth on.

⌐ Number-One Tennis Player ⌐

My dad decided when I was eight years old that he was going to teach me to play tennis. I was not at all enthusiastic about his offer. My dad didn't mess around when he decided to teach me something. I knew it meant drill and sweat and blisters. I would rather have played cowboys with my friends in the neighborhood. But my dad wanted me to play tennis, and I respected him too much to turn him down. So we spent several agonizing Saturdays on the court. He would hit me a ball, and I'd whack it over the fence and then have to go get it. I couldn't have been less motivated, but I tried to act involved. "You think I'm getting it, Dad?" I asked as another ball flew straight up.

About a month later, however, things began to click. I started to feel good when I hit the ball correctly. One afternoon a fellow my age came up and asked if I'd play him a game. Well, I'd never thought about it, but I didn't see why not. So we played a set of tennis—and I beat him—and I liked that. I slowly began to realize what this game had to offer me. A spark of enthusiasm turned into a source of self-confidence. If asked to write, "Who am I?" during the trials of adolescence, I would have begun, "I am the number-one tennis player in the high school." If my dad had not planted his thumb in my back, urging me to try something new, I'd have never known what I missed. I am thankful that he helped me compensate. Have you done as much for your child?

⌐ Lessons of Life ⌐

When my daughter was five years old, she was given a baby hamster for Christmas. Being an incurable animal lover, she became extremely fond of the furry little creature. I noticed at once, however, that she lacked the responsibility to take care of the pet properly. Repeatedly I warned her to keep the door closed on its cage and to provide enough food and water for its survival. Despite my intervention, I returned home one day to find my daughter exhausted and red-eyed from crying. Sure enough, she had left the cage door open, and our world-famous dachshund, Siggie (Sigmund Freud), had sent the hamster on to its untimely reward. When my daughter found its stiff, bloody little body near its cage, she was brokenhearted.

What, then, was to be my response? I had told her repeatedly to care for the hamster, but she had failed to do so. Nevertheless, it would have been wrong for me to lash out at her for this mistake. Instead, I took her in my arms and held her until she stopped crying. Then I talked softly to her in these terms: "Danae, you know that I told you what would happen if you didn't take care of your hamster. But you were thinking about something else, and now he's dead. I'm not mad at you, because you haven't done anything mean. You have just behaved like a child. However, I want you to understand something. I warned you about taking care of your hamster because I didn't want to see you get hurt. It was to keep you from feeling like you do today that made me urge you to do the job properly. Now, there will be many other times when I will warn you and teach you and urge you to do something, and I'll also be doing that to keep you from being hurt by life. It is very important for you to see me as your friend, and when I tell you to do something, it is because I love you and can see dangers that you don't see. If you'll learn to listen to what I say, you'll have fewer times like today when you are so sad."

My response to Danae's behavior was dictated by her intention. She did not deliberately defy me, and she deserved no punishment. Likewise, every parent should know individual personalities well enough to make an instantaneous appraisal of this important factor, acting accordingly.

～ The Power of a Praying Mother ～

Shirley and I prayed this prayer for our son and daughter throughout their developmental years: "Be there, Father, in the moment of decision when two paths present themselves to our children. Especially during that time when they are beyond our direct influence, send others who will help them do what is righteous and just."

I believe God honors and answers that kind of intercessory prayer. I learned that from my grandmother, who seemed to live in the presence of God. She had prayed for her six children throughout their formative years, but her youngest son (my father) was a particularly headstrong young man. For seven years following his high-school graduation, he had left the church and rejected its teachings. Then, as it happened, an evangelist came to town and a great spiritual awakening swept their local church. But my father would have no part of it and refused even to attend.

One evening as the rest of the family was preparing to go to church, my father (who was visiting his parents' home) slipped away and hid on the side porch. He could hear his brothers chatting as they boarded the car. Then one of them, Willis, said suddenly, "Hey, where's Jim? Isn't he going tonight?"

Someone else said, "No, Willis. He said he isn't ever going to church again."

My father heard his brother get out of the car and begin searching for him all over the house. Willis had experienced a personal relationship with Jesus Christ when he was nine years old, and he loved the Lord passionately. He had held tightly to his faith throughout adolescence when his brothers (including my father) mocked him unmercifully. They had called him "Preacher Boy," "Sissy," and "Goody-Goody." It only made him more determined to do what was right.

My dad remained silent as Willis hurried through the house calling his name. Finally, he found my father sitting silently in the swing on the side porch.

"Jim," he said, "aren't you going with us to the service tonight?"

My dad said, "No, Willis. I'm through with all of that. I don't plan to ever go back again."

Willis said nothing. But as my father sat looking at the floor, he saw big tears splashing on his brother's shoes. My father was deeply moved that Willis would love him that much, after the abuse he had taken for his Christian stand.

I'll go just because it means that much to him, my dad said to himself.

Because of the delay my father had caused, the family was late arriving at the church that night. The only seats left were on the second row from the front. They streamed down the aisle and were seated. A song evangelist was singing, and the words began to speak to my dad's heart. Just that quickly, he yielded. After seven years of rebellion and sin, it was over. He was forgiven. He was clean.

The evangelist at that time was a man named Bona Fleming, who was unusually anointed of God. When the singer concluded, Reverend Fleming walked across the platform and put his foot on the altar rail. He leaned forward and pointed his finger directly at my dad.

"You! Young man! Right there! Stand up!"

My father rose to his feet.

"Now, I want you to tell all these people what God did for you while the singer was singing!"

My dad gave his first testimony, through his tears, of the forgiveness and salvation he had just received. Willis was crying, too. So was my grandmother. She had prayed for him unceasingly for more than seven years.

To the day of his death at sixty-six years of age, my father never wavered from that decision. His only passion was to serve the God with whom he fell in love during a simple hymn. But where would he have been if Willis had not gone to look for him? How different life would have been for him . . . and for me. God answered the prayers of my grandmother by putting a key person at the critical crossroads.

He will do as much for your children, too, if you keep them in your prayers. But until that moment comes, pray for them in confidence—not in regret. The past is the past. You can't undo your mistakes. You could no more be a perfect parent than you could be a perfect human being. Let your guilt do the work God intended and then file it away forever. I'll bet Solomon would agree with that advice.

⤳ Success Where It Matters ⤳

It occurred first in 1969, when *Dare to Discipline* was being written. I was running at an incredible speed, working myself to death like every other man I knew. I was superintendent of youth for my church and labored under a heavy speaking schedule. Eight or ten "unofficial" responsibilities were added to my full-time commitment at USC School of Medicine and Children's Hospital of Los Angeles. I once worked seventeen nights straight without being home in the evening. Our five-year-old daughter would stand in the doorway and cry as I left in the morning, knowing she might not see me until the next sunrise.

Although my activities were bringing me professional advancement and the trappings of financial success, my dad was not impressed. He had observed my hectic lifestyle and felt obligated to express his concern. While flying from Los Angeles to Hawaii one summer, he used that quiet opportunity to write me a lengthy letter. It was to have a sweeping influence on my life. Let me quote one paragraph from his message that was especially poignant:

Danae [referring to our daughter] is growing up in the wickedest section of a world much farther gone into moral decline than the world into which you were born. I have observed that the greatest delusion is to suppose that our children will be devout Christians simply because their parents have been, or that any of them will enter into the Christian faith in any other way than through their parents' deep travail of prayer and faith. But this prayer demands time, time that cannot be given if it is all signed and conscripted and laid on the altar of career ambition. Failure for you at this point would make mere success in your occupation a very pale and washed-out affair, indeed.

Those words, written without accusation or insult, hit me like the blow from a hammer.

Having been confronted with these spiritual obligations and responsibilities, the Lord then gave me an enormous burden for my two children. I carry it to this day. There are times when it becomes so heavy that I ask God to remove it from my shoulders, although the concern is not motivated by the usual problems or anxieties. Our kids are apparently healthy and seem to be holding their own emotionally and academically. (Update: Danae finished college in 1990 and Ryan was entering his junior year at the time of the revision.) The source of my burden derives from the awareness that a "tug of war" is being waged for the hearts and minds of every child on earth, including these two precious human beings. Satan would deceive and destroy them if given the opportunity, and they will soon have to choose the path they will take.

The urgency of this mission has taken Shirley and me to our knees since before the birth of our first child. Furthermore, from October 1971 until early 1978, I designated one day a week for fasting and prayer specifically devoted to the spiritual welfare of our children. (Shirley then accepted the responsibility and continues it to this day.) This commitment springs from an intense awareness of our need for divine assistance in the awesome task of parenthood. There is not enough knowledge in the books—not enough human wisdom anywhere on earth—to guarantee the outcome of parenting. There are too many factors beyond our control—too many evil influences—

that mitigate against the Christian message. That is why we find ourselves in prayer, week after week, uttering this familiar petition:

Lord, here we are again. You know what we need even before we ask, but let us say it one more time. When You consider the many requests we have made of You through the years . . . regarding our health and my ministry and the welfare of our loved ones . . . please put this supplication at the *top* of the list: Keep the circle of our little family unbroken when we stand before You on the Day of Judgment. Compensate for our mistakes and failures as parents, and counteract the influences of an evil world that would undermine the faith of our children. And especially, Lord, we ask for Your involvement when our son and daughter stand at the crossroads, deciding whether or not to walk the Christian path. They will be beyond our care at that moment, and we humbly ask You to *be there*. Send a significant friend or leader to help them choose the right direction. They were Yours before they were born, and now we give them back to You in faith, knowing that You love them even more than we do. Toward that end, we dedicate this day of fasting and prayer.

Not only has God heard this prayer, but He has blessed it in ways that we did not anticipate in the beginning. First, it has represented a project that Shirley and I have enjoyed *together*, drawing us closer to one another as we drew closer to God. Second, this act of fasting each week serves to remind us continually of our system of priorities. It is very difficult to forget your highest values when one day out of seven is spent concentrating on them. Finally, and most important, the children have seen this act of discipline every Tuesday and have been influenced by it. Conversations similar to the one below occurred throughout the critical years of childhood:

"Why are you not eating dinner with us tonight, Dad?"

"This is Tuesday, and I'm fasting today."

"Oh, yeah—what did you say 'fasting' meant?"

"Well, some Christians go without food during a short time of special prayer. It's a way of asking God for a blessing, or of expressing love to Him."

"What are you asking for?"

"Your mother and I are praying for you and your brother today. We're asking God to lead and direct your lives; we want Him to help you choose a profession and to find the right person to marry, if that is His will. We're also asking Him to walk with you every day of your lives."

"You must love us a lot to fast and pray like that."

"We *do* love you. And God loves you even more."

I suppose there's another explanation behind my concern for the spiritual welfare of our two children. I'm told that George McCluskey, my great-grandfather on the maternal side, carried a similar burden for his children through the final decades of his life. He invested the hour from eleven to twelve o'clock each morning to intercessory prayer for his family. However, he was not only asking God to bless his children; he extended his request to generations not yet born! In effect, my great-grandfather was praying for *me*.

Toward the end of his life, the old man announced that God had made a very unusual promise to him. He was given the assurance that *every* member of four generations of our family would be Christians, including those yet to be born. He then died and the promise became part of the spiritual heritage that was passed to those of us in George McCluskey's bloodline.

Since I represent the fourth generation subsequent to the one that included my great-grandfather, his promise assumes added significance. It has, in fact, been fulfilled in a fascinating way. McCluskey and his wife were ministers and charter members in their church denomination. They brought two daughters into the world, one eventually becoming my grandmother and the other my great-aunt. Those two girls married men who were ministers in the same denomination as their parents. Between them, they produced a boy and four girls, one becoming my mother. The girls all married ministers in the same denomination, and the boy became one. Then came my generation. My cousin H. B. London and I were the first two members to reach the age for college, where we were roommates. During the first semester of our sophomore year, he announced that God had called him to be a minister in (you guessed it) the same denomination as his great-grandfather. And believe me, I began to get very *nervous* about the entire proposition!

I now represent the first, though not the only, member of four generations from the time of my great-grandfather who has not felt specifically "called" into the ministry. But considering the hundreds of times I have stood before audiences, talking about the gospel of Jesus Christ and its application to family life, I have to ask, "What's the difference?" God has marvelous methods of implementing His purposes in our lives. There have been times as I have sat on the platform of a large church, waiting to speak, that I have felt the presence of the old man . . . and it seemed as though he was smiling mischievously from the beyond.

Though my great-grandfather is long dead, having died a year before my birth, he still provides the richest source of inspiration for me. It staggers the mind to realize that the prayers of this one man, spoken more than fifty years ago, reach across four generations of time and influence developments in my life today. That is the power of prayer and the source of my hope and optimism. Don't tell me God is dead . . . or that He doesn't honor His commitments. George McCluskey and I know that He lives!

The men in my family have transmitted a spiritual heritage that is more valuable than any monetary estate they could have accumulated. And I am determined to preserve it on behalf of my children. There is no higher calling on the face of the earth.

Are All the Children In

> I think at times as the night draws nigh
>   of an old house on the hill
> And of a yard all wide and blossomed-starred
>   where the children play at will
> And when the night at last came down hushing
>   the merry din
> Mother would look around and ask—
>   are all the children in
> Oh, it's many, many a year since then
>   and the old house on the hill
> No longer echoes to childish feet and the
>   yard is still, so still
> But I see it all as the shadows creep
>   and though many the year since then
> I can hear Mother ask—are all the children in

I wonder if when the shadows fall on the last short
   earthly day
When we say good-bye to the world outside
All tired with our childish play
When we step out into the other land where
   Mother so long has been
Will we hear her ask just as of old
   are all the children in

                —Anonymous

∼ Cat's in the Cradle ∼

A popular song beautifully portrays the cost of overcommitment in family life. It was written by Sandy and Harry Chapin, who titled it "Cat's in the Cradle." I've obtained permission to reproduce the lyrics, as follows, specifically for the fathers who are reading this book:

Cat's in the Cradle

My child arrived just the other day
he came to the world in the usual way—

But there were planes to catch and bills to pay
he learned to walk while I was away
and he was talkin' 'fore I knew it and as he grew he'd say

I'm gonna be like you, Dad
you know I'm gonna be like you.

and the cat's in the cradle and the silver spoon
Little boy blue and the man in the moon
when you comin' home, Dad
I don't know when
but we'll get together then—
you know we'll have a good time then

70

My son turned 10 just the other day
he said, Thanks for the ball, Dad, com'on let's play
Can you teach me to throw?
I said not today, I got a lot to do
He said, That's okay
and he walked away but his smile never dimmed
it said I'm gonna be like him, yeah
you know I'm gonna be like him

and the cat's in the cradle and the silver spoon
Little boy blue and the man in the moon
when you comin' home, Dad

I don't know when
but we'll get together then—
you know we'll have a good time then

Well he came home from college just the other day
so much like a man I just had to say
Son, I'm proud of you, can you sit for awhile
He shook his head and said with a smile—
what I'd really like, Dad, is to borrow the car keys
see you later, can I have them please?

When you comin' home, Son?
I don't know when
but we'll get together then
you know we'll have a good time then

I've long since retired, my son's moved away
I called him up just the other day
I said I'd like to see you if you don't mind
He said, I'd love to, Dad—if I can find the time
You see my new job's a hassle and the kids have the flu
but it's sure nice talkin' to you, Dad
It's been nice talking to you

And as I hung up the phone, it occurred to me—
he'd grown up just like me; my boy was just like me

and the cat's in the cradle and the silver spoon
Little boy blue and the man in the moon
when you comin' home, Son?

I don't know when
but we'll get together then, Dad,
we're gonna have a good time then[1]

Do those words strike home to anyone but me? Have *you* felt the years
slipping by with far too many unfulfilled promises to your children? Have
you heard yourself saying, "Son, we've been talking about that wagon we
were going to build one of these Saturdays, and I just want you to know that
I haven't forgotten it. But we can't do it this weekend 'cause I have to make
an unexpected trip to Indianapolis. However, we *will* get to it one of these
days. I'm not sure if it can be next weekend, but you keep reminding me, and
we'll eventually work together. And I'm going to take you fishing, too. I *love*
to fish and I know a little stream that is jumping with trout in the spring.
But this just happens to be a very busy month for your mom and me, so let's
keep planning and before you know it, the time will be here."

Then the days soon become weeks, and the weeks flow into months and
years and decades . . . and our kids grow up and leave home. Then we sit in
the silence of our family rooms, trying to recall the precious experiences that
escaped us there. Ringing in our ears is that haunting phrase, "We'll have a
good time . . . then. . . ."

Oh, I know I'm stirring a measure of guilt into the pot with these words.
But perhaps we need to be confronted with the important issues of life, even
if they make us uncomfortable. Furthermore, I feel *obligated* to speak on
behalf of the millions of children around the world who are reaching for
fathers who aren't there. The names of specific boys and girls come to my
mind as I write these words, symbolizing the masses of lonely kids who
experience the agony of unmet needs. Let me acquaint you with two of those
children whose paths I have crossed.

I think first of the mother who approached me after I had spoken some years ago. She had supported her husband through college and medical school, only to have him divorce her in favor of a younger plaything. She stood with tears in her eyes as she described the impact of his departure on her two sons.

"They miss their daddy every day," she said. "They don't understand why he doesn't come to see them. The older boy, especially, wants a father so badly that he reaches for every man who comes into our lives. What can I tell him? How can I meet the boy's needs for a father who will hunt and fish and play football and bowl with him and his brother? It's breaking my heart to see them suffer so much."

I gave this mother a few suggestions and offered my understanding and support. The next morning I spoke for the final time at her church. Following the service, I stood on the platform as a line of people waited to tell me good-bye and extend their greetings. Standing in the line was the mother with her two sons.

They greeted me with smiles, and I shook the older child's hand. Then something happened which I did not recall until I was on my way back to Los Angeles. The boy did not let go of my hand! He gripped it tightly, preventing me from welcoming others who pressed around. To my regret, I realized later that I had unconsciously grasped his arm with my other hand, pulling myself free from his grip. I sat on the plane, realizing the full implications of that incident. You see, this lad *needed* me. He needed a man who could take the place of his renegade father. And I had failed him, just like all the rest. Now I'm left with the memory of a child who said with his eyes, "Could you be a daddy to me?"

Another child has found a permanent place in my memory, although I don't even know her name. I was waiting to catch a plane at Los Angeles International Airport, enjoying my favorite activity of "people-watching." But I was unprepared for the drama about to unfold. Standing near me was an old man who was obviously waiting for someone who should have been on the plane that arrived minutes before. He examined each face intently as the passengers filed past. I thought he seemed unusually distressed as he waited.

Then I saw the little girl who stood by his side. She must have been seven years old, and she, too, was desperately looking for a certain face in the crowd. I have rarely seen a child more anxious than this cute little girl. She clung to the old man's arm, who I assumed to be her grandfather. Then as the last passengers came by, one by one, the girl began to cry silently. She was not merely disappointed in that moment; her little heart was broken. The grandfather also appeared to be fighting back the tears. In fact, he was too upset to comfort the child, who then buried her face in the sleeve of his worn coat.

Oh, God! I prayed silently. *What special agony are they experiencing in this hour? Was it the child's mother who abandoned her on that painful day? Did her daddy promise to come and then change his mind?*

My great impulse was to throw my arms around the little girl and shield her from the awfulness of that hour. I wanted her to pour out her grief in the protection of my embrace, but I feared that my intrusion would be misunderstood. So I watched helplessly. Then the old man and the child stood silently as the passengers departed from two other planes, but the anxiety on their faces had turned to despair. Finally, they walked slowly through the terminal and toward the door. Their only sound was the snuffling of the little girl who fought to control her tears.

Where is this child now? God only knows.

⌁ Dad Coming Home Was Real Treat ⌁

This touching article appeared in a June 1985 issue of the *Los Angeles Times*:

When I was a little boy I never left the house without kissing my parents good-bye.

I liked kissing my mother because her cheek felt mushy and warm and because she smelled of peppermints. I liked kissing my father because he felt rough and whiskery and smelled of cigars and witch hazel.

About the time I was 10 years old, I came to the conclusion that I was now too big to kiss my father. A mother, OK. But with a father, a big boy should shake hands—man to man, you see.

He didn't seem to notice the difference or to mind it. Anyway, he never said anything about it. But then he never said much about anything, except his business.

In retrospect, I guess it was also my way of getting even with him. Up until then, I had always felt I was something special to him. Every day, he would come home from that mysterious world of his with a wondrous treat, just for me. It might be a miniature baseball bat, engraved with Babe Ruth's signature.

It might be a real honeycomb with waffle-like squares soaked in honey. Or it might be exotic rahat, the delectable, jellied Turkish candies, buried in powdered sugar and crowded into a little wooden crate.

How I looked forward to his coming home each night! The door flung open and there he stood. I would run to him, hug him while he lifted me high in his arms.

I reached my peak the day of my seventh birthday. I woke up before anyone else in the family and tiptoed into the dining room. There, on the heavy mahogany table, was a small, square wristwatch with a brown leather strap, stretched out full length in a black velvet box. Could it really be for me? I picked it up and held it to my ear. It ticked! Not a toy watch from the 5-and-10, but a real watch like grown-ups wore. I ran into his bedroom, woke up Father, and covered him with kisses. Could any boy possibly be as happy as me?

Later, it began to change. At first, I wasn't aware it was happening. I supposed I was too busy with school and play and having to make new friends all the time. (We moved every two years, always seeking a lower rent.)

The flow of treats dried up. No more bats or honeycombs. My father gradually disappeared from my life. He would come home late, long after I had gone to sleep. And he would come home with his hands empty. I missed him very much, but I was afraid to say anything. I hoped that he would come back to me as strangely as he had left. Anyhow, big boys weren't supposed to long for their fathers.

Years after he died, my mother talked about how the Depression had "taken the life out of him." It had crushed his dream of being a "big man." He no longer had money for treats. He no longer had time for me.

I am sorry now. I look at his picture and his crinkly hazel eyes and wish that he were here today. I would tell him what is happening with me now and talk about things that he might like to hear—politics, foreign events, and how business is doing. And I would put my arms around his neck and say, "Pop, you don't have to bring me anything—just come home early." And I would kiss him.[2]

⟶ Manhood at Its Best ⟵

How can we get a handle on the ephemeral qualities of character and strength in a man of God? It is understood most readily by observing a good *model,* and I crossed paths momentarily with one of the finest a few years ago.

My family had joined me at Mammoth, California, for a weekend ski outing. The kids were still young, and I was working frantically to teach them the fundamentals of the sport. That's a tough assignment, as every skiing father knows. You can guess who gets to carry *all* the skis, boots, and poles, and then park the car, stand in line to buy the lift tickets, herd the clan toward the ski slopes, and get everyone zipped up and ready to go. At that precise moment, inevitably, one of the children announces that he or she has to go to the bathroom. Upon hearing that important news, Dad clomps back down the hill with his child in tow and then goes through the zippety-zip process twice more. Then he trudges back up the mountain. That is how the system works on a *good* day.

On a bad morning, some of the most frustrating experiences in living can occur. Children are fully capable of announcing this need to visit the "john" one at a time, sending Dad up and down the mountain like a yo-yo. By the time he and the last child get back, the first one has to go again. Kids seem to delight in losing valuable equipment, too, such as leather gloves, designer wool hats, ski jackets, etc. They're also good at bickering, which drives their harried parents crazy.

On the particular day in question, it was a *bad* morning for my family. Our children did everything wrong. There we were on a family vacation to produce a little togetherness, but I couldn't stand either one of my kids. They complained and dawdled and spread clothes all over the city of Mammoth. Maybe it will make other families feel better to know that the Dobsons have nerve-wracking days like that. By the time I transported the family to the ski lodge, I was well on my way to total irritation. Danae and Ryan climbed out of the car with a grumble, and I headed toward a parking lot a mile or so away. On the way down the hill, I muttered a brief prayer. Actually, it was more an expression of exasperation than anything else.

"What am I going to do with these kids You've given to me?" I said to the Lord, as though it were His fault. He did not reply.

I parked the car and walked back to an assembly area where a flatbed truck comes by every ten minutes to pick up passengers. About fifteen skiers stood awaiting a ride up the mountain, and I quietly joined them. Then I noticed a "different" young lady standing with the others. She turned to look at me, and I observed the unmistakable appearance of mental retardation in her eyes. This late teenager was behaving in a very strange way. She stood facing the mountain, quoting the word *whomever* over and over. "Whomever!" she said in a loud voice. A few seconds later, she repeated the word nonsensically.

Having worked with developmentally disabled individuals for years, I felt an instant empathy for this girl. It was apparent, however, that the other skiers didn't share my concern. They were young, attractive, and beautifully outfitted. I watched them glance in the direction of the girl and then take a step or two backward. They rolled their eyes at each other as if to say, "Who's the 'crazy' we have with us?"

About that time the truck arrived, and all of us began climbing onto its bed. As the driver took us toward the ski lodge, the retarded girl continued to face the mountain and say the word *whomever*. By this time she stood alone, as the "in crowd" left her isolated at the center of the bed. She was alone, that is, except for a big man who stood nearby. Suddenly, I realized that he was her father.

It was at that point that this man with the kind face did something I will never forget. He walked over to his daughter and wrapped his arms around her. He put his big hand on the back of her head and gently pressed it to his chest. Then he looked down at her lovingly and said, "Yeah, babe. Whomever."

I must admit that I had to turn my head to conceal the moisture in my eyes. You see, that father had seen the same rejection from the beautiful people that I had observed. He saw their smiles . . . their scorn. His act of love to the girl was only partially done for her benefit. The father was actually speaking to all of us.

He was saying, "Yes, it's true. My daughter is retarded. We can't hide that fact. She is very limited in ability. She won't sing the songs. She won't write the books. In fact, she's already out of school. We've done the best we could for her. But I want you all to know something. This young lady is my girl, and I love her. She's the whole world to me. And I'm not ashamed to be identified with her. 'Yeah, babe. Whomever!'"

The selfless love and tenderness of that father flooded out from his soul and engulfed mine. Instantly, I felt compassion and love for our two children.

"All right, Lord!" I said. "I get the message."

Two weeks later, I was a guest on a national television show, and the moderator gave me four and a half minutes to answer such questions as "How did the institution of the family get into such a mess, and how can we correct the problem?"

I couldn't have answered the question in four and a half hours . . . but I can say this: One of the solutions to family disintegration has something to do with what that father was feeling for his handicapped girl, there in the back of that flatbed truck. That kind of unconditional love will heal a troubled home. It will resolve conflicts between parent and child. It will even help us cope with a tragedy like mental retardation.

CHAPTER FOUR

Parenting Teens

The task of raising kids is rather like trying to fly a kite on a day when the wind doesn't blow. Mom and Dad run down the road pulling the cute little device at the end of a string. It bounces along the ground and shows no inclination of flying.

Eventually and with much effort, they manage to get it fifteen feet in the air, but great danger suddenly looms. The kite dives toward electrical lines and twirls near trees. It is a scary moment. Will they ever get it safely on its way? Then, unexpectedly, a gust of wind catches the kite, and it sails upward while Mom and Dad feed out line as rapidly as they can.

Then the moment of release comes. The string slips through his fingers, and the kite soars majestically into God's beautiful sky.

Mom and Dad stand gazing at their precious "baby," who is now gleaming in the sun, a mere pinpoint of color on the horizon. They are proud of what they've done—but sad to realize that their job is finished. It was a labor of love. But where did the years go?

∼ The Worst Punishment ∼

My mother, I might note, was a master at trench warfare during my own stubborn adolescent years. My father was a full-time minister and frequently on the road, so Mom had the primary responsibility of raising me. I was giving my teachers a hard time during this year and on several occasions was sent to the principal's office, where I received stern lectures and a few swats with an infamous rubber hose (which was permissible back then). This discipline did not change my bad attitude, however, and my mother became increasingly frustrated with my irresponsibility and dropping grades. It wasn't long before she reached her limit.

One day after school, she sat me down and said firmly, "I know you have been fooling around in school and ignoring your assignments. I also know you've been getting in trouble with your teachers." (She always seemed to have a team of detectives who told her every detail of my private life, although today I think it was little more than a keen mind, good eyes, and an unbelievable intuitive skill.) She continued, "Well, I've thought it over, and I've decided that I'm not going to do anything about what is going on. I'm not going to punish you. I'm not going to take away privileges. I'm not even going to talk about it anymore."

I was about to smile in relief when she said, "I do want you to understand one thing, however. If the principal ever calls *me* about your behavior, I promise you that the next day I'm going to school with you. I'm going to walk two feet behind you all day. I will hold your hand in front of all your friends in the hall and at lunch, and I'm going to enter into all your conversations throughout the whole day. When you sit in your seat, I'm going to pull my chair alongside you, or I'll even climb into the seat with you. For one full day, I will not be away from your side."

That promise absolutely terrified me. It would have been social suicide to have my "mommy" following me around in front of my friends. No punishment would have been worse! I'm sure my teachers wondered why there was such a sudden improvement in my behavior and a remarkable jump in my grades near the end of my freshman year in high school. I simply couldn't run the risk of Mom getting that fatal phone call.

My mother knew that the threat of spanking is not the best source of motivation to a teenager. She had a better idea.

We Dare Not Try to Make It on Our Own

I'll never forget the time some years ago when our daughter had just learned to drive. Danae had been enrolled in Kamikaze Driving School, and the moment finally arrived for her to take her first solo flight in the family car. Believe me, my anxiety level was climbing off the chart that day. Someday you will know how terrifying it is to hand the car keys to a sixteen-year-old kid who doesn't know what she doesn't know about driving. Shirley and I stood quaking in the front yard as Danae drove out of sight. We then turned to go back into the house, and I said, "Well, babe, the Lord giveth and the Lord taketh away." Fortunately, Danae made it home safely in a few minutes and brought the car to a careful and controlled stop. That is the sweetest sound in the world to an anxious parent!

It was during this era that Shirley and I covenanted between us to pray for our son and daughter at the close of every day. Not only were we concerned about the risk of an automobile accident, but we were also aware of so many other dangers that lurk out there in a city like Los Angeles, where we lived at that time. That part of the world is known for its weirdos, kooks, nuts, ding-a-lings, and fruitcakes. That's one reason we found ourselves on our knees each evening, asking for divine protection for the teenagers whom we loved so much.

One night we were particularly tired and collapsed into bed without our benedictory prayer. We were almost asleep before Shirley's voice pierced the night. "Jim," she said. "We haven't prayed for our kids yet today. Don't you think we should talk to the Lord?"

I admit it was very difficult for me to pull my six-foot-two frame out of the warm bed that night. Nevertheless, we got on our knees and offered a prayer for our children's safety, placing them in the hands of the Father once more.

Later we learned that Danae and a girlfriend had gone to a fast-food establishment and bought hamburgers and Cokes. They drove up the road a few miles and were sitting in the car eating the meal when a city policeman drove by, shining his spotlight in all directions. He was obviously looking for someone but gradually went past.

In a few minutes, Danae and her friend heard a "clunk" from under the car. They looked at one another nervously and felt a sharp bump. Before they could leave, a man crawled out from under the car and emerged on the passenger side. He was very hairy and looked as if he had been on the street for weeks. The man immediately came over to the door and attempted to open it. Thank God, it was locked. Danae quickly started the car and drove off . . . no doubt at record speed.

Later, when we checked the timing of this incident, we realized that

Shirley and I had been on our knees at the precise moment of danger. Our prayers were answered. Our daughter and her friend were safe!

It is impossible for me to overstate the need for prayer in the fabric of family life. Not simply as a shield against danger, of course. A personal relationship with Jesus Christ is the cornerstone of marriage, giving meaning and purpose to every dimension of living. Being able to bow in prayer as the day begins or ends gives expression to the frustrations and concerns that might not otherwise be ventilated. On the other end of that prayer line is a loving heavenly Father who has promised to hear and answer our petitions. In this day of disintegrating families on every side, we dare not try to make it on our own.

⟿ Parents Pulling for You ⟾

When I was sixteen years old, I began to play some "games" that my parents viewed with alarm. I had not yet crossed the line into all-out rebellion, but I was definitely leaning in that direction. My father was a minister who was traveling consistently during that time, and when my mother informed him of my sudden defiance, he reacted decisively. He canceled his three-year speaking schedule and accepted a pastoral assignment that permitted him to be home with me for my last two years in high school. He sold our home and moved the family seven hundred miles south to give me a fresh environment, new friends, and the opportunity to hunt and fish. I didn't know that I had motivated this relocation, but now I understand my parents' reasoning and appreciate their caring enough to sacrifice their home, job, friends, and personal desires, just for my welfare. This was one way they revealed their love for me at a critical stage of my development.

The story does not end there, of course. It was difficult making new friends in a strange high school at the beginning of my junior year. I was lonely and felt out of place in a town that failed to acknowledge my arrival. My mother sensed this feeling of friendlessness and, in her characteristic way, was "hurting" with me. One day after we had been in the new community for about two weeks, she took my hand and pressed a piece of paper into the palm. She looked in my eyes and said, "This is for you. Don't tell anybody. Just take it and use it for anything you want. It isn't much, but I want you to get something that looks good to you."

I unfolded the "paper," which turned out to be a twenty-dollar bill. It was money that my mother and father didn't have, considering the cost of the move and the small salary my dad was to be paid. But no matter. I stood at the top of their list of priorities during those stormy days. We all know that money won't buy friends, and twenty dollars (even then) did not change my life significantly. Nevertheless, my mother used that method of saying to me, "I feel what you feel; I know it's difficult right now, but I'm your friend and I want to help." Every troubled teen should be so fortunate as to have parents who are still pulling for him and praying for him and feeling for him, even when he has become most unlovable.

The Doctor Doesn't Always Know Best

The pace of living has become so frantic that we don't have time for our kids. That situation makes us willing to accept surrogate parenting uncritically from the "experts" who meander through our lives. Some parents resist the cultural mind-set, but the pressure to get out of the way and let various authorities take over for them can be quite severe.

I'm reminded of a mother who told me that she took her fourteen-year-old daughter to their pediatrician for a routine physical exam. The mother was aware that her daughter was beginning to develop physically and might be sensitive to her being in the examining room with her. She offered to remain in the waiting room, but the girl objected.

"I don't want to go in there by myself," she said. "Please come with me." After arguing with her daughter for a moment, the mother agreed to accompany her to the examining room.

When the exam was over, however, the doctor turned to the mother and criticized her for intruding. He said to the mother in front of the girl, "You know, you really had no business being in the examining room. It is time I related directly to your daughter. You should not even be aware of the care that I give her or the medication I prescribe. You shouldn't even know the things that are said between us. My care of your daughter should now be a private matter between her and me."

The girl had been going through a period of rebellion, and the mother felt her authority was weakened by the doctor's comments. It was as though he were saying, "Your day of supervision of your daughter has now passed. She should now make her own decisions." Fortunately, that mother was unwilling to do as she was told and promptly found a new doctor. Good for her!

I have discussed this conversation with several pediatricians, and they have each agreed with the doctor in this case. They emphasized the importance of a youngster having someone to talk with in private. Perhaps. But I disagree with the autonomy demanded by the physician.

Fourteen-year-old boys and girls are not grown, and their parents are still the best people to care for them and to oversee their development. It is appropriate for a physician to have some private moments with his young patient, but he should never forget to whom he is accountable!

Furthermore, if greater authority is to be granted to the doctor, the parent had better find out just what he believes about contraceptives for minors, premarital sex, spiritual matters, and the like. Be careful whom you choose to trust with the body and the soul of your child. Educators, youth ministers, athletic coaches, music instructors, psychologists, counselors, and physicians are there to assist parents in raising their kids, not to replace them.

～ Fatherly Wisdom ～

I've spent more than half my life studying children, yet my own kids continue to surprise and fascinate me. I remember calling home some years ago from a city in Georgia where I had traveled for a speaking engagement. Danae, who was then thirteen years of age, picked up the phone, and we had a warm father-daughter chat. Then she said, "Oh, by the way, Dad, I'm going to be running in a track meet next Saturday."

"Really?" I said. "What distance have you chosen?"

"The 880," she replied.

I gasped. "Danae, that is a very grueling race. Do you know how far 880 yards is?"

"Yes," she said. "It's a half-mile."

"Have you ever run that far before?" I asked.

She said that she hadn't, even in practice. I continued to probe for information and learned that nine schools would be competing in the meet, which was only three days away. My daughter intended to compete against a field of other runners who presumably had been training for weeks. I was concerned.

"Danae," I said, "you've made a big mistake. You're about to embarrass yourself and I want you to think it over. You should go to your coach and ask to run a shorter race. At that speed 880 yards will kill you!"

"No, Dad," she said with determination. "No one else signed up for the 880, and I want to run it."

"Okay," I replied, "but you're doing it against my better judgment."

I thought about that beloved kid the rest of the week and wondered what humiliation was in store for her. I called again on Saturday afternoon.

"Guess what, Dad!" Danae said cheerfully. "I won the race today!" She had indeed finished in first place, several yards ahead of her nearest competitor. The following year, also without training, she won the same race by fifty yards and set a school record that may still be standing.

Wow! I said to myself. *The kid has talent. She'll be a great runner someday.* Wrong again. She ran and won two races in the ninth grade, came in second in the next, and then lost interest in track. End of story.

So much for fatherly wisdom in all its glory.

∽ Robin Hood II ∽

The shoulder muscle is a surprisingly useful source of minor pain. It can be utilized in those countless situations where face-to-face confrontations occur between adult and child. One such incident happened to me back in the days when my own kids were young. I had come out of a drugstore, and there at its entrance was a stooped, elderly man, approximately seventy-five or eighty years of age. Four boys, probably ninth graders, had cornered him and were running circles around him. As I came through the door, one of the boys had just knocked the man's hat down over his eyes, and they were laughing about how silly he looked, leaning on his cane.

I stepped in front of the elderly fellow and suggested that the boys find someone else to torment. They called me names and then sauntered off down the street. I got in my car and was gone about fifteen minutes. I returned to get something I had forgotten, and as I was getting out of my car I saw the same four boys running from a nearby hardware store. The proprietor raced after them, shaking his fist and screaming in protest. I discovered later that they had run down the aisles in his store, raking cans and bottles off the shelves and onto the floor. They also made fun of the fact that he was Jewish and rather overweight.

When the boys saw me coming, I'm sure they thought I viewed myself as Robin Hood II, protector of the innocent and friend of the oppressed. One of the young tormentors ran straight up to my face and stared defiantly in my eyes. He was about half my size, but obviously felt safe because he was a teenager. He said, "You just hit me! I'll sue you for everything you're worth!"

I have rather large hands to go with my six-foot-two, 195-pound frame. It was obviously time to use them. I grasped his shoulder muscles on both sides, squeezing firmly. He immediately dropped to the ground, holding his neck. He rolled away and ran off with his friends, screaming insults back at me.

I reported the incident and later that evening received a phone call from the police. I was told the four young thugs had been harassing merchants and customers along that block for weeks. Their parents refused to cooperate with authorities, and the police felt hamstrung. Without the parents' help, they didn't know what to do. As I reflect now on that incident, I can think of no better way to breed and cultivate juvenile delinquency than for society to allow such early defiance to succeed with impunity. Leonardo da Vinci is quoted as saying, "He who does not punish evil commands it to be done."

⟶ Everyone Loves Mr. Lyndon ⟵

Near my home in Arcadia, California, is a tan gentleman who certainly understands the way children think. He owns and operates Bud Lyndon's Swim School. Mr. Lyndon must be approaching sixty years of age now, and he has been working with youngsters most of his life. He has a remarkable comprehension of the principles of discipline, and I enjoy sitting at poolside just to watch the man work. However, there are few child developmentalists who could explain why he is so successful with the little swimmers in his pool. He is not soft and delicate in his manner; in fact, he tends to be somewhat gruff. When the kids get out of line, he splashes water in their faces and says sternly, "Who told you to move? Stay where I put you until I ask you to swim!" He calls the boys "Men of Tomorrow," and other pet names. His class is regimented, and every minute is utilized purposefully. But would you believe it, the children *love* Bud Lyndon. Why? Because they know that he loves them. Within his gruff manner is a message of affection that might escape the adult observer. Mr. Lyndon never embarrasses a child intentionally, and he "covers" for the youngster who swims more poorly. He delicately balances his authority with a subtle affection that attracts children like the Pied Piper. Mr. Bud Lyndon understands the meaning of discipline with love.

When I was in the ninth grade, I had an athletic coach who affected me the same way. He was the master of the moment, and no one *dared* challenge his authority. I would have fought wild lions before tackling Mr. Ayers. Yes, I feared him. We all did. But he never abused his power. He treated me courteously and respectfully at a time when I needed all of the dignity I could get. Combined with his acceptance of the individual was an obvious self-confidence and ability to lead a pack of adolescent wolves who had devoured less capable teachers. And that's why my ninth-grade gym coach had a greater influence on me than any other person during my fifteenth year. Mr. Craig Ayers understood discipline with love.

Not every parent can be like Mr. Lyndon or Mr. Ayers, and I would not suggest that they try. Nor would it be wise for a mother to display the same gruffness at home that is appropriate on the athletic field or at the pool. Each person must fit his approach to discipline within his own personality patterns and the responses that feel natural. However, the overriding principle remains the same for men and women, mothers and fathers, coaches and teachers, pediatricians and psychologists: It involves discipline with love, a reasonable introduction to responsibility and self-control, parental leadership with a minimum of anger, respect for the dignity and worth of the child, realistic boundaries that are enforced with confident firmness, and a judicious use of rewards and punishment to those who challenge and resist. It is a system that bears the approval of the Creator Himself.

⁓ Declaration of Independence ⁓

Let me tell you what I have said to my son and daughter with regard to the matter of independence.

87

First, I want you to know how much I love you. One of the greatest privileges of my life has been the opportunity to raise you . . . to be your father and watch you grow. However, you're now entering a new phase of life known as adolescence, which sometimes puts a strain on a loving relationship like ours. There may be times during the next few years when you will want me to give you more freedom than I feel you can handle. You may want to be your own boss and make all of your own decisions before I feel you are ready for that independence. This situation may create some friction between us, although I don't expect the conflict to be major.

If it occurs, however, I want you to know that I'm going to compromise as much as I can on each issue. I'll listen to your point of view and then try to understand your feelings and attitudes. I will not be a "dictator" who doesn't care about the needs or desires of the other person. In other words, my love for you will lead me to try to make you happy, if possible.

On the other hand, you can expect me to say "no" when my better judgment requires it. The easiest thing in the world would be to say, "Go ahead and do what you want. I don't care what friends you're with or what kind of grades you make in school. I'll stay off your back and you can do whatever you please." That would be a simple way to avoid all conflict and bad feelings between us.

But love demands that I do what is right, even if it is unpleasant. You'll soon learn that I have the courage to make those decisions when I must. Therefore, a moment of tension may occur in the coming years. But when it happens, I want you to remember that I love you and you love me, and we're going to remain friends through these difficult times. The world can be a cold and lonely place without the support of loving family members; that's why we're going to continue to care for one another in this home. And I think when you've reached your twenties and look back on these small conflicts, you'll appreciate the fact that I loved you enough to set you free gradually and as you were ready for additional responsibility.

⟋ Love Mixed with Discipline ⟋

When mothers and fathers fail to take charge in moments of challenge, they create for themselves and their families a potential lifetime of heartache.

That's what happened in the case of the Holloways, who were the parents of a teen named Becky (not their real names). Mr. Holloway came to see me in desperation one afternoon and related the cause of this concern. Becky had never been required to obey or respect her parents, and her early years were a strain on the entire family. Mrs. Holloway was confident Becky would eventually become more manageable, but that never happened. She held her parents in utter contempt from her youngest childhood and was sullen, disrespectful, selfish, and uncooperative. Mr. and Mrs. Holloway did not feel they had the right to make demands on their daughter, so they smiled politely and pretended not to notice her horrid behavior.

Their magnanimous attitude became more difficult to maintain as Becky steamrolled into puberty and adolescence. She was a perpetual malcontent, sneering at her family in disgust. Mr. and Mrs. Holloway were afraid to antagonize her in any way because she would throw the most violent tantrums imaginable. They were victims of emotional blackmail. They thought they could buy her cooperation, which led them to install a private telephone in her room. She accepted it without gratitude and accumulated a staggering bill during the first month of usage.

They thought a party might make her happy, and Mrs. Holloway worked very hard to decorate the house and prepare refreshments. On the appointed evening, a mob of dirty, profane teens swarmed into the house, breaking and destroying the furnishings. During the course of the evening, Mrs. Holloway said something that angered Becky. The girl struck her mother and left her lying in a pool of blood in the bathroom.

Away from home at the time, Mr. Holloway returned to find his wife helpless on the floor; he located his unconcerned daughter in the back-yard, dancing with friends. As he described for me the details of their recent nightmare, he spoke with tears in his eyes. His wife, he said, was still in the hospital contemplating her parental failures as she recovered from her wounds.

Parents like the Holloways often fail to understand how love and discipline interact to influence the attitudes of a child. These two aspects of a relationship are not opposites working against each other. They are two dimensions of the same quality. One demands the other. Disciplinary action is not an assault on parental love; it is a function of it. Appropriate punish-ment is not something parents do *to* a beloved child; it is something done *for* him or her. That simple understanding when Becky was younger could have spared the Holloways an adolescent nightmare.

Their attitude when Becky rebelled as a preschooler should have been, "I love you too much to let you behave like that."

⟜ I Wanted to Know Your God ⟊

Not only do I remember the emotional conflicts of my own early adolescence, but I have had ample opportunity since then to observe this troubled time of life in others. I was privileged to teach in public schools from 1960 to 1963, and two of those profitable years were spent at the junior high level. I taught science and math to 225 rambunctious troops each day, although I learned much more from them than they did from me. There on the firing line is where my concepts of discipline began to solidify. The workable solutions were validated and took their place in a system I know to be practical. But the lofty theories dreamed up by my grandmotherly educators exploded like so much TNT when tested on the battlefield each day.

One of the most important lessons of those years related to the matter of low self-esteem, which we have been discussing. It became clear to me very early that I could impose all manner of discipline and strict behavioral requirements on my students, provided I treated each young person with genuine dignity and respect. I earned their friendship before and after school, during lunch, and through classroom encounters. I was tough, especially when challenged, but never discourteous, mean, or insulting. I defended the underdog and tenaciously tried to build each child's confidence and self-respect. However, I never compromised my standards of deportment. Students entered my classroom without talking each day. They did not chew gum, or behave disrespectfully, or curse or stab one another with ballpoint pens. I was clearly the captain of the ship, and I directed it with military zeal.

The result of this combination of kindness and firm discipline stands as one of the most pleasant memories of my professional life. I *loved* my students and had every reason to believe that I was loved in return. I actually missed them on weekends (a fact my wife never quite understood). At the end of the final year when I was packing my books and saying good-bye, there were twenty-five or thirty teary-eyed kids who hung around my gloomy room for several hours and finally stood sobbing in the parking lot as I drove away. And yes, I shed a few tears of my own that day. (Please forgive this self-congratulatory paragraph. I haven't bothered to tell you about my failures, which are far less interesting.)

One young lady to whom I said good-bye in the school parking lot in 1963 called me on the telephone during 1975. I hadn't seen Julie for more than a decade, and she had become a grown woman in the ensuing years. I remembered her as a seventh grader whose crisis of confidence was revealed in her sad brown eyes. She seemed embarrassed by her Latin heritage and the fact that she was slightly overweight. She had only one friend, who moved away the following year.

Julie and I talked amiably on the phone about old times at Cedarlane Junior High School, and then she asked me a pointed question: "Where do you go to church?"

I told her where we attended, and she replied, "I wonder if you'd mind my visiting there some Sunday morning?"

I said, "Julie, I'd be delighted."

The next week, my wife and I met Julie in the vestibule of the sanctuary, and she sat with us during the service. Through a process of growth and guidance in subsequent months, this young woman became a vibrant Christian. She now participates in the choir, and many members of the congregation have commented on the radiant glow she seems to transmit when singing.

I stopped her as we were leaving the church a few months later and said, "Julie, I want to ask you a question. Will you tell me why you went to so much trouble to obtain my unlisted phone number and call me last fall? Why did you want to talk to me after all those years, and why did you ask what church I attended?"

Julie thought for a moment and then paid me the highest compliment anyone has ever sent my way. She said, "Because when I was a seventh-grade student in junior high school, you were the *only* person in my life who acted like you respected and believed in me . . . and I wanted to know your God."

If you can communicate that kind of dignity to oppressed and harassed teenagers, then many of the characteristic discipline problems of adolescence can be circumvented. That is, after all, the best way to deal with people of *any* age.

Letting Him Go

A mother came to me recently in regard to her twenty-year-old son, Paul. He was not obeying her as she thought he should, and the conflict was literally making her sick. Paul rented an apartment against her will, with a roommate she disliked, and he was seen with girls of questionable reputation. He threatened to transfer from a Christian college to a local university and more or less denounced his faith.

"What can I do? What can I possibly do to get him straightened out?" she asked.

I told her that Paul's day-to-day behavior was no longer her responsibility. She had completed her task as his mother and should set him free. I explained that her nagging and begging were probably accentuating Paul's defiance, since she was playing an inappropriate "mothering" role he resented. I suggested that this woman sit down and write her son a polite and loving letter, telling him emphatically that she was letting him go—once and for all.

Several days later the woman brought for my approval a rough draft of a letter she had written. It was not what I had in mind. Her composition turned out to be a finger-wagging indictment, warning of the future and urging the wayward boy back to his senses. It was impossible to edit what she had written, so I wrote a letter for her. She sent my letter to her son over her own signature, and I have printed it below with her permission:

> Dear Paul:
>
> This is the most important letter I have ever written to you, and I hope you will take it as seriously as it is intended. I have given a great amount of thought and prayer to the matter I want to convey and believe I am right in what I've decided to do.
>
> For the past several years, you and I have been involved in a painful tug-of-war. You have been struggling to free yourself of my values and my wishes for your life. At the same time, I have been trying to hold you to what we both know is right. Even at the risk of nagging, I have been saying, "Go to church," "Choose the right friends," "Make good grades in school," "Live a Christian life," "Prepare wisely for your future," etc. I'm sure you've gotten tired of this urging and warning, but I have only wanted the best for you. This is the only way I knew to

keep you from making some of the mistakes so many others have made.

However, I've thought all of this over during the last month, and I believe that my job as your mother is now finished. Since the day you were born, I have done my best to do what was right for you. I have not always been successful—I've made mistakes, and I've failed in many ways. Someday you will learn how difficult it is to be a good parent, and perhaps then you'll understand me better than you do now. But there's one area where I have never wavered: I've loved you with everything that is within me. It is impossible to convey the depth of my love for you through these years, and that affection is as great today as it's ever been. It will continue to be there in the future, although our relationship will change from this moment. As of now, you are free! You may reject God or accept Him, as you choose. Ultimately, you will answer only to Him anyway. You may marry whomever you wish without protest from me. You may go to UCLA or USC or any other college of your selection. You may fail or succeed in each of life's responsibilities. The umbilical cord is now broken.

I am not saying these things out of bitterness or anger. I still care what happens to you and am concerned for your welfare. I will pray for you daily, and if you come to me for advice, I'll offer my opinion. *But the responsibility now shifts from my shoulders to yours.* You are a man now, and you're entitled to make your own decisions—regardless of the consequences. Throughout your life I've tried to build a foundation of values that would prepare you for this moment of manhood and independence. That time has come, and my record is in the books.

I have confidence in you, son. You are gifted and have been blessed in so many ways. I believe God will lead you and guide your footsteps, and I am optimistic about the future. Regardless of the outcome, I will always have a special tenderness in my heart for my beloved son.

Sincerely,
Your mother

We are given eighteen or twenty years to interject the proper values and attitudes; then we must take our hands off and trust in divine leadership to influence the outcome. And surprisingly, the chances of a young adult making the right decisions are greatly increased when no fight is under way for adulthood and independence.

CHAPTER FIVE

Lifelong Love

The essential investment of commitment is sorely missing in so many modern marriages. "I love you," they seem to say, "as long as I feel attracted to you—or as long as someone else doesn't look better—or as long as it is to my advantage to continue the relationship." Sooner or later, this unanchored love will certainly vaporize.

"For better or worse, for richer for poorer, in sickness and in health, to love, and to cherish, till death us do part . . ." That familiar pledge from the past still offers the most solid foundation upon which to build a marriage, for therein lies the real meaning of genuine romantic love, and the key to finding lifelong love.

∽ The Ups and Downs of Courtship ∽

When I first met my wife, Shirley, she was a lowly sophomore in college and I was a lofty senior. I viewed myself as a big man on campus, and I wasn't very enthusiastic about the new kid on the block. But she felt very differently. She had been very successful with boys and was challenged by the independence she saw in me. She wanted to win me because she wasn't sure she could. I understood that and held our friendship very loosely.

After my graduation, Shirley and I had one of those tension-filled conversations known to lovers the world over. I said I wanted her to date other guys while I was in the army because I didn't plan to get married soon. I liked her a lot, but I just didn't think I loved her. We could still be friends in the future, but the relationship was basically over.

It was a bombshell for which Shirley had no preparation. She hadn't seen it coming. We had been dating for more than a year and had built many warm memories together. That's why I thought she would be devastated. Although I didn't want to hurt her, I fully expected her to cry and hold on to me. Instead, Shirley said quietly and confidently, "I've been thinking the same thoughts, and I would like to date other guys. Why don't we just go our separate ways for now?"

Her answer rocked me. Was she really going to let me go without a struggle? I walked her to her dorm and asked if I could kiss her good-bye. She said no and went inside. Who would have believed it?

What I didn't learn for many months was that Shirley went up to her room, closed the door, and cried all night. But she knew intuitively that she could not let me see her pain. She let me go with such dignity and respect that I immediately began wondering if I had done the right thing. I had been hoping to escape gracefully, but now I questioned whether I really wanted to go. The next day I wrote her a letter and apologized, asking to continue the relationship. Shirley waited two weeks to answer.

I went away to the army and later returned to the University of Southern California to begin my graduate training. By this time, Shirley was an exalted senior and I was a collegiate has-been. She was homecoming queen, senior class president, a member of Who's Who in American Colleges and Universities, and one of the most popular girls in her class. And I have to tell you, she began to look very good to me. I began calling her several times a day, complaining about whom she was spending her time with and trying to find ways to please her.

What happened next should have been predictable. When Shirley saw that I was anxious about losing her, she began to get bored with me. Gone was the challenge that had attracted her two years before. Instead, I had become just another guy pounding on her door and asking for favors. Our relationship was on the rocks.

One day after a particularly uninspiring date, I sat down at a desk and spent two solid hours thinking about what was happening. This girl had been wrapped around my finger two years ago, and now she was rapidly slipping away from me. What had gone wrong?

Suddenly, I realized the mistake I was making. I was treating myself with disrespect, groveling and hoping for a handout. I grabbed a pen and wrote ten changes I was going to make in our relationship.

First, I decided to demonstrate self-respect and dignity, even if I lost the girl I now loved so deeply. Second, I determined to convey this attitude every time I got the chance: "I am going somewhere in life, and I'm anxious to get there. I love you and hope you choose to go with me. If you do, I'll devote myself to you and try to make you happy. However, if you decide not to make the journey with me, then I'll find someone else. The decision is yours, and I'll accept it." There were other elements to my plan, but they all centered on self-confidence and independence.

The first night that I applied the new approach was one of the most exhilarating experiences of my life. The girl who is now my wife saw me starting to slip away, and she reacted with alarm. We were riding in my car without talking. Shirley asked me to pull over to the curb and stop. When I did, she put her arms around my neck and said, "I'm afraid I'm losing you, and I don't know why. Do you still love me?" I noticed by the reflected light of the moon that she had tears in her eyes.

She obviously didn't hear my thumping heart as I made a little speech about my solitary journey in life. Our relationship was sealed that night, and we were married shortly thereafter. You see, I had reestablished the challenge for Shirley, and she responded predictably.

The psychological force that produced our seesaw relationship is an important one, since it is almost universal in human nature. We crave what we can't attain, but we disrespect what we can't escape. This axiom is particularly relevant in romantic matters and will probably influence your love life, too.

⁓ We'll Marry ⁓

This is a generation who worries about the odds against successful marriages. That concern showed up in a popular song sung a few years ago by Carly Simon. The lyrics are devastating. They say, in effect, "It is impossible to achieve intimacy in marriage, and our life together will be lonely, meaningless, and sterile. But if that's what you want . . . we'll marry." Read them for yourself:

My father sits at night with no lights on:
His cigarette glows in the dark.
The living room is still
I walk by, no remark.
I tiptoe past the master bedroom where
My mother reads her magazines.
I hear her call sweet dreams.
But I forget how to dream.

But you say it's time we moved in together
And raise a family of our own, you and me.
Well, that's the way I've always heard it should be:
You want to marry, we'll marry.

My friends from college they're all married now.
They have their houses and their lawns.
They have their silent noons.
Tearful nights, angry dawns.

Their children hate them for the things they're not:
They hate themselves for what they are.
And yet they drink, they laugh.
Close the wound, hide the scar.

But you say it's time we moved in together
And raise a family of our own, you and me.
Well, that's the way I've always heard it should be:
You want to marry, we'll marry.

You say that we can keep our love alive;
Babe, all I know is what I see.
The couples cling and claw
And drown in love's debris.
You say we'll soar like two birds through the clouds,
But soon you'll cage me on your shelf.
I'll never learn to be just me first by myself.

Well, OK, it's time we moved in together
And raise a family of our own, you and me.
Well, that's the way I've always heard it should be:
You want to marry me, we'll marry.
We'll marry.[1]

While I understand the pessimism expressed in this song, I disagree emphatically with its message. The family was God's idea, not our own, and it is still a wonderful institution.

Stay Away from Pink Champagne

Erma Bombeck went so far as to recommend separate honeymoons for husbands and wives. That's crazy, of course, but the first week or two of married life *can* produce some hilarious experiences. The best honeymoon story I've heard came from some friends close to Shirley and me. After a fancy wedding, they drove to a local hotel and checked into the bridal suite. The new husband glided into the bathroom to freshen up, and his wife awaited his grand entrance. During that interlude, she noticed that a large bottle of champagne had been delivered to their room, compliments of the hotel. The bride had never tasted an alcoholic beverage, but she did recall that her doctor recommended a small quantity of wine to settle her honeymoon jitters. *Why not?* she thought. She poured herself a glass of bubbly and found she liked it quite well. She quickly poured and drank another glass and continued guzzling until the bottle was almost empty. That's when it hit her. The groom stepped out of the bathroom expectantly and found his bleary-eyed bride clutching a champagne bottle and grinning from ear to ear. She was stone-cold drunk. He smelled like aftershave lotion, and she smelled like a skid-row bum. The young wife then became deathly ill and "tossed her cookies"—including the awful wedding cake—for several hours. That cooled down the groom considerably. He sat up with her through the night and helped her get dressed the next morning. They had to catch an early plane to Hawaii, although the bride was in poor condition to travel. She was still drunk and had to be led, weaving and groaning, to the airport. She did not regain her equilibrium for two more days. By then, the groom had forgotten what he came for. This delightful couple has now been married for twenty-two years, and neither has been drunk since. But they will tell you, if you ask, that honeymoons are made for trouble!

If your honeymoon is also a tragicomedy, take heart. Things will get better. You *will* learn. Amazingly, sex can still be exciting and new after thirty or forty years of marriage because individuals are continuing to learn how to please themselves and one another. The critical thing is not to panic if initial disappointments are encountered. Fears and failures, if experienced early in the relationship, can cause the sexual response to shut down in order to prevent any further emotional pain. That need not happen if one's level of expectations can be lowered going into marriage. You have a lifetime to enjoy one another. But don't demand too much too soon . . . and stay away from pink champagne.

Men and women differ significantly in their sexual appetites, and those differences should be comprehended by both the husband and wife. For a man, intercourse is much more physiological than it is for a woman. This means that he is more easily stimulated visually and typically becomes excited more quickly than she. Within moments, the idea of sexual relations can enter his mind, and four or five minutes later the act might be finished and he is asleep again. She lies awake resenting him and regretting the brief episode. One woman even told me that her sex life with her husband reminded her of an old silent movie . . . not a word was exchanged between them. The movie might well be titled *Romancing the Stone*.

A husband and wife must understand that she doesn't function that way. First, the way she feels about her husband sexually is a by-product of their romantic relationship at that time. If she feels close to him . . . loved by him . . . protected by him . . . then she is more likely to desire him physically. Merely seeing his body does not do that much for her. Yes, she is interested in how he looks, but the surge of passion comes not from a stolen glance, but from the quality of their interaction. It derives from his touch and his tenderness toward her.

Newlywed Nonsense

Not long ago, I was flipping through the channels on our television and paused momentarily to watch one of those "newlywed" game shows. It was a bad decision. The leering host posed a series of dumb questions to a lineup of flaky brides whose husbands were sequestered backstage in a soundproof room. He challenged the women to predict their husbands' responses to inquiries that went something like this:

"Where was the exact spot your husband saw you stark naked for the first time?"

"If you and your husband ever separated, which of his friends would be the first to make a pass at you?"

"How would you describe the first time you and your husband made 'whoopee' using these TV terms: 'First Run,' 'Rerun,' or 'Canceled'?"

"Where is the last place you would have, if you could have, made love?"

Without the least hesitation, the women blurted out frank answers to these and other intimate questions. At times I felt I shouldn't be watching, and indeed, past generations would have blushed and gasped at the candor. But the host was undaunted. He then asked the women to respond to this question: "What kind of insect does your husband remind you of when he's feeling romantic?" If you think the question was ridiculous, consider the answer given by one female contestant. She replied, "A bear." When her husband realized she couldn't tell an insect from a mammal, he pounded her frantically with his answer card. She said, "Welllll . . . I didn't know!"

A few minutes later, the men were given an opportunity to humiliate their wives. They grabbed it. Among other questions designed to produce hostility between the sexes, they were asked to complete this sentence: "You haven't seen ugly until you've seen my wife's _____." What fun to watch the brides squirm as their husbands described their anatomical deficiencies to millions of viewers! Throughout the program, the men and women continued to club one another on the head with their answer cards and call each other "stupid." That did it. I couldn't watch any more.

It has been said that television programming reflects the values held widely within the society it serves. Heaven help us if that is true in this instance. The impulsive responses of the newlyweds revealed their embarrassing immaturity, selfishness, hostility, vulnerability, and sense of inadequacy. These are the prime ingredients of marital instability, and too commonly, divorce. An army of disillusioned ex-husbands and ex-wives can attest to that fact all too well.

⟿ The Cost of Overcommitment ⟾

I was a third-year student in college, hoping to earn a Ph.D., get married, have children, buy a home, and earn a living in the next few years. Because I was young, I thought there were no limits to what I could accomplish. But then my aunt, Lela London, heard a Christian psychologist named Clyde Narramore speak one day, and he offered to spend an afternoon with any promising student who wanted to enter the field of mental health. "We need Christians in this work," he said, "and I'll help those who are interested." I called Dr. Narramore a few days later, and he graciously agreed to see me. This busy man gave me two hours of his time in the living room of his home. I still remember his words thirty years later. Among other things, he warned me not to get married too quickly if I wanted to get through school and become a practicing psychologist.

He said, "A baby will come along before you know it, and you will find yourself under heavy financial pressure. That will make you want to quit. You'll sit up nights caring for a sick child and then spend maybe $300 in routine medical bills. Your wife will be frustrated, and you will be tempted to abandon your dreams. Don't put yourself in that straitjacket."

I accepted Dr. Narramore's advice and waited until I was twenty-four years old and had almost finished my master's degree before Shirley and I were married. We then delayed our first child for five more years until I had completed the coursework for my doctorate. It was a wise choice, although today I am listed in the *Guinness Book of World Records* as "Oldest Living Father of a Teenager." Life is a trade-off, as they say.

Though Dr. Narramore did not say so, I assure you that marital problems are almost inevitable when couples overcommit themselves during the early years. The bonding that should occur in the first decade requires time together—time that cannot be given if it is absorbed elsewhere. My advice to you is to hold on to your dreams, but take a little longer to fulfill them. Success will wait, but a happy family will not. To achieve the former and lose the latter would be an empty victory, at best.

Let me toss in this afterthought. I read an article in the *Los Angeles Times* recently about a man named J. R. Buffington. His goal in life was to produce lemons of record-breaking size from the tree in his backyard. He came up with a formula to do just that. He fertilized the tree with ashes from the fireplace, some rabbit-goat manure, a few rusty nails, and plenty of water. That spring, the scrawny little tree gave birth to two gigantic lemons, one weighing over five pounds. But every other lemon on the tree was shriveled and misshapen. Mr. Buffington is still working on his formula.

Isn't that the way it is in life? Great investments in a particular endeavor tend to rob others of their potential. I'd rather have a tree covered with juicy lemons than a record-breaking but freakish crop, wouldn't you? Balance is the word. It is the key to successful living . . . and parenting.

Keep trying, Mr. Buffington. Have you thought about using licorice?

Viva La Difference

My wife, Shirley, and I have been blessed with a wonderful relationship. She is literally my best friend, and I would rather spend an evening with her than anyone on earth. But we are also unique individuals and have struggled at times with our differences. Our most serious conflict has raged now for thirty-plus years with no solution in sight. The problem is that we operate on entirely different internal heating mechanisms. I am very hot-blooded and prefer a Siberian climate if given a choice. Shirley has ice in her veins and even shivers in the California sunshine. She has concluded that if we can have only one flesh between us, she's going to make it sweat! She will slip over to the thermostat at home and spin the dial to at least eighty-five degrees. All the bacteria in the house jump for joy and begin reproducing like crazy. In a few minutes I am starting to glow and begin throwing open doors and windows to get relief. That ridiculous tug-of-war has been going on since our honeymoon and will continue till death do us part. In fact, there have been a few times when I thought death would surely part us over this difficulty.

What is interesting to me is how many other husbands and wives struggle with this problem. It also plagues bosses and their secretaries who fight over the office thermostat. Obviously, temperature is a common pressure point between men and women. Why? Because women typically operate at a lower rate of metabolism than men. It is only one of the countless physiological and emotional differences between the sexes. It is important to understand some of the other ways men and women are unique if we hope to live together in harmony. Genesis tells us that the Creator made *two* sexes, not one, and that He designed each gender for a specific purpose. Take a good look at male and female anatomy, and it becomes obvious that we were created to "fit" together. This is not only true in a sexual context but psychologically as well. Eve, being suited to Adam's particular needs, was given to him as a "help-meet." How unfortunate has been the recent effort to deny this uniqueness and homogenize the human family! It simply won't square with the facts.

⟶ Collision Course for Conflict ⟵

I had been through six weeks of incredible pressure, involving obligations that should have been spread over six months. I still don't know what wave of stupidity caused me to yield to such nonsense. I wasn't forced. No one threatened my life. I was not financially pressed. I can recall having *no* excuse. I simply relaxed my guard for a few weeks and found myself in a race for survival.

I had agreed to speak at various functions around the country on five out of six consecutive weekends. That, in itself, was ridiculous, meaning I would not see my children on a Saturday for more than a month. But at the same time, I was facing deadlines on a new book, three new tape albums, a weekly radio broadcast, and a random IRS audit (lucky me). To compound matters, the San Antonio trip and near death of my dad, mentioned earlier, occurred in the middle of this period. Fatigue mounted week by week as I ran to catch planes and write speeches and search for tax receipts.

The climax occurred in early October when I flew to Cincinnati to participate in a praise gathering, sponsored by Bill Gaither. I lost a night of sleep going in, due to the time change, and then spent two days standing before crowds ranging from two hundred to eight thousand people. It was an exhilarating time of teaching and sharing and counseling, but it squeezed the last drop of energy from my frame. I staggered toward the airport in a state of utter exhaustion. One thought pulsed through my head as the plane headed west: *It's over!*

For six weeks I had had no time to myself. My great desire was to crawl through the front door of my house and remain in isolation for at least seven days. Above all, I wanted to watch the USC-Alabama football game on television the next day. That, to me, is therapy at its best (provided USC wins!).

Let's leave that westbound plane for a moment and journey to a home in Arcadia, California, where my wife, Shirley, is also approaching the end of a siege. For six long weeks, she has run the home without benefit of a man. It has been her task to discipline and train and guide and feed and medicate and bathe two rambunctious kids. Needless to say, she is *also* nearing the point of exhaustion. Furthermore, Shirley has hardly seen her husband since the first of September, and her emotional needs have been on a prolonged "hold." One thought gives her strength to continue: *At last, Jim is coming home, and he'll take over!*

It takes no great analyst to observe that Shirley and I approached that final weekend on a collision course! An explosion was just a matter of time, because each of us was too exhausted to consider the needs of the other.

I should pause to explain the relationship that Shirley and I enjoy as husband and wife. God has blessed our marriage in such a beautiful way. Shirley is, truly, my very best friend on the face of the earth. As I have already mentioned, if I had one free evening that I could spend with any person of my choice, there is no one in the world who would outrank my own wife. It is amazing that two people could live together for thirty-one years and yet find so much to talk about and share day by day. We have also grown in mutual understanding so that it is rarely necessary to quarrel and argue at this stage in our lives. The "power struggle" of earlier years is largely over. Nevertheless, I'm here to tell you that Shirley and I had a dandy fight on the weekend following the praise gathering.

I arrived home on Friday night, and Shirley greeted me warmly at the door. We chatted about recent events and the kids and routine matters before sleep overtook us. The next morning went smoothly enough . . . at least until breakfast was over. We ate on the patio in the backyard. But as we were finishing the meal, our attitudinal differences suddenly blew up in our faces.

"Uh, Jim," said Shirley, "as you know, seventy-five members from the singles department at our church will be using our house tonight, and I need you to help me get ready for them. First, I want you to wash down the patio umbrella for me."

My blood pressure immediately shot up to about 212, and steam began to curl from my ears. *Doesn't Shirley know how hard I worked? What kind of a slave driver is this woman? Doesn't she understand how badly I need this day? Well, I'll tell you something! I'm watching that football game, and if Shirley doesn't like it she can just lump it!*

I don't recall what words I used to convey these thoughts, but I must have gotten the idea across. Shirley stood startled for a moment, then she went in the house and slammed the door. I sat under the dirty umbrella for a few minutes, filled with righteous indignation. I never felt so justified in my life. "After all, you know, I'm not an iron man. I need rest, too, and I'm gonna have it!"

So I had my way. I watched the USC-Alabama game in my study, but the tension around me was incredible. Silence prevailed between husband and wife. Not a word had been spoken since our terse interchange in the backyard. Then our anger began to turn into mutual hurt, which is even more damaging to communication.

The seventy-five church members came that evening and were served refreshments on the patio. They didn't seem to notice the dirty umbrella. They eventually departed, leaving me in the company of a mute female who still acted like the entire episode was my fault. Isn't that just like a woman!

Then came the awkward time of day called bedtime. I climbed into my side of the king-size bed and parked as close to the edge as possible without plunging over the precipice. Shirley did likewise, clinging tenaciously to her "brink." At least eight feet of mattress separated us. No words were spoken. There were, however, frequent sighs from both parties, accompanied by much rolling and tossing. Shirley finally got up to take two aspirin and then returned to bed. Fifteen minutes later I turned on the light to put some nose drops in my nostrils. What followed was one of the worst nights of sleep in my life.

The next morning was Sunday, which presented more uncomfortable moments. We dressed and went to our adult class, still bearing deep wounds and resentment. And wouldn't you know, the teacher chose that morning to talk about marital harmony and God's plan for husbands and wives. Shirley and I nodded and smiled in agreement, but we felt like kicking each other under the table. It made me suspect that many other couples were also putting on a good front to hide their real feelings. (I later told this story to the same class and found that my suspicions were accurate.)

I wish I could say that the problem was resolved on Sunday afternoon, but such was not the case. Nor did it end on Monday or Tuesday. By Wednesday morning, we were sick to death of this silent warfare. We were both more rested by that time, and the issue began to lose some of its fire. I told Shirley I wanted her to join me for breakfast at a restaurant and announced my intention of going to work late.

What occurred was a beautiful time of communication and love. I began to see that Shirley was in the same state of need that I had been. She began to understand the depths of my fatigue. We talked it out and reestablished the closeness that makes life worth living. Not only did we survive the crisis, but we learned several valuable lessons and grew from the experience.

I have not written the details of this conflict for the purpose of entertaining you. Rather, it is my conviction that *most* couples have fought over the same issue, and the lessons that Shirley and I learned from it can be helpful to others. Three distinct concepts emerged that may assist you in handling a similar episode in your marriage. Let me enumerate them.

1. All miscommunication results from differing assumptions.

It is now clear that my battle with Shirley resulted entirely from our differing assumptions about the approaching weekend and our failure to clarify those attitudes before they collided. I assumed that my responsibilities as husband and father would not resume until I had been given a chance to rest and recuperate. That was a reasonable expectation, but it happened to differ with Shirley's assumption. She felt that her lonely tour of duty at home was to end with my return from the wars, and that I would accept the burden from her weary shoulders with the rise of the Saturday sun. It was a reasonable supposition, but it was not in harmony with mine. We could have avoided the conflict by a five-minute conversation prior to the umbrella incident.

I should have said, "Shirley, I know you've had it rough here at home these past six weeks, and I intend to help you pull things together. But I'm going to ask you to understand me for a few more days. I'm more tired than I ever remember being, and I find it difficult even to engage in conversation. If you'll let me hole up for a few days . . . watch some football games on television and sleep a lot . . . I'll pick up my domestic responsibilities the first part of next week."

Shirley would have understood this request and honored it. That's the kind of woman she is. Likewise, if she had said to me, "Jim, these past six weeks have been extremely hectic here at home. I know you couldn't help it, but we've missed your presence here. Just as soon as possible, I need you to get involved with the kids, and for that matter, I want to be with you, too. And besides, there's *one* task I can't do that I would appreciate your handling Saturday morning. You see, the umbrella is dirty and—"

The brief explanation would have helped me understand Shirley's situation. But in reality, we allowed our differing assumptions to remain unspoken . . . and you know the rest of the story.

2. The hostility in many marriages is a direct expression of deep hurt between husband and wife.

Returning to my conflict with Shirley, remember that neither of us sought to hurt the other person. Our initial anger was not motivated by malice or vindictiveness, but by a sense of having been wronged. That situation often underlies marital conflict. Being wounded in spirit gives birth to anger and resentment, leading to destructive words between husbands and wives.

3. Overcommitment is the number-one marriage killer.

This third lesson growing out of our conflict is the most important. Not only are fatigue and time pressure destructive to parent-child relationships, but they undermine even the healthiest of marriages. How can a man and woman communicate with each other when they're too worn out even to talk? How can they pray together when every moment is programmed to the limit? How can they enjoy a sexual relationship when they are exhausted at the end of every day? How can they "date" one another or take walks in the rain or sit by a fire when they face the tyranny of an unfinished "to do" list?

From this vantage point, I have to admit that my fight with Shirley was primarily *my* fault. Not that I was wrong in wanting to rest after arriving home. But I was to blame for foolishly overcommitting my time during that period. The conflict would never have occurred if I had not scheduled myself wall to wall for six weeks. My lack of discipline in my work caused Shirley and me to become exhausted, which brought a chain reaction of negative emotions: irritability, self-pity, petulance, selfishness, and withdrawal. Few marriages can survive a long-term dose of that bitter medicine.

⌒ **Couldn't We Just Cuddle?** ⌒

There has been ample evidence that men and women differ in their sexual appetites, both scientific and pragmatic. Ann Landers was contacted a few years ago, for example, by a female reader who posed this challenge:

Dear Ann Landers:

Often I have been tempted to write to you and express another viewpoint when letters appeared that I did not agree with. The motivation was never strong enough—until now.

I cannot rest until I respond to the man who wanted a penis implant. He said his anxiety over not being able to complete the sex act with the woman he loves was driving him crazy because he knew she must feel deprived and unfulfilled.

For him I have only one word: *hogwash*. It's his ego talking. That man is totally ignorant of the workings of the female mind and heart. If you were to ask 100 women how they feel about sexual intercourse, 98 would say, "Just hold me close and be tender. Forget about the act."

If you don't believe it, why not take a poll? Your readership is phenomenal and people tell you things they would never tell anyone else. How about it, Ann? Will you ask them?

Longtime Faithful in Oregon

Ann replied:

Dear Faithful:

You're on! I am asking the women in my reading audience to send a postcard or letter with a reply to the question: Would you be content to be held close and treated tenderly and forget about "the act"? Reply YES or NO and please add one line. "I am over (under) 40 years of age." No signature is necessary.

A few months later, Ann published this follow-up comment in her column.

Well dear readers, to date I have received more than 90,000 responses and they are still pouring in. The mail room looks like a disaster area. We have put on extra help. The employees are working double shifts and weekends, yet the mailbags seem to multiply like rabbits. Since I have been writing this column, the only time the response was heavier was when I asked my readers to clip the column, sign it and send it to President Reagan. That column was about nuclear war. This sex survey beats the meatloaf recipe, the lemon pie and the poll asking parents, "If you had it to do over again, would you have children?" (Seventy percent said no.)

Mercifully, the vast majority of respondents sent postcards, but a surprising number of women felt compelled to write letters. Some went on for three and four pages, explaining why they felt as they did.

I believe the intense interest in this poll makes a statement about what goes on behind closed doors in the bedrooms of the world. Keep in mind my column appears in Canada, Europe, Tokyo, Hong Kong, Bangkok, Mexico City, and a variety of other places around the world. And the mail came from everywhere. It also says something about communication and fulfillment (or lack of it) among great numbers of couples who are having sexual relations—both married and unmarried.

Was I surprised at the outcome of the poll? Yes—but not very. I could have guessed the way it would go. But I never dreamed that more than 90,000 women would be moved to express themselves on this highly intimate subject. Nor would I have predicted the percentages or the passion with which so many women described their sex lives.

The greatest revelation, to me at least, is what the poll says about men as lovers. Clearly there is trouble in paradise.

Tomorrow I will print the results as well as excerpts from letters. That column is sure to be a topic of conversation in bars, drawing rooms, beauty shops and sociology classes for a long time to come.

The next day she released the results of the poll. These were her findings:

More than 90,000 women cast their ballots. Seventy-two percent said yes they would be content to be held close and treated tenderly and forget about the act. Of those 72 percent who said yes, 40 percent were under 40 years old. That was the most surprising aspect of the survey.

Many women who voted no said they needed the sexual climax to relieve physical tension. Almost as many said they wanted the ultimate in gratification—that anything less would make them feel exploited and used.

A 32-year-old from Atlanta put it this way: He insists on getting his satisfaction so why shouldn't I have mine?

Columbus, Ohio. I am under 40 and would be delighted to settle for tender words and warm caresses. The rest of it is a bore and can be exhausting. I am sure the sex act was designed strictly for the pleasure of males.

Anchorage, Alaska. I am under 40, 26 to be exact. I want three children, so obviously I need more than conversation. After I have my family, I would happily settle for separate rooms. Sex doesn't do a thing for me.

Westport, Connecticut. I vote yes. My husband is a diabetic and hasn't been able to perform for 10 years. I would have voted yes 20 years ago. He never bothered to satisfy me when he had his health. His illness was a blessing.

Kansas City. I am 55 and vote yes. The best part is the cuddling and caressing and the tender words that come with caring. My first husband used to rape me about five times a week. If a stranger had treated me like that I would have had him arrested.

Chicago. I don't want either his tender words or the act. My husband became impotent from alcoholism 10 years ago. The only word I'd like from him is "good-bye," but he won't leave.

Helena, Montana. No. I am 32. To say that touching and tender words are sufficient is like settling for the smell of fresh baked bread and ignoring the nourishment it provides. Such people must be crazy.

Texarkana. Yes. Without the tender embrace the act is animalistic. For years I hated sex and felt used. I was relieved when my husband died. My present mate is on heart pills that have made him impotent. It's like heaven to be held and cuddled.

Washington, D.C. Yes, yes a million times yes. I would love to be spoken to tenderly. It would be enough. My boyfriend never says a word. If I say anything he says, "Be quiet. You're spoiling things."

Eureka. I am 62 and voting no. If my old man was over the hill I would settle for high-school necking, but as long as he's able to shake the walls and wake up the neighbors downstairs, I want to get in on the action. And I'll take an encore anytime I can get it.[2]

Would you have believed that 72 percent of the women who responded care only about loving closeness and tenderness? I would, after having surveyed more than ten thousand women in polls of my own. It boils down to this: Women often give sex to get intimacy, and men give intimacy to get sex. Believe me, that difference has enormous implications. A man can enjoy a quick romp in bed, even if he and his wife have argued and bickered all evening. In some ways it is even more exciting for him to "conquer" this woman who has engaged him in a verbal battle. For her, sex under those circumstances makes her feel "used" by her husband . . . almost like a prostitute. This difference in orientation has set off a million fiery-tempered confrontations between husbands and wives who didn't really understand why the other was frustrated. Because women are more romantically inclined, the man who wants an exciting sexual relationship with his wife should focus on the *other* twenty-three and a half hours in the day. He should compliment her, bring her flowers, and tell her that he cares. These are the ingredients of genuine passion. Author Kevin Leman has gone a step further. He said the greatest of all aphrodisiacs is for a man to take out the garbage for his wife. I agree.

To make the most of the physical dimension of marriage, a man must pursue his wife's *mind* as well as her body. They cannot be separated. Turning the coin over, the woman should make herself as attractive to her husband as possible. Forget the curlers, cold cream, and flannel pajamas. He is a creature of vision, and she is a lover of touch. By a little unselfish fore-thought, each can learn to excite the other. The differences between them are what makes the game interesting.

～ Nothing Is Forever ～

John F. Whitaker, M.D., has written "A Personal Marriage Contract," which was published in *Woman's Day,* of all places, and bore this headline: "A set of contemporary guidelines for the young couple who are contemplating marriage today." Whitaker then provided a contract to be signed, witnessed, and dated by the parties involved. If you can read the conditions of the contract without becoming indignant, you're made of different stuff than I. Let me quote a few of the items:

I understand that nothing is forever; that there are no absolute guarantees, and that NOW is the only real forever.

I cannot make you happy or unhappy, but I can make myself happy. My happiness will be an invitation for you to join me in happiness, joy and love.

I will set my own standards and ultimately depend upon myself for approval.

I give up the myth that there is a "one and only" who will make me happy.

When I make commitments to do what I want to do, then I am being free. . . . There is no freedom without responsibility.

Since I understand that we cannot be everything to each other, I will respect and value the importance of your having separate play and work activities with separate friends and co-workers.

I understand that there will be pain as well as joy, and I accept the risk of a brief period when we part. [Notice that the author does not say "*if* we part."] I know that I must ultimately give up everyone I love unless he dies first.

I will love, honor, and respect you (but not obey or subjugate myself to you) until either of us changes his mind and maintains a change of attitude for a period of one year or until the termination date of the contract.

Don't expect me to accept you as you are when you fail to maintain mental attractiveness and fail to take care of your mind.

Don't expect me to accept you as you are when you fail to maintain physical attractiveness and fail to take care of your body.

I will put myself first. By keeping myself full, satisfied, and not hungry, I will have an abundance of joy, love, and caring to give you.

I will own my separate money and property, and enjoy sharing ownership with you of our common money and property.

Whenever we are confronted with a problem, I will resolve my feelings first, and then, with a cool mind, rationally solve any mutual problems with you.

While I reserve the right to have private areas of my life that I will not share with you, I will not lie to you either by word or action or by failure to share relevant information that affects our relationship.

I will not give come-on signals to others for sexual relations when I see that you feel threatened. I will count on you to recognize, admire and stroke me for my sexuality and attractiveness as a man or woman.[3]

A place is provided on the contract for the designated term of the agreement. The instructions read, "On the date of termination, we will reconfirm or renegotiate the contract; or we will cease being WITH each other, will part in a friendly manner and will go on with our lives separately."

Isn't that a sweet basis on which to build a marriage? The author is proposing that a straight life be established, but that the newlyweds agree in advance not to stay on it very long. And you can be assured that they won't. One basic flaw runs through the easy-out concept: It underestimates the power of sex and marriage to make us "one flesh" and fails to anticipate the ripping and tearing of that flesh at the moment of disintegration. It will only bring pain to those who apply its godless philosophy.

The Meaning of Commitment

Simply put, the stability of marriage is a by-product of an iron-willed determination to make it work. If you choose to marry, enter into that covenant with the resolve to remain committed to each other for life. Never threaten to leave your mate during angry moments. Don't allow yourself to consider even the possibility of divorce. Calling it quits must not become an option for those who want to go the distance!

That was the attitude of my father when he married my mother in 1935. Forty years later, he and I were walking in a park and talking about the meaning of commitment between a husband and wife. With that, he reached in his pocket and took out a worn piece of paper. On it was written a promise he had made to my mother when she agreed to become his wife. This is what he had said to her:

> I want you to understand and be fully aware of my feelings concerning the marriage covenant we are about to enter. I have been taught at my mother's knee, and in harmony with the Word of God, that the marriage vows are inviolable, and by entering into them I am binding myself absolutely and for life. The idea of estrangement from you through divorce for any reason at all (although God allows one—infidelity) will never at any time be permitted to enter into my thinking. I'm not naive in this. On the contrary, I'm fully aware of the possibility, unlikely as it now appears, that mutual incompatibility or other unforeseen circumstances could result in extreme mental suffering. If such becomes the case, I am resolved for my part to accept it as a consequence of the commitment I am now making, and to bear it, if necessary, to the end of our lives together.
>
> I have loved you dearly as a sweetheart and will continue to love you as my wife. But over and above that, I love you with a Christian love that demands that I never react in any way toward you that would jeopardize our prospects of entering heaven, which is the supreme objective of both our lives. And I pray that God Himself will make our affection for one another perfect and eternal.

If that is the way you approach the commitment of marriage, your probabilities of living happily together are vastly improved. Again, the Scripture endorses the permanence of the marital relationship: "Therefore what God has joined together, let man not separate" (Mark 10:9).

That's the Way Life Goes Sometimes

If the reader will bear with me, I must introduce you to one other child whose family experience has become so common in the Western world. I was waiting at Shawnee Mission Hospital for word on my dad's heart condition, after he was stricken in September. There in the waiting room was an *American Girl* magazine, which caught my attention. (I must have been desperate for something to read to have been attracted to the *American Girl*.)

I opened the cover page and immediately saw a composition written by a fourteen-year-old girl named Vicki Kraushaar. She had submitted her story for publication in the section of the magazine entitled "By You." I'll let Vicki introduce herself and describe her experience.

That's the Way Life Goes Sometimes

When I was ten, my parents got a divorce. Naturally, my father told me about it, because he was my favorite. [Notice that Vicki did not say, "I was *his* favorite."]

"Honey, I know it's been kind of bad for you these past few days, and I don't want to make it worse. But there's something I have to tell you. Honey, your mother and I got a divorce."

"But, Daddy—"

"I know you don't want this, but it has to be done. Your mother and I just don't get along like we used to. I'm already packed and my plane is leaving in half an hour."

"But, Daddy, why do you have to leave?"

"Well, honey, your mother and I can't live together anymore."

"I know that, but I mean why do you have to leave town?"

"Oh. Well, I got someone waiting for me in New Jersey."

"But, Daddy, will I ever see you again?"

"Sure you will, honey. We'll work something out."

"But what? I mean, you'll be living in New Jersey, and I'll be living here in Washington."

"Maybe your mother will agree to you spending two weeks in the summer and two in the winter with me."

"Why not more often?"

"I don't think she'll agree to two weeks in the summer and two in the winter, much less more."

"Well, it can't hurt to try."

"I know, honey, but we'll have to work it out later. My plane leaves in twenty minutes and I've got to get to the airport. Now I'm going to get my luggage, and I want you to go to your room so you don't have to watch me. And no long good-byes either."

"Okay, Daddy. Good-bye. Don't forget to write."

"I won't. Good-bye. Now go to your room."

"Okay. Daddy, I don't want you to go!"

"I know, honey. But I have to."

"Why?"

"You wouldn't understand, honey."

"Yes, I would."

"No, you wouldn't."

"Oh well. Good-bye."

"Good-bye. Now go to your room. Hurry up."

"Okay. Well, I guess that's the way life goes sometimes."

"Yes, honey. That's the way life goes sometimes."

After my father walked out that door, I never heard from him again.[4]

Vicki speaks eloquently on behalf of a million American children who have heard those shattering words, "Honey, your mother and I are getting a divorce." Throughout the world, husbands and wives are responding to the media blitz that urges and goads them to do their own thing, to chase impulsive desires without regard for the welfare of their families.

"The kids will get over it," goes the rationalization.

I'm so sorry, Vicki, that you had to go through this heartache at such a young age. Thank you for sharing your pain with us. Maybe it will help others avoid the errors of your parents. If we can prevent just one marriage from disintegrating—or just one child from suffering the loss of a family—our effort will be justified.

⟶ The Failure of Feminism ⟵

The now-defunct Women's Liberation Movement left its mark before disappearing from the scene, but the general public quickly realized that anger between the sexes and lesbian ideologies, even the Equal Rights Amendment, were not in society's best interests. Unfortunately, many gullible people were sucked into the web before their eyes were opened. Some are still paying the price for mistakes made during that era.

The best testimonial I have read to this effect was written by Kay Ebeling and published in the "My Turn" section of *Newsweek* magazine. I will let her speak from the vantage point of the 1990s:

> The other day I had the world's fastest blind date. A Yuppie from Eureka penciled me in for 50 minutes on a Friday and met me at a watering hole in the rural northern California town of Arcata. He breezed in, threw his jammed daily planner on the table and shot questions at me, watching my reactions as if it were a job interview. He eyed how much I drank. Then he breezed out to his next appointment. He had given us 50 minutes to size each other up and see if there was any chance for romance. His exit was so fast that as we left he let the door slam back in my face. It was an interesting slam.
>
> Most of our 50-minute conversation had covered the changing state of male-female relationships. My blind date was 40 years old, from the Experimental Generation. He is "actively pursuing new ways for men and women to interact now that old traditions no longer exist." That's a real quote. He really did say that, when I asked him what he liked to do. This was a man who'd read *Ms.* magazine and believed every word of it. He'd been single for 16 years but had lived with a few women during that time. He was off that evening for a ski weekend, meeting someone who was paying her own way for the trip.
>
> I too am from the Experimental Generation, but I couldn't even pay for my own drink. To me, feminism has backfired against women. In 1973 I left what could have been a perfectly good marriage, taking with me a child in diapers, a 10-year-old Plymouth and Volume 1, Number One of *Ms.* magazine. I was convinced I could make it on my own. In the last 15 years my ex has married or lived with a succession of women. As he gets older, his women stay in their 20s. Meanwhile, I've stayed unattached. He drives a BMW. I ride buses.

Today I see feminism as the Great Experiment That Failed, and women in my generation, its perpetrators, are the casualties. Many of us, myself included, are saddled with raising children alone. The resulting poverty makes us experts at cornmeal recipes and ways to find free recreation on weekends. At the same time, single men from our generation amass fortunes in CDs and real-estate ventures so they can breeze off on ski weekends. Feminism freed men, not women. Now men are spared the nuisance of a wife and family to support. After childbirth, if his wife's waist doesn't return to 20 inches, the husband can go out and get a more petite woman. It's far more difficult for the wife, now tied down with a baby, to find a new man. My blind date that Friday waved good-bye as he drove off in his RV. I walked home and paid the sitter with laundry quarters.

The main message of feminism was: woman, you don't need a man; remember, those of you around 40, the phrase: "A woman without a man is like a fish without a bicycle"? That joke circulated through "consciousness raising" groups across the country in the '70s. It was a philosophy that made divorce and cohabitation casual and routine. Feminism made women disposable. So today a lot of females are around 40 and single with a couple of kids to raise on their own. Child-support payments might pay for a few pairs of shoes, but in general, feminism gave men all the financial and personal advantages over women.

What's worse, we asked for it. Many women decided: you don't need a family structure to raise your children. We packed them off to day-care centers where they could get their nurturing from professionals. Then we put on our suits and ties, packed our briefcases and took off on this Great Experiment, convinced that there was no difference between ourselves and the guys in the other offices.

"Biological thing": How wrong we were. Because like it or not, women have babies. It's this biological thing that's just there, these organs we're born with. The truth is, a woman can't live the true feminist life unless she denies her childbearing biology. She has to live on the pill or have her tubes tied at an early age. Then she can keep up with the guys with an uninterrupted career and then, when she's 30, she'll be paying her own way on ski weekends too.

The reality of feminism is a lot of frenzied and overworked women dropping kids off at day-care centers. If the child is sick, they just send along some children's Tylenol and then rush off to underpaid jobs that they don't even like. Two of my working-mother friends told me they were mopping floors and folding laundry after midnight last week. They live on five hours of sleep, and it shows in their faces. And they've got husbands! I'm not advocating that women retrogress to the brainless housewives of the '50s who spent afternoons baking macaroni sculptures and keeping Betty Crocker files. Post–World War II women were the first to be left with a lot of free time, and they weren't too creative in filling it. Perhaps feminism was a reaction to that bored housewife, especially as she was portrayed in the media. In that respect, feminism has served a purpose.

Women should get educations so they can be brainy in the way they raise their children. Women can start small businesses, do consulting, write free-lance out of the home. But women don't belong in 12-hour-a-day executive office positions, and I can't figure out today what ever made us think we would want to be there in the first place. As long as that biology is there, women can't compete equally with men. A ratio cannot be made using dis-proportionate parts. Women and men are not equal; we're different. The economy might even improve if women came home, opening up jobs for unemployed men, who could then support a wife and children, the way it was, pre-feminism.

Sometimes on Saturday nights I'll get dressed up and go out club-hopping or to the theater, but the sight of all those other women my age, dressed a little too young, made up to hide encroaching wrinkles, looking hope-fully into the crowds, usually depresses me. I end up coming home, to spend my Saturday night with my daughter asleep in her room nearby. At least the NBC Saturday-night lineup is geared demographically to women at home alone.[5]

A former editor-in-chief and government public information officer, Kay Ebeling is now a single mother of a three-year-old daughter. Her eighteen-year-old son has lived with his father since age five, when Ebeling went to work full-time. "It was really ironic," Ebeling says. "I gave up custody of my son so I could pursue the feminist dream of an 'unfettered' career. Then I became a workaholic, trying to find the gratification on the job that I lost by giving up my son." She now writes freelance out of her home and does occa-sional childcare so she can earn a living and still be a full-time "stay-at-home" mother.

⟶ **I Am Committed to You** ⟵

To My Darlin' Little Wife, Shirley

on the occasion of our eighth anniversary

I'm sure you remember the many, many occasions during our eight years of marriage when the tide of love and affection soared high above the crest—times when our feeling for each other was almost limitless. This kind of intense emotion can't be brought about voluntarily, but it often accompanies a time of particular happiness. We felt it when I was offered my first professional position. We felt it when the world's most precious child came home from the maternity ward of Huntington Hospital. We felt it when the University of Southern California chose to award a doctoral degree to me. But emotions are strange! We felt the same closeness when the opposite kind of event took place; when threat and potential disaster entered our lives. We felt an intense closeness when a medical problem threatened to postpone our marriage plans. We felt it when you were hospitalized last year. I felt it intensely when I knelt over your unconscious form after a grinding automobile accident.

I'm trying to say this: Both happiness and threat bring that overwhelming appreciation and affection for a person's beloved sweetheart. But the fact is, most of life is made up of neither disaster nor unusual hilarity. Rather it is composed of the routine, calm, everyday events in which we participate. And during these times, I enjoy the quiet, serene love that actually surpasses the effervescent display, in many ways. It is not as exuberant, perhaps, but it runs deep and solid. I find myself firmly in that kind of love on this eighth anniversary. Today I feel the steady and quiet affection that comes from a devoted heart. I am committed to you and your happiness, now more than I've ever been. I want to remain your "sweetheart."

When events throw us together emotionally, we will enjoy the thrill and romantic excitement. But during life's routine, like today, my love stands undiminished. Happy Anniversary to my wonderful wife.

Jim

The key phrase in my note to Shirley is, "I am committed to you." My love for my wife is not blown back and forth by the winds of change, by circumstances and environmental influences. Even though my fickle emotions jump from one extreme to another, my commitment remains solidly anchored. I have chosen to love my wife, and that choice is sustained by an uncompromising will.

~ A Kiss That Still Works ~

There is nothing so ugly as a husband or wife who bitterly attacks and demeans his mate. But nothing is so beautiful as a loving relationship that conforms to God's magnificent design. We'll conclude with a brilliant example of this divinely inspired love. It was written by the surgeon who experienced it. Perhaps you will be deeply moved by his words, as was I:

I stand by the bed where a young woman lies, her face postoperative, her mouth twisted in palsy, clownish. A tiny twig of the facial nerve, the one to the muscles of her mouth, has been severed. She will be thus from now on. The surgeon had followed with religious fervor the curve of her flesh; I promise you that. Nevertheless, to remove the tumor in her cheek, I had to cut the little nerve.

Her young husband is in the room. He stands on the opposite side of the bed, and together they seem to dwell in the evening lamplight, isolated from me, private. Who are they, I ask myself, he and this wry-mouth I have made, who gaze at and touch each other so generously, greedily? The young woman speaks.

"Will my mouth always be like this?" she asks.

"Yes," I say, "it will. It is because the nerve was cut."

She nods and is silent. But the young man smiles.

"I like it," he says. "It is kind of cute."

All at once I *know* who he is. I understand, and I lower my gaze. One is not bold in an encounter with a god. Unmindful, he bends to kiss her crooked mouth, and I so close I can see how he twists his own lips to accommodate to hers, to show her that their kiss still works. I remember that the gods appeared in ancient Greece as mortals, and I hold my breath and let the wonder in.[3]

CHAPTER SIX

Life Lessons

The temporal things of this world, even vast riches and power, will not deliver the satisfaction they advertise! There must be something more substantial on which to base one's values, purposes, and goals. And of course, there is. Jesus said it succinctly: "But seek ye first the kingdom of God, and his righteousness; and all these things shall be added unto you."

Jesus Christ is the source—the only source—of meaning in life. He provides the only satisfactory explanation for why we're here and where we're going. Because of this good news, the final heartbeat for the Christian is not the mysterious conclusion to a meaningless existence. It is, rather, the grand beginning to a life that will never end.

~ An Overcomer ~

My friend David Hernandez was born to illegal immigrants from Mexico who were trying to start a new life in this country. Unfortunately, they couldn't find work for months, and the children were hungry for weeks at a time. Finally, the family was hired as migrant farmworkers helping to harvest the potato crop in the state of California. They lived under trees and used a big oil drum as a stove. They owned nothing and had very little chance of escaping the suffocating grip of poverty.

Despite their depressing circumstances, the Hernandez family had a certain dignity and strength about them. They were Christians, and they taught their children that God loved them and had a plan for their lives. Their little boy, David, internalized that message of hope. He never thought of himself as a victim even though he had every reason to feel cheated. His family was at the bottom of the social ladder without even a house to live in, but his worth as an individual was rooted in his faith.

David began attending public schools, and he proved to be an outstanding student. As he grew older, he was given a scholarship to attend a private school, where he continued to excel academically. To make a long story short, he went on to graduate from college near the top of his class and was granted admission to Loma Linda University School of Medicine. He earned his medical degree and went into a surgical residency in obstetrics and gynecology. Dr. David Hernandez then became a professor at both Loma Linda University and the University of Southern California schools of medicine.

Who would have thought that the little Mexican boy in the potato fields would become a highly respected physician and medical educator? It would never have happened if David had seen himself as a helpless victim—a loser whom life had shortchanged. Because he refused to adopt a defeatist attitude, he overcame the obstacles in his path.

But life was to deal David Hernandez yet another challenge. He called one day to tell me that he had been diagnosed with a terrible liver disease. He was still in his thirties at the time. A few years later, David died from this rare disorder called sclerosing cholangitis.

I went to see him in the hospital a few days before the end. Though very sick, David did not whine or ask, "Why me?" Even in that difficult hour when he knew death was imminent, he never indulged in self-pity. He knew intuitively that a person is only a victim if he accepts himself as one.

I strongly advise you to follow Dr. David Hernandez's model—to resist the temptation to see yourself as a victim. Fight it with all your might. It is one of Satan's most powerful weapons against you, and it is a lie. God made you with His own hands, and He makes no junk. He will help you overcome the circumstances that present themselves as obstacles lying in your path.

∼ Life Will Trash Your Trophies ∼

I have lived long enough to see some of my early dreams of glory come unstitched. One of them began shortly after I graduated from high school and went off to college. I arrived on campus several days before classes started and walked around looking at the place that would be my home for the next four years. I was like a tourist on holiday.

Of greatest interest to me that morning was the trophy case standing in the main administration building. There behind the glass were the glitzy symbols of past athletic victories. Basketball, track, and baseball were well represented there. Then I saw it. Standing majestically at the center of the case was the perpetual tennis trophy. It was about two feet tall and had a shiny little man on top. Engraved on the shaft were the names of all the collegiate tennis champions back to 1947. Every one of those heroes was burned into my memory. I could name most of them today.

As I stood there before that historic trophy, I said to myself, *Someday! Some fine day I'm going to add my name to that list of legends.* I set my jaw and determined to show the world.

As strange as it may seem today, becoming our college tennis champ was my highest goal in living at that time. Nothing could have mattered more to me. Tennis had been my passion in high school.

I had played six days a week and eleven months per year. When I graduated and headed for college, it was with the intention of riding this sport into the record books.

Well, I did have a certain amount of success with my tennis career. I lettered all four years, captained the team as a senior, and yes, I got my name inscribed on the big trophy. In fact, I did it twice during each of my last two seasons. I left the college with the satisfaction of knowing that future generations of freshmen would stand at the display case and read my name in admiration. Someday they might be great like me.

Alas, about fifteen years later, a friend had reason to visit the college I attended. He was dumping something in the trash behind the administration building, and what do you suppose he found? Yep, there among the garbage and debris was the perpetual tennis trophy! The athletic department had actually thrown it away! What a blow! There I was, a legend in my own time, and who cared? Some universities retire the jersey numbers of their greatest athletes. My school didn't retire my number. They retired my memory!

The friend, Dr. Wil Spaite, who had been one of my teammates in college, took the tennis trophy home and cleaned it up. He put a new shiny man on the top and bought a new base for it. Then he gave it to me to commemorate our "prime," which everyone appeared to have forgotten. That trophy stands in my office today. I'll show it to you if you come by for a visit. My name is on it twice. You'll be impressed. It was a big deal at the time. Honest.

This brief encounter with fame has taught me a valuable lesson about success and achievement. Pay attention now, because this could be on the mid-term: *If you live long enough, life will trash your trophies, too.* I don't care how important something seems at the time, if it is an end in itself, the passage of time will render it old and tarnished. Who cares today that Zachary Taylor or William Henry Harrison won their elections for president of the United States? Can you name three U.S. senators in the year 1933? Probably not, and who cares anyway? What difference did it make that the Brooklyn Dodgers defeated the Yankees in the 1955 World Series? The hero of that series, Sandy Amoros, made a game-saving catch that a nation cheered, but he was soon penniless, forgotten, and living on the streets.

John Gilbert was the biggest romantic male movie star of the 1920s. He was by far the highest-paid actor in Hollywood, and his name was given top billing in every movie in which he starred. Almost everyone in the country knew his name. But within two years, no studio would hire him. Gilbert died in 1936 from a heart attack brought on by alcohol and drug abuse. He was just thirty-six years old. Have you ever heard of him? I doubt it. My point is that even the most awesome triumphs lose their sizzle in time.

Let me bring the matter closer to home. In November 1974, the University of Southern California's football team played its historic rival, Notre Dame, at the Coliseum in Los Angeles. It was one of the most exciting games in history, especially for USC fans. I attended graduate school at USC, and I still get very jazzed about its football games. And there are very few pleasures more gratifying for me than beating the socks off Notre Dame! (Supporters of the Irish will just have to forgive me.)

Well, that November day in 1974 produced one of the greatest football games of all times. Notre Dame ripped through the Trojans in the first half, leading 24–6 at halftime. I don't know what Coach John McKay said to his team in the locker room, but something set USC on fire. They were an entirely different club in the second half. A tailback named Anthony

(A. D.) Davis took the opening kickoff eighty-five yards for a touchdown. That started one of the most unbelievable comebacks in the history of the series. By the final gun, A. D. had scored four touchdowns, and USC had put 54 points on the board.

I was watching the game on television that afternoon. There I was in my study, cheering and screaming as though I were surrounded by a hundred thousand fans in the Coliseum. I never sat down through the second half! It was some kind of day.

A. D. Davis was the hero of the game, of course. He was on talk shows, and his picture was on virtually every sports page in the country the next morning. He had his day in the sun, to be sure. Football fans everywhere were talking about Anthony and his four explosive touchdowns.

Well, many years went by, and USC was again engaged in another make-or-break football game. This time the opponent was UCLA, and the winner would be going to the Rose Bowl on January 1, 1990. I was on the sidelines that day as the Trojans pulled off another miracle and scored a last-minute touchdown to win. The athletic director at that time, Mike McGee, is a friend of mine, and he invited me into the locker room after the game. It was another wonderful victory in the history of USC football. The two heroes of the day, Rodney Peete and Eric Afhaulter, were hoisted to the shoulders of their teammates, and everyone was singing the Trojan fight song. It was a fine experience just being there.

Then I was distracted momentarily and looked to my left. There in the shadows was A. D. Davis, the superstar of 1974. He was watching the hulla-baloo from the sidelines. I don't mean to be disrespectful to him because it happens to all of us, but A. D. didn't look like the finely tuned athlete I remembered from the past. He had put on some weight and had acquired a little belly that wasn't there in his prime. Here was "Mr. Yesterday," watch-ing the new whiz kids and probably remembering what it was like to be in the spotlight. But his time on center stage had come and gone, and now—what did it really matter?

That's the way the system works. Your successes will fade from memory, too. That doesn't mean you shouldn't try to achieve them. But it should lead you to ask, Why are they important to me? Are my trophies for me, or are they for Him? Those are critical questions that every believer is obli-gated to answer.

∼⊙ The Orientation Blues ⊙∼

When I first joined the staff at Children's Hospital in Los Angeles, I had to go through an "orientation session." An orientation session is a meeting that employees are required to attend when they begin a new job. It's a training period prepared by the employer to acquaint each person with the organization that has hired him. But unfortunately, these meetings are usually boring—it almost seems that they're planned to be dull! The speakers talk endlessly about health insurance and retirement programs and the proper use of the telephone and similar topics that are terribly monotonous. Knowing this, I dreaded going through the orientation session at the hospital.

Nevertheless, I arrived as expected at 9:00 A.M. There were twelve new employees in the room that day, and it just happened that I was the only man there. The eleven women appeared to be young, and I guessed that most of them were secretaries or clerks, probably starting their first jobs. The atmosphere between the people that morning was "icy." In other words, the women were strangers to each other, and they seemed frightened and tense. They came in quietly and sat around a large, horseshoe-shaped table, but no one talked unless spoken to. If one of the young ladies had anything to say, she leaned over and covered her mouth so others would not hear.

I could see that there was one possibility of keeping us all awake for the next two hours, and that was for the director to offer us plenty of coffee—it was our only hope! And sure enough, a large coffeepot was percolating on a table in a corner. However, nothing was said about coffee. I can only guess that the pot had not been plugged in until a few minutes earlier, and it was not ready. However, it was obvious that all eleven women were thinking about that coffeepot, because every time it chugged, they would turn and look at it. What's more, there were colorful donuts arranged on the table, and the aroma filled the room. But the goodies were never mentioned.

The orientation lady stepped to the front of the room and began her long-winded speech. She spoke in a dry, monotonous voice, and attacked the first subject on a forty-two-item list. She talked for over an hour, but still nothing was said about coffee. The women yawned sleepily, leaned on one elbow, and glanced periodically in the direction of the coffeepot.

Finally, after an endless presentation, the leader said, "Okay, we're going to take a break and get some coffee now." However, she wasn't about to send all eleven ladies to the coffee table at the same time. Instead, she thought she had a better idea. She turned to a lady at one end of the table and said, "How would you like to slip back and get a cup of coffee?"

Well, this young lady was very shy, and she wasn't sure she wanted to be the first to go. She obviously knew that there are many ways a person can get "hurt" doing anything in front of eleven other people. She could trip on her way to the coffee table, or the spigot could stick on the coffeepot, or she could burn herself coming back. I watched her as she looked around the room and considered the risks of accepting the coffee. In a moment, she dropped her eyes and said, "No, thank you, I don't believe I'll have any."

I *knew* she wanted a cup of coffee. What she planned to do, it was clear, was to wait until everybody else had gone to the refreshment table, and then she could quietly get a cup of coffee with no risk! That way her ego wouldn't be in any danger. I found her amusing, but just watched her quietly from the opposite side of the table where I sat.

The orientation lady then turned to the next girl and said, "Well, okay, how about you? Would you like to have a cup of coffee?"

But you see, the second girl faced all the same risks that scared the first young lady, plus a new one. The group had now "spoken" through that first individual and said, "We're not drinking coffee today." Only one "vote" had been cast, but it was unanimous. This pressure on the second girl was also too great, so she said, "No, thank you." That made the vote two to nothing!

The coffee invitation was then extended to the third girl. "Will you have a cup of coffee?" said the leader.

"No, thank you," said the employee.

The pressure then became enormous. It was clear that no one was expected to drink coffee or eat donuts. To my amazement, all the other women refused the offer of refreshments one at a time. Each said, "No, thanks" when their turn came to reply. But when the invitation was made to me, I said, "I believe I'll have a cup."

Would you believe that when I got up to get my cup of coffee, *eleven women followed me to the table!* I looked over my shoulder and here they came. As a gentleman, I felt I should step back and let the ladies go first, and it took me fifteen minutes to reach the goodies table!

Isn't it amazing how terrified we are of each other? We won't even get a cup of coffee if it's not socially acceptable at a given moment! We're terrified that somebody will laugh at us or ridicule us, or that we might make a mistake in front of others. Even such a completely insignificant thing as getting a cup of coffee can be frightening if we think the rest of the group doesn't want us to do it. This causes us to limit our behavior to those acts which are completely safe and totally beyond ridicule. We do that to eliminate the chance of anyone laughing at us.

⌒ **Come and Gone** ⌒

Everything in this life is temporary. That thought occurred to me one day when I was taking a commercial airline flight. We taxied out to the end of the runway and waited for clearance to take off. I looked out the window and saw the remains of two huge 747 airplanes sitting on the field. All the paint had been stripped off the fuselage, and rust was spreading down from the top. The insides had been gutted, and the windows were sealed. Then I saw a tiny bit of blue paint on the tail of one plane and realized these had been proud ships in the fleet of Pan American Airways.

The empty hulks looked pitiful sitting out there alone, shorn of their beauty. For some reason, they reminded me of the poem entitled "Little Boy Blue" by Eugene Field (1850–1895). The first stanza reads:

> The little toy dog is covered with dust,
> But sturdy and staunch he stands.
> And the little toy soldier is red with rust,
> And his musket molds in his hands.
> Time was when the little toy dog was new,
> And the soldier was passing fair;
> And that was the time when our Little Boy Blue
> Kissed them and put them there.[1]

I might have composed my own poem as I sat looking out the window:

> Time was when these two airplanes were new
> And they flew to great heights in the sky.
> But now they are rusty, forgotten, and old
> And they seem to be questioning, "Why?"

I imagined the day these magnificent craft were rolled out of the Boeing plant with shiny new enamel and the proud Pan Am insignia on their tails. They were christened with champagne amid cheers and laughter. Then they were taken on their maiden voyages. Little boys and girls craned their necks skyward to watch these beautiful birds come in for a landing. What excitement they must have generated for passengers and crew.

Now the company that owned them has gone bankrupt, and the planes are grounded forever. How could it happen in fewer than twenty years? Who would have thought these multimillion-dollar aircraft would come to such a quick and ignoble end?

As we taxied past the shells, I thought about the impermanence of everything that now looks so stable. Nothing lasts very long. And we are the ones who are passing through, on our way to another life of far greater significance.

You Cannot Outgive God

I learned to give a tenth of my income to the church when I was a preschool lad. My grandmother would give me a dollar every now and then, and she always instructed me to place a dime of it in the church offering the next Sunday morning. I have tithed from that day to this. I also watched my father give of his limited resources, not only to the church, but to anyone in need.

My dad was the original soft touch to those who were hungry. He was an evangelist who journeyed from place to place to hold revival meetings. Travel was expensive, and we never seemed to have much more money than was absolutely necessary. One of the problems was the way churches paid their ministers in those days. Pastors received a year-round salary, but evangelists were paid only when they worked. Therefore, my father's income stopped abruptly during Thanksgiving, Christmas, summer vacation, or any time he rested. Perhaps that's why we were always near the bottom of the barrel when he was at home. But that didn't stop my father from giving.

I remember Dad going off to speak in a tiny church and coming home ten days later. My mother greeted him warmly and asked how the revival had gone. He was always excited about that subject. Eventually, in moments like this she would get around to asking him about the offering. Women have a way of worrying about things like that.

"How much did they pay you?" she asked.

I can still see my father's face as he smiled and looked at the floor. "Aw . . . ," he stammered. My mother stepped back and looked into his eyes.

"Oh, I get it," she said. "You gave the money away again, didn't you?"

"Myrt," he said. "The pastor there is going through a hard time. His kids are so needy. It just broke my heart. They have holes in their shoes, and one of them is going to school on these cold mornings without a coat. I felt I should give the entire fifty dollars to them."

My good mother looked intently at him for a moment and then she smiled. "You know, if God told you to do it, it's okay with me."

Then a few days later the inevitable happened. The Dobsons ran completely out of money. There was no reserve to tide us over. That's when my father gathered us in the bedroom for a time of prayer. I remember that day as though it were yesterday. He prayed first.

"Oh Lord, You promised that if we would be faithful with You and Your people in our good times, then You would not forget us in our time of need. We have tried to be generous with what You have given us, and now we are calling on You for help."

A very impressionable ten-year-old boy named Jimmy was watching and listening very carefully that day. *What will happen?* he wondered. *Did God hear Dad's prayer?*

The next day an unexpected check for $1,200 came for us in the mail. Honestly! That's the way it happened, not just this once but many times. I saw the Lord match my dad's giving stride for stride. No, God never made us wealthy, but my young faith grew by leaps and bounds. I learned that you *cannot* outgive God!

My father continued to give generously through the mid-life years and into his sixties. I used to worry about how he and Mom would fund their retirement years because they were able to save very little money. If Dad did get many dollars ahead, he'd give them away. I wondered how in the world they would live on the pittance paid to retired ministers by our denomination. (As a widow, my mother received just $80.50 per month after Dad spent forty-four years in the church.) It is disgraceful how poorly we take care of our retired ministers and their widows.

One day my father was lying on the bed, and Mom was getting dressed. She turned to look at him and he was crying.

"What's the matter?" she asked.

"The Lord just spoke to me," he replied.

"Do you want to tell me about it?" she prodded.

"He told me something about you," Dad said.

She then demanded that he tell her what the Lord had communicated to him.

My father said, "It was a strange experience. I was just lying here thinking about many things. I wasn't praying or even thinking about you when the Lord spoke to me and said, 'I'm going to take care of Myrtle.'"

Neither of them understood the message but simply filed it away in the catalog of imponderables. But five days later my dad had a massive heart attack, and three months after that he was gone. At sixty-six years of age, this good man whose name I share went out to meet the Christ whom he had loved and served all those years.

It was thrilling to witness the way God fulfilled His promise to take care of my mother. Even when she was suffering from end-stage Parkinson's disease and required constant care at an astronomical cost, God provided. The small inheritance that Dad left to his wife multiplied in the years after his departure. It was sufficient to pay for everything she needed, including marvelous and loving care. God was with her in every other way, too, tenderly cradling her in His secure arms until He took her home. In the end, my dad never came close to outgiving God.

May I urge you to give generously not only to your church, but also to the needy people whom God puts in your path? There is no better way to keep material things and money in proper perspective. You can hardly become selfish or greedy when you are busily sharing what you have with others. You see, God does not need your money. He could fund His ministries from an annual beef auction alone (He owns the cattle on a thousand hills). But you and I *need* to give! Those who comprehend and respond to this biblical principle will find that He is faithful to "open you the windows of heaven, and pour you out a blessing, that there shall not be room enough to receive it" (Malachi 3:10 KJV). And don't forget the greatest blessing of all: The curly-headed, impressionable children around your feet will be watching and will someday pass the good news on to *their* kids! That may be your greatest legacy on this earth.

⟶ **Miracle at Yellowstone** ⟵

I have been privileged to witness some incredible evidences of God's power in my life and in the experiences of those with whom I am close. One of the most miraculous events happened to my friend Jim Davis when he and his family visited Yellowstone National Park in 1970. Jim was a guest on the Focus on the Family broadcast some time later, and he shared that experience with our listeners. These are his approximate words on that occasion:

My wife and I were both raised in Christian families, and we were taught the power of prayer. But we were not living very godly lives. We did not pray together or have a family altar in our home. About that time, she made a wonderful commitment to the Lord and began praying for me. She bought me a research Bible, and I began to get into the Word. Things started to change in my heart, but I still wasn't mature spiritually.

That summer, we went on a vacation to Yellowstone Park with four other couples. Several of these friends went fishing the next day in an aluminum boat, and one of the ladies hooked a trout. She leaned over to net the fish, and her glasses fell off. They immediately sank to the bottom of the lake. She was very disturbed by the loss because it was the beginning of their vacation, and she could not drive or read without the glasses. She also got severe headaches when she didn't wear them.

That night, everyone was talking about the glasses and how unfortunate it was that they were lost. Then my wife said, "No sweat. Jim is a great scuba diver. He'll go out and find them for you."

"Hey, thanks a lot," I said. "Do you know that Yellowstone Lake has 172 miles of shoreline, and every tree is coniferous and looks exactly the same? There's no way I can get a fix on where you guys were when the glasses went overboard. Besides, the water is very, very cold—50 degrees. They won't even allow you to water-ski out there. And I don't have a wet suit—just a pair of fins and snorkel."

My objections fell on deaf ears. She told me privately that she intended to pray that the Lord would help me find those glasses.

Yeah, sure, I thought.

The next morning we got in the boat and headed about a half mile out from shore.

"Uh, where do you think you dropped them?" I asked.

"It seems like about here," someone said.

Well, I got in the water, and it was freezing. I took hold of a rope, and the boat dragged me along the surface as I looked at the bottom. The water was about ten feet deep and crystal-clear. We made a swath about fifty feet long and then turned and worked our way back. After about twenty minutes of this search, I was just chilled to the bone. I prayed a little prayer and said, "Lord, if You know where those glasses are, I sure wish You'd tell me." I wasn't convinced He knew. It's a very big lake.

But a little voice in my mind said, *I know exactly where they are. Get in the boat, and I'll take you to them.* Well, I didn't tell anyone about this message because I was too embarrassed to say it. But about twenty minutes later I was just shivering, and I said, "Lord, if You still know where those glasses are, I'll get in the boat."

I called out to my friends and said, "We're in the wrong place. They're over there."

I got in the boat and pointed to a spot that I thought the Lord was telling me about. The driver said, "No, we weren't out that far." But we kept going, and I said, "Stop. Right here. This is the place."

I jumped back in the water and looked down. We were right on top of those glasses. I dove to the bottom and came up with the prize. It was one of the clearest answers to prayer I've ever experienced, and it set me on fire spiritually. It was also an incredible witness to my wife and all my friends. And I'll never forget those sparkling glasses at the bottom of Yellowstone Lake.

As dramatic as this story is, I can personally vouch for its authenticity as Jim told it. There are many witnesses who remember that remarkable day on Yellowstone Lake. What I don't know is why the Lord chose to reveal Himself that way, or why He doesn't do it more often. Clearly, He has plans and purposes to which we are not privy.

∼ Study While You Sleep ∽

When I was in college, there was a malicious little rumor going around that an amazing discovery had been made about human learning. A new technique called "sleep teaching" made it possible to cram one's head full of facts while sawing the logs. I have to tell you that idea was very appealing to me. It would have fit into my program perfectly to do the big-man-on-campus thing during the day and accomplish my studying while dreaming. Also, being a psychology major, I was interested in brain functions and promptly set out to test the hypothesis.

I selected a class in which three tests were given during the semester with the lowest score being dropped by the professor. I studied hard on the first two exams and earned respectable grades, which permitted me to experiment with the third. When the exam was scheduled, I recorded all the necessary factual information on my tape machine, being careful not to learn the details as I spoke into the microphone. In all, about sixty minutes of data were packed on one side of an old reel-to-reel tape. Then I went out and enjoyed myself the night before the test. While my brighter friends were grinding away in the library, I was shooting the breeze in a restaurant with some guys who never studied much anyway. It felt wonderful.

At bedtime that night, I plugged the tape recorder into my clock radio so that my own voice would begin speaking to my unconscious mind at 2:00 A.M. One hour later, I was awakened by the flopping of the tape at the end of the reel, and I reset the timer for 4:00. The tape played for another hour and awakened me again at 5:00. The final "hearing" occurred between 6:00 and 7:00. So passed the restless night.

The examination was scheduled for 8:00, and I was there, yawning and bleary-eyed. The first thing I noted was that the questions on the printed test were not even vaguely familiar to me (always a bad sign). But I was still confident that the information was stored down deep in my brain, somewhere. I turned in the test and stood waiting for a proctor to calculate my score. It only took a few minutes.

There were seventy-three people in the class, and I got the seventy-second lowest score. I managed to beat the class dummy by one point, but he appealed to the professor over a disputed answer and was granted two additional points. I came in dead last! The only thing I got from that experiment was a terrible night's sleep and the wrath of a roommate who had lain there in the moonlight learning junk he didn't want to know.

Many years have passed since those days of my callow youth when I still thought getting something for nothing was possible. I was dead wrong. Everything worth having comes with a price.

⤳ A Man and His Animals ⤝

Proverbs 12:10 says, "A righteous man cares for the needs of his animal[s], but the kindest acts of the wicked are cruel." It makes sense, doesn't it? Anyone who would care about the welfare of a helpless dog or cat or cow is likely to have a soft spot for hurting people, as well. My dad was such a man. He loved everything God made, especially furry little canines called toy terriers.

Penny was a brilliant representative of that breed. We adopted him into our family when I was thirteen years of age, and the two of us grew up together. By the time I left for college, he was established as a full-fledged member of the Dobson household, with all the rights and privileges thereof. He and my dad had a special understanding for one another, like two old friends who could communicate deep feelings without uttering a word. Only dog lovers will fully comprehend what I mean.

But alas, Penny grew old and decrepit. At seventeen years of age, he was afflicted with a terminal case of cancer and was obviously experiencing severe pain. He would walk the fence and moan hour after hour. My dad knew the time had come to put his little friend to sleep, but he couldn't bring himself to do it.

"How can I kill my dog?" he would ask.

But it was more cruel to let Penny suffer. So Dad made an appointment with the veterinarian at the humane society to discuss the matter. The doctor was a perceptive man and recognized how painful this event was for my father. He shared a similar situation with reference to his own dog, and these two grown men sat and wept together.

The decision was made to end Penny's life, and the day was chosen. Throughout the prior afternoon, a man and a dog sat together under the vine-covered arbor in their backyard. Neither spoke. (Penny communicated his thoughts with his ears and eyes and tail.) I suspect they both cried. Then they said good-bye for the final time.

When the moment came, Penny was given five barbiturates to prevent him from recognizing the despised smell of the animal hospital. My mother handed him to the attendant and then hurried back to the car. Dad was visibly shaken. For nearly a week, he sat alone under the arbor, going there immediately after fulfilling his teaching responsibilities at the college each day. He continued to grieve for Penny for several years.

During this time, we encouraged my father to get another dog, but he was reluctant to expose himself to another painful loss. Nine years passed before he considered trying to replace the memory of Penny.

But wait, why don't I let him tell you the story in his own words. The following narrative was written by my dad, shortly before his death:

Guaranteed Healthy

I like dogs. Some of my best friends are dogs! I sometimes think that I can communicate better with dogs than I can with people. At least I have never had a dog misunderstand me to the point of breaking up a friendship once it was established! I had grieved for my little toy terrier, Penny, for nine years. I said I would never get another dog. Some of this was due to the Judas Iscariot kind of guilt I was carrying. You see, I was forced by my very love for him to end his hopeless agony. I, his trusted keeper, betrayed him to his executioner! Penny, so gentle, so obedient, so intelligent! Gone was my constant companion of seventeen years! I miss him still and always will, but "Nine years is enough," I told my wife. "I will get me another dog."

"You are just asking for more pain," she said. "A dog's life usually averages about eight to ten years—then you will have to go through this sorrow again."

"Maybe not," I said. "I have thought a lot about this decision. I will soon be over the hill myself. It could be that we will arrive at the Golden Gate at about the same time."

I decided to take great care in selecting this new pet. I wanted the same kind of dog, a toy terrier, but he would have to be pedigreed. Penny had been a lucky accident—a throwback more like his fox terrier ancestors. I know the breed and know, too, that beyond the AKC papers, you have to select the individual dog for intelligence and other desirable qualities. You have to get a pup by six weeks of age, to be sure he hasn't been ruined by someone else. Then he would have to be in perfect health, having had the necessary shots, etc.

All these thoughts were getting settled in my mind as I started watching the papers for dog advertisements. No luck. Someone would always beat me to the best dogs, since I wouldn't answer an ad on Sunday, and that's when thoroughbreds were offered. Finally, I saw a notice from a pet shop about a toy terrier, but I didn't take it seriously.

"There's something funny about this," I told my wife. "The ad says the dog is a nine-month-old thoroughbred, but he has no papers. Nine months in a pet shop and nobody wants him! It doesn't sound good to me. I wouldn't buy an unregistered dog anyway!" But later, I said, "Let's just drive out and see him."

We found the shop in a rundown section of the city. My wife was almost afraid to get out of the car. The business was in one room of an old abandoned house. When I stepped through the front door, the stench almost over-whelmed me. I spotted the dog in question at once. He was crowded into a cubicle with other larger puppies who were bumping him and stepping on his tiny body. They were a motley assortment of mongrels of various kinds, all yapping and defecating; some were trying to sleep away their misery, curled up on the wire bottom of their filthy enclosure!

When the saleslady brought the little toy terrier out and put him down on the floor he seemed to be in a wall-eyed trance.

This dog has been through some traumatic emotional experience, I thought. He looked up at me with pitiful glazed eyes that reflected unspeakable sadness. Far from considering him, I couldn't believe anyone would offer an animal for sale in this condition. His skinny little frame, all four pounds of it, was trembling, and every few seconds he would cough and gag from some kind of chest infec-tion. I thought I recognized this as a case of the dreaded distemper. Between coughs, he would dig frantically at his ears, which were infested with mites. He would follow me about the room, meekly, his tiny tail clamped tightly down—a picture of dejection.

Nobody knows what other disease he has got—maybe incurable, I thought. *Oh, no! I'm not getting into that!* But in spite of myself I wanted to cry. He seemed to be saying, "You look like a nice man, but I know you will be like all the rest." He was so little and helpless and hopeless. While I was hardening myself to his unhappy fate with such reasoning as "It's not my fault . . . I can't turn my home into a dog hospital," he put out his warm pink tongue and licked my hand, as if to say, "Thanks, anyway, for coming to see me." I had to get out of there quick!

We were silent as we drove away. When we had gone a few blocks I made an instant decision. I guess it was the effect of that lick on the hand—the intuitive longing it expressed! Wheeling the car around, I started back. I turned stone deaf to the neatly logical reasoning my wife poured into my ear. In a split second, instead of a nameless wart of a dog in a rotten pet shop, that had become my little dog in there, suffering and lonely and sick! I was bursting with compassion that should rightfully have been expended on a more worthy object: I know, God, please forgive me. I wrote the check and received in exchange a receipt for the money. On it were the incredible words, "*Guaranteed Healthy!*"

I folded the shivering form into my arms, stink and all. A warm bath soon removed the nauseating smell; then I took him to the best veterinarian I could find. He took one look and shook his head.

"I'll try, but I can't promise he will make it," he said. It was days of anti-biotics for the cough, weeks of application of drops for the ear mites, worm medicine, shots of various kinds, a tonic to regulate that wildly beating little heart, and love made warm and tender by years of grieving for Penny. And to the astonishment of the doctor, most of all, we have a dog to be proud of, fit and sound.

And talk about gratitude! My pup, whom we named Benji, expresses it in the blasphemous, idolatrous way he worships me. He thinks I am God Almighty when he comes to meet me in the morning, twisting and wiggling like he will tear himself in two. It is as though he will never allow himself to forget his private hell in the pet shop!

Three years after this happy beginning, Benji was to lose his beloved master. He had seen my mother and father leave in the car one morning, but only one of them returned. No one could explain to him the meaning of death, of course. So Benji sat waiting month in and out, straining to hear the sound of that familiar voice. The shutting of a car door would bring him hope and excitement . . . followed by obvious disappointment. Wrong person, again.

I visited my mother several months after the funeral to help pack my father's possessions and give away his clothes. As I busily folded coats and pants and placed them in a suitcase, Benji jumped on the bed. He reverently approached the clothes and sniffed them carefully on all sides. He climbed into the suitcase and curled up within one of my father's most familiar coats. Then he looked up at me.

"I understand, Benji. I miss him, too," I said.

⤙ Forgiving Your Parents ⤚

My mother closed her eyes for the last time on June 26, 1988, and went to be with the Lord. She had been so vibrant—so important to each member of our family. I couldn't imagine life without her just a few years earlier. But time passed so quickly, and before we knew it, she had grown old and sick and incompetent. This human experience is like that. In just a brief moment, it seems, our fleeting days are gone, and as King David said, "The place thereof will know it no more."

As I sat at the memorial service for my good mother, I was flooded with memories and a profound sense of loss. But there was not the slightest hint of regret, remorse, or guilt. There were no hurtful words I wished I could have taken back. There were no brawls—no prolonged conflicts—that remained unresolved between my parents and me.

Why not? Was I a perfect son, born to flawless parents? Of course not. But in 1962, when Shirley and I had been married two years and I was twenty-six years old, I remember saying to her, "Our parents will not always be with us. I see now the incredible brevity of life that will some-day take them from us. We must keep that in mind as we live out our daily lives. I want to respond to both sets of parents in such a way that we will have no regrets after they are gone. This is what I believe the Lord wants of us."

To those of you who are in need of this advice, I urge you not to throw away these good, healthy times. Your parents will not always be there for you. Please think about what I have written and be careful not to create bitter memories that will hang above you when the record is in the books. No conflict is worth letting that happen.

⤙ Don't Let It End This Way ⤚

Sue Kidd tells a powerful story that will make its own case. I hope you'll read it carefully. There's a message here for all of us.

> The hospital was unusually quiet that bleak January evening, quiet and still like the air before a storm. I stood in the nurses' station on the seventh floor and glanced at the clock. It was 9:00 P.M.

I threw a stethoscope around my neck and headed for room 712, last room on the hall. Room 712 had a new patient. Mr. Williams. A man all alone. A man strangely silent about his family.

As I entered the room, Mr. Williams looked up eagerly but dropped his eyes when he saw it was only me, his nurse. I pressed the stethoscope over his chest and listened. Strong, slow, even beating. Just what I wanted to hear. There seemed little indication he had suffered a slight heart attack a few hours earlier.

He looked up from his starched white bed. "Nurse, would you—" He hesitated, tears filling his eyes. Once before he had started to ask me a question but had changed his mind.

I touched his hand, waiting.

He brushed away a tear. "Would you call my daughter? Tell her I've had a heart attack. A slight one. You see, I live alone and she is the only family I have." His respiration suddenly speeded up.

I turned his nasal oxygen up to eight liters a minute. "Of course I'll call her," I said, studying his face.

He gripped the sheets and pulled himself forward, his face tense with urgency. "Will you call her right away—as soon as you can?" He was breathing fast—too fast.

"I'll call her the very first thing," I said, patting his shoulder.

I flipped off the light. He closed his eyes, such young blue eyes in his fifty-year-old face.

Room 712 was dark except for a faint night-light under the sink. Oxygen gurgled in the green tubes above his bed. Reluctant to leave, I moved through the shadowy silence to the window. The panes were cold. Below a foggy mist curled through the hospital parking lot.

"Nurse," he called, "could you get me a pencil and paper?"

I dug a scrap of yellow paper and a pen from my pocket and set it on the bedside table.

I walked back to the nurses' station and sat in a squeaky swivel chair by the phone. Mr. Williams's daughter was listed on his chart as the next of kin. I got her number from information and dialed. Her soft voice answered.

"Janie, this is Sue Kidd, a registered nurse at the hospital. I'm calling about your father. He was admitted tonight with a slight heart attack and—"

"No!" she screamed into the phone, startling me. "He's not dying, is he?"

"His condition is stable at the moment," I said, trying hard to sound convincing.

Silence. I bit my lip.

"You must not let him die!" she said. Her voice was so utterly compelling that my hand trembled on the phone.

"He is getting the very best care."

"But you don't understand," she pleaded. "My daddy and I haven't spoken in almost a year. We had a terrible argument on my twenty-first birthday, over my boyfriend. I ran out of the house. I—I haven't been back. All these months I've wanted to go to him for forgiveness. The last thing I said to him was, 'I hate you.'"

Her voice cracked, and I heard her heave great agonizing sobs. I sat, listening, tears burning my eyes. A father and a daughter, so lost to each other. Then I was thinking of my own father, many miles away. It had been so long since I had said, "I love you."

As Janie struggled to control her tears, I breathed a prayer. "Please, God, let this daughter find forgiveness."

"I'm coming. Now! I'll be there in thirty minutes," she said. *Click.* She had hung up.

I tried to busy myself with a stack of charts on the desk. I couldn't concentrate. Room 712; I knew I had to get back to 712. I hurried down the hall nearly in a run. I opened the door.

Mr. Williams lay unmoving. I reached for his pulse. There was none.

"Code 99, Room 712. Code 99. Stat." The alert was shooting through the hospital within seconds after I called the switchboard through the intercom by the bed.

Mr. Williams had had a cardiac arrest.

With lightning speed I leveled the bed and bent over his mouth, breathing air into his lungs. I positioned my hands over his chest and compressed. One, two, three. I tried to count. At fifteen I moved back to his mouth and breathed as deeply as I could. Where was help? Again I compressed and breathed. Compressed and breathed. He could not die!

"O God," I prayed. "His daughter is coming. Don't let it end this way."

The door burst open. Doctors and nurses poured into the room pushing emergency equipment. A doctor took over the manual compression of the heart. A tube was inserted through his mouth as an airway. Nurses plunged syringes of medicine into the intravenous tubing.

I connected the heart monitor. Nothing. Not a beat. My own heart pounded. "God, don't let it end like this. Not in bitterness and hatred. His daughter is coming. Let her find peace."

"Stand back," cried a doctor. I handed him the paddles for the electrical shock to the heart. He placed them on Mr. Williams's chest. Over and over we tried. But nothing. No response. Mr. Williams was dead.

A nurse unplugged the oxygen. The gurgling stopped. One by one they left, grim and silent.

How could this happen? How? I stood by his bed, stunned. A cold wind rattled the window, pelting the panes with snow. Outside—every-where—seemed a bed of blackness, cold and dark. How could I face his daughter?

When I left the room, I saw her against the wall by a water fountain. A doctor who had been inside 712 only moments before stood at her side, talk-ing to her, gripping her elbow. Then he moved on, leaving her slumped against the wall.

Such pathetic hurt reflected from her face. Such wounded eyes. She knew. The doctor had told her that her father was gone.

I took her hand and led her into the nurses' lounge. We sat on little green stools, neither saying a word. She stared straight ahead at a pharmaceutical calendar, glass-faced, almost breakable-looking.

"Janie, I'm so, so sorry," I said. It was pitifully inadequate.

"I never hated him, you know. I loved him," she said.

God, please help her, I thought.

Suddenly she whirled toward me. "I want to see him."

My first thought was, *Why put yourself through more pain? Seeing him will only make it worse.* But I got up and wrapped my arm around her. We walked slowly down the corridor to 712. Outside the door I squeezed her hand, wishing she would change her mind about going inside. She pushed open the door.

We moved to the bed, huddled together, taking small steps in unison. Janie leaned over the bed and buried her face in the sheets.

I tried not to look at her at this sad, sad good-bye. I backed against the bedside table. My hand fell upon a scrap of yellow paper. I picked it up. It read:

My dearest Janie,

I forgive you. I pray you will also forgive me. I know that you love me. I love you too.

Daddy

The note was shaking in my hands as I thrust it toward Janie. She read it once. Then twice. Her tormented face grew radiant. Peace began to glisten in her eyes. She hugged the scrap of paper to her breast.

"Thank You, God," I whispered, looking up at the window. A few crystal stars blinked through the blackness. A snowflake hit the window and melted away, gone forever.

Life seemed as fragile as a snowflake on the window. But thank You, God, that relationships, sometimes fragile as snowflakes, can be mended together again—but there is not a moment to spare.

I crept from the room and hurried to the phone. I would call my father. I would say, "I love you."[2]

Why Do They Do It?

One Sunday afternoon, my wife and I visited my elderly aunt in the nursing home where she is confined. When we arrived, an informal church service was in progress.

A family of six, including two children, had come to the institution to sing and share the Scriptures with the sick and dying patients. Arrayed in front of them were about twenty white-haired, aged women slumped in their wheelchairs. Most were senile or too weak to respond. It made no difference. The young family had come to comfort and entertain them with music and truths from God's Word.

I stood watching from the doorway and struggled to hold back the tears. I felt a great love for this little band of servants who had given their time unselfishly to care for such a pitiful flock of women who could not even express their appreciation. Though I did not know the singers, I thanked God for the compassion and kindness I heard in their voices.

This, I thought, represents the best of the Christian ethic. Sure, we've heard about a few ministers visiting prostitutes and absconding with God's money. The media flood us with the details when Christians fail. But there is another side. It will not be told in the newspapers tomorrow morning. It is a story of kindness and love expressed by caring people in countless quiet ways.

The Pain of Powerlessness

There is reason to be concerned about those who have been stripped of all social power in this day. The elderly, the handicapped, the poverty-stricken, the homeless, the sick, and the dying are often among that number.

My father was given a glimpse of their plight toward the end of his life. I'll never forget visiting him in the hospital for the final time after his massive heart attack. I flew in from Cincinnati that night and rushed to his bedside. I sat with him through the late hours and talked about his circumstances. He was in a contemplative mood. Dad told me that the medical staff had given him good care, but they somehow managed to convey disrespect for him. He was not angry, and he didn't ask me to intercede on his behalf. That was not his point. He had simply made an observation that troubled him. He said the young doctors and nurses responded to him as though he were an old man. He was only sixty-six years of age then and was still engaged full-time as a college professor. He had been a very energetic man until the pruning knife of time did its dastardly work. Now, life was rapidly winding down, and he seemed to know it.

Then he said, "I have seen during these past few days what it is like to experience the absolute powerlessness of old age—where you are totally dependent on someone who does not value you as a person. I understand for the first time the disrespect that accompanies advanced age in this country. It is a frightening thing."

Millions of older people know precisely what my dad was trying to express. Being powerless is difficult even when accompanied by love and acceptance. Dependency is terrifying when surrounded by disrespect. I believe this is why Jesus came to help the down-and-outers—the wounded, lame, and sick. He touched the leper who had not been approached in years.

And He told His disciples, "It is not the healthy who need a doctor, but the sick . . ." (Mark 2:17). He admonished us all, "I tell you the truth, whatever you did for one of the least of these brothers of mine, you did for me" (Matthew 25:40). What incredible compassion He had for those who hurt— for the powerless people of the world. I wish I could point them all to Him. He is a friend who will stick closer than a brother.

My Own Mid-Life Crisis

It is almost impossible to bridge the awesome gap between the thirties and the fifties without wandering for a time through a dark valley. My journey was no exception. For at least seven years, I went through a period best described as a time of "contemplative reassessment." I was busily dealing in that decade with the many disturbing thoughts that echo through the mind of a man who realizes suddenly that he will not live forever. Whether he is a Christian, an atheist, an agnostic, or a New Ager, he *must* come to terms with these kinds of questions: "Who am I, *really?*" and "What am I doing here?" and "Is this the way I want to spend the rest of my life?" and "What really matters to me?" and "Who put me here?" and "What did He have in mind for me to accomplish?" and "Is Someone keeping score?" and "Is there life after death?" and "What will it be like to die?" These and many related questions seem to descend on men in rapid succession in mid-life.

As a deeply committed believer in Jesus Christ, I had already answered the questions related to my faith and my relationship with my Maker. Nevertheless, I needed to transform my beliefs from a youthful abstraction to a personal reality. I also needed to get a new fix on my circumstances and objectives. Have you arrived at that point in life? Have you ever felt like you were running so fast and were so involved and entangled with the task of living that you were failing to notice about 90 percent of what was happening around you? That's what was going on in my mind. By the time I had paid my taxes, fixed the leak in the roof, changed the tires on the car, raised my kids, and done my job and all the other stuff expected of me, an entire decade had gone by and it was only a blur in my memory. There are times like these for all of us when we need to pull back and say, "Just a minute, here, I need to do some thinking. Stop shouting at me, world, until I can get myself together."

That process of reevaluation took about seven years to complete. I emerged from it with a stronger dedication to the fundamentals of what I had been taught . . . and to a determination to "stay the course." Specifically, there were two conclusions that jumped out at me and that now serve as centerpieces of my system of values. Neither is new or particularly unique, but perhaps my readers will find it helpful to review the basics on which family and spiritual stability are grounded.

The first realization that has shaped my attitude toward everything else has already been mentioned. I came face to face with the breathtaking brevity of life. The passage of time seemed like a well-greased string that was sliding through my taut fingers. I was but a short-term visitor on this planet. It is a tremendous shock to the system when it first sinks in that you are simply "passin' through."

I remember sitting in church one day when I was forty-eight years old, and I was thinking about what it would be like to be fifty. Then I thought of my father's death at sixty-six. "Wow," I said to myself. "I may only have eighteen years left." Then I began calculating the meaning of those figures. (The sermon that morning must have been uninspiring.) I quickly realized that if I had lived forty-eight years and had eighteen to go, I had already "burned" 72 percent of my allotted time. What a stomach-grabber for a man who still thought of himself as "Joe College"! Nine years earlier, I had been in my thirties . . . still considered youthful . . . but two years hence I would be in my fifties . . . with only 24 percent of a lifetime left. Furthermore, there was not the slightest guarantee that I would be granted even one more hour.

I thought again about the meaning of the term *mid-life*. It is a seductive lie for most of us; the middle *thirties* are the mid-life years and the forties are the "two-thirds" years. In my case, I had hit the three-fourths years by age forty-eight. A humorous notion, perhaps, but a hammer blow to this guy who thought of himself as a very young man.

There were other insults. In an incident that has now become almost a "trademark" for me, I went to the YMCA one day to play basketball. I was an out-of-towner and unfamiliar with the guys who routinely played there in Dallas. I must have looked eighty years old to the teenagers on the court that day. They couldn't figure why a decrepit dude like me would think he could play a young man's game. But what could they do? I was there, and they had to include me.

We divided the troops that day into a four-on-four arrangement, and I was assigned to guard a seventeen-year-old black athlete. This kid was loaded with natural talent, and he knew it. He was as smooth as silk. Despite the mismatch, however, I rose to the challenge. I reached back about twenty years and pulled up some moves long forgotten. Adrenaline surged through my body, and the old thrill came back. Through luck and pluck, I scored about three quick baskets in the face of this young hotshot. With that, he took a step back, put his hands on his hips, and said, "Man! You must have been sompin' in yo' prime!"

His words stuck in my heart. My prime?! I couldn't even remember my prime! I soon grabbed my warmup jacket and headed back to the hotel. My self-concept wobbled violently for a few days.

Many writers have attempted to describe this emotional impact of comprehending life's brevity for the first time. One of my favorites is a lady named Erma Bombeck. I saw her as a guest on the *Phil Donahue Show* when she was asked if she was sensitive about her age.

"Not at all," she replied.

"Then how old are you?" Phil asked.

"I'm somewhere between estrogen and death," she answered.

Erma went on to say that her next-door neighbor wore a pacemaker, and every time he sneezed, her garage door opened.

Some of Mrs. Bombeck's pronouncements are not intended to be funny, however. In fact, they contain striking observations about life. One such statement about the aging process appeared in her book, *If Life Is a Bowl of Cherries, What Am I Doing in the Pits?* Included in that collection of writings was a short piece entitled, "When Does the Mother Become the Daughter and the Daughter Become the Mother?" It focused on her relationship with her own mom, which underwent a radical role reversal with the passage of time. Her mother had always been so strong, independent, and secure. Erma admired her and attempted to model herself after the one who had brought her into the world. But in recent years, the mother was undeniably becoming more childlike.

Erma first noticed the change when they were riding in a car one day. She was driving, and her mom was sitting near the right front door. Suddenly, an emergency occurred, causing Erma to slam on the brakes. Instinctively, she reached out to keep her mother from hitting the windshield. When the crisis had passed, the two women sat looking at one another. Each realized that something had changed in their relationship . . . for in prior years Mom would have attempted to protect Erma.

Then there was the following Thanksgiving when Erma baked the turkey and her mother set the table. Clearly, the mother was becoming the daughter, and the daughter was becoming the mother. As time passed, the transformation became more dramatic. When the two women were going shopping, it was Erma who said, "My goodness, don't you look nice in that new dress" and, "Don't forget to wear your sweater so you won't be cold in the department stores." Echoing in her mind was the advice of a concerned mother, "Button up your coat, Erma. Wear your galoshes, stay warm, take care of yourself."

Erma understood the new role she was asked to play, but resisted it vigorously. She didn't want to see this strong, noble woman become dependent . . . childlike . . . insecure. Nevertheless, the inexorable march of time could not be resisted. She had to get her mother up at night to take her to the bathroom and to care for most of her physical needs. How different the relationship had become. When Erma was a kindergartner, she had made a plaster-of-Paris "hand," which decorated the kitchen for years. Forty years later, mom was sent to a senior citizens' crafts class where she made a macramé. It eventually hung in her room in the Bombeck home.

As senility began to creep in, Erma found her own frustration rising to a crescendo. She said, "Mom! Will you *please* quit talking about seeing Dad last night. You *know* he's been gone for ten years." But Mom couldn't help it because she was no longer mentally competent. That completed the transformation. The mother had become the daughter, and the daughter became the mother.

Shortly thereafter, Erma and her own daughter were riding in a car one day. There was a sudden stacking of cars and the illumination of brake lights. Instinctively, the daughter reached out to protect Erma from hitting the windshield. They looked at each other for a moment, and Erma said, "My Lord! How quickly!!"

How quickly, indeed! One of the most wrenching experiences of the forties for me was watching my mother become my daughter and beginning to look at me as her father. She and my dad had been best friends, and his loss was devastating to her. She never fully recovered from his sudden death. It was as though she had been cut in half.

I remember making a fatherly visit to see my mother one day in her little condo. After leaving, I wrote down a portion of our conversation as a reminder of that period of her life. This is the exact interchange that took place:

"How you doing today?"

"I'm holding my own."

"Are you missing Dad today?"

(pause) "I miss him every day."

"I know. What do you suppose he's doing right now?"

"I wish I knew. He's probably off on Mars or Jupiter learning about how they're made."

"You loved him, didn't you, Mom?"

"I loved him, Jim."

"Mom, I worry about you staying in this condo too much. You really need to get out and mix with people—get involved in something."

"No, I'm all right. I just don't have any desire to go anymore."

"I love you, Mom."

"I love you, Jim."

The son was becoming the father, and the mother was becoming the daughter. Her mind then began to slip and many of the experiences of Erma Bombeck became my own. Mom was soon afflicted with Parkinson's disease and slowly began a long descent toward her death in 1988. Another conversation occurred twenty-one months before her passing that proved to be historic. I recorded the following comments on a pocket Dictaphone immediately after a remarkable encounter had transpired:

Shirley and I just visited my mother in the nursing home where she resides. She has been rather deeply into senility in recent weeks and has been unable either to understand what we say or to communicate with us. Yet today the Lord granted us a brief reprieve. She was asleep when we arrived, and we gently sat on her bedside and awakened her. She instantly recognized us, and for the first time in weeks she was able to express her thoughts and understand the love that we gave to her. I took that opportunity, not knowing if it would return, to stroke her forehead and pat her hand and thank her for being a good mother. I thanked her for being a good wife to my father—a good pastor's wife, even though it was he who was called to the ministry. I thanked her for living according to the principles of Christianity and staying true to the Christ whom she accepted when she was twenty years old. I stroked her face and thanked her for sacrificing to help me through college, doing without things that she needed. I thanked her for coming to our house when we were on our honeymoon and putting twenty dollars' worth of groceries and staples in our cupboard when I knew she didn't have those same items in hers. I told her how she was loved, not only by us, but by the Lord Himself. She smiled—she understood. She took my hand and said, "You know I've been thinking." And I said, "What have you been thinking about?" And she said, "That it's almost over. I've almost made it. It's almost done." I said, "Mom, when you make that crossing, you know my dad is going to be waiting for you on the other side." She smiled and understood. Then I said, "Jesus is waiting for you, too. And He's going to say, 'Well done! Thou good and faithful servant.'" Then I prayed for her and thanked the Lord for the influence of a good woman, and for her love in my life. She returned our love, and we said good-bye. At this stage of life, we never know when the last opportunity to communicate soul to soul has occurred. If this proves to be that last window of opportunity, I am grateful for the Lord's presence in that room today.

As it turned out, that *was* the final rational conversation I had with my mother. I will always be thankful for those concluding moments at the close of her time on earth.

This rapid passage of time that we have discussed is not just relevant to those in the mid-life years, although it becomes more apparent as we get older. For those who are younger, let me suggest that you conduct your own investigation. Look carefully at your family, and especially at the changing relationships with your own children. It is there, up close and personal, that the pace of life will come into focus. If you were riding on a passenger train and wished to judge the speed at which you and it were traveling, the distant mountains would be of little help. You'd get a better approximation by looking at the ground nearest the train. Likewise, those loved ones closest to you are the best measure of the dramatic changes in process. Children remain children for a brief moment, and hardly a day is the same as the next. It is in their growth and development that the dynamic nature of living is seen.

I can almost hear your thoughts as I write. *What morbid ideas! Why would anyone want to contemplate the passage of time and focus on the brevity of life?* The answer comes directly from Scripture. The temporary quality of this life is a very important biblical concept! King David said, "As for man, his days are as grass: as a flower of the field, so he flourisheth. For the wind passeth over it, and it is gone; and the place thereof shall know it no more" (Psalm 103:15–16 KJV). Moses shared that perspective and said, "So teach us to number our days, that we may apply our hearts unto wisdom" (Psalm 90:12 KJV). Wisdom, you see, comes from understanding the temporary nature of this life. Jesus, on the other hand, referred to a rich man who thought he had years to live and called him a "fool." We would also be foolish to assume that things will always be as they are, or that eternal matters can be dealt with later. For all we know, "This night thy soul shall be required of thee" (Luke 12:20 KJV). If that is the nature of this human existence, then we would do well to acknowledge it and to live our lives accordingly.

The Game of Life

Shirley and I have seen the material world from the bottom up, to be sure. We had absolutely nothing when we were married, and it looked for about ten years like we were destined to keep it. We didn't have any financial problems because we had no finances. I finally clawed my way through the doctoral program at the University of Southern California and escaped the oppressive tuition that had strangled us. After graduation, I immediately joined the faculty of the USC School of Medicine and began earning a livable salary. Then I wrote my first book, and we were finally able to purchase and furnish the house in which we still live.

I would not be truthful if I denied the satisfaction derived from this establishment of a home and a "place" for our kids. During the mid-life years, however, we realized how temporary and how empty those things can be if not kept in proper perspective. The Lord seemed to use some everyday object lessons to emphasize this truth to Shirley and me. On one occasion it was a simple table game that caught my attention. I had been a dedicated game player as a kid, and especially loved Monopoly by Parker Brothers. I could wheel and deal with the best of 'em! But those days were gone and almost forgotten by the time our sixteen-year-old daughter came home raving about a new game called Monopoly. She begged Shirley and me to take her on, and we consented.

We sat down to play one evening after Ryan had gone to bed, and very quickly I caught the old excitement of the game. And why not? I began prospering almost from the beginning. Before long I owned Boardwalk and Park Place, Illinois, Kentucky, Indiana, and even Baltic and Mediterranean. I started putting little green houses everywhere, and soon they were traded in for big red hotels. It was wonderful. My family was squirming like crazy, and I was loving it. I had $500 bills stuffed in my pockets, under the board, and even in my shoe. What I was experiencing was green-eyed greed, pure and simple.

The game ended precipitously when Shirley and Danae landed on my hotels in quick succession and suffered irreversible financial collapse. Suddenly, it was over. I had won. My family was pretty disgusted with my unsportsmanlike conduct by that point, so they went off to bed in a huff and left me to put away the game. There I was sitting alone in the family room around midnight, feeling strangely empty and unfulfilled. All of my earlier excitement and competitive energy were left with nowhere to go. I had won the game. So what? I began sorting all my money and laboriously putting it back in the box. My beautiful $500 bills were begrudgingly returned to the "bank." Then I stacked and replaced my coveted property . . . Boardwalk and Park Place included. My amassed fortune was disappearing in front of my eyes.

That's when it seemed that the Lord spoke to me. No, it was not an audible voice, but these were my thoughts in the family room on that night:

Jim, pay attention now. I'm about to teach you a lesson. That's not just the game of Monopoly you've been playing. It's very much like the game of life. You sweat and struggle to acquire things . . . to build and grow . . . to get bank accounts, property, retirement programs, and a piece of the rock. You spend a lifetime accumulating . . . in search of security. Then one day, it suddenly ends. You're going along minding your own business, when a strange pain develops gradually in your chest

and then extends down your left arm. "Could this be . . . ?" you ask yourself. Or
you're taking a morning shower and inadvertently discover a protrusion in the area
of your abdomen. "I've never noticed a bump there before. Maybe I ought to check
it out." Or you're driving your car and make a sudden lane change without looking
in your rearview mirror. Just that quickly, the great quest for security and posses-
sions is over. The game ends and everything must be returned to the box. The rules
specify that nothing can be taken with you. Not one dime. There are no U-Haul
trailers that follow the hearse to the cemetery. We come into the world with a
clenched fist, and we die with an open hand. That's what life does to us. Each per-
son must then answer the question asked of the rich fool, "Whose shall those things
be, which thou hast provided?" (Luke 12:20 KJV).

"True enough," a critic might reply, "but I'm not trying to accumulate
wealth for my own use. My goal is to pass it along to my children and future
generations. I want them to have it easier than I did . . . to enjoy a head start
that only money can give."

Shirley and I have spent many hours thinking and talking about that
objective with reference to our own children. Even it if were possible for us
to leave them a large estate, would that be a wise thing to do? I think not. It
takes a steady hand to hold a full cup, and many young people have been
destroyed by money that burned its way through their lives.

Perhaps it is clear now why I emerged from the mid-life years with some
concepts firmly in place. My children (and other people) are the *only* things
I can take to heaven with me. That's why I left the medical school back in
1977 and declined almost all speaking invitations that came my way. It
became clear to me that Danae and Ryan were temporary residents in our
home . . . that they would soon be grown and on their own. Parenthood is a
short-term affair, and the opportunity to lead and influence them was a "now
or never" proposition. Thus, I retooled my professional responsibilities and
focused heavily on my own family. I've made some bad decisions in my life
and a few rather good ones, but this was my most brilliant moment. The
empty nest did indeed come quickly, and I thank God I have not squandered
my most precious privilege of participating in the lives of my children.

Let me leave you with a letter I wrote the day our son Ryan went off to
college. Perhaps it will serve to punctuate this update on one of the most
important topics I've ever addressed. Incorporated in this letter are all the

primary conclusions I drew during the mid-life years and which I wish I had understood fully when I first entered manhood.

Twenty-three precious years have come and gone since the morning of October 6, 1965, when our first child came into the world. An instant and irrational love affair was born that day between this new dad and his baby daughter, Danae Ann, who took center stage in the Dobson household. How deeply I love that little girl! She would stand in the doorway each morning and cry as I left for work and then run giggling and breathless to meet me at the end of the day. You would have thought we had been separated for months. *Could I ever love another child as much as this one?* I wondered.

Then five years later a little lad named James Ryan made his grand entrance, and it all happened again. He was my boy—the only son I would ever be privileged to raise. What a joy it was to watch him grow and develop and learn. How proud I was to be his father—to be trusted with the well-being of his soul. I put him to bed every night when he was small, and we laughed and we played and we talked about Jesus. I would hide his sister's stuffed animals around the house, and then we would turn out the lights and hunt them with flashlights and a toy rifle. He never tired of that simple game. But the day for games has passed.

This morning, you see, marked the official beginning of the "empty nest" for Shirley and me. Danae graduated from college a year ago and is now building an exciting life of her own. It was difficult for us to let her go, back in 1983, but we took comfort in Ryan's six remaining years at home. How quickly those months have flown, and today, our formal years of parenthood came suddenly to an end. We took Ryan to the airport and sent him off to Colorado for a five-week summer program. Then in August, he plans to enter his freshman year at a college in the Midwest. Though he will be home periodically for years to come, our relationship will not be the same. It might be even better, but it will certainly be different. And I have never liked irreversible change.

Though for many years I knew this moment was coming, and though I had helped others cope with similar experiences, I admit freely that Ryan's departure hit me hard. For the past two weeks, we have worked our way through a massive accumulation of junk in his room. Ryan is a collector of things no one else would want—old street signs, broken models, and favorite fishing rods. The entire family took tetanus shots, and we plunged into the debris. Finally last night, Shirley and Ryan packed the remaining boxes and emptied the last drawer. The job was finished. His suitcases were packed. Our son was ready to go.

Ryan came into my study about midnight, and we sat down for another of the late-night chats that I have cherished. He has always liked to talk at the end of the day. I won't tell you what we said in that final conversation. It is too personal to share with anyone. I can only say that the morning came too quickly, and we drove as a family to the airport. There I was, driving down the freeway, when an unexpected wave of grief swept over me. I thought I couldn't stand to see him go. It was not that I dreaded or didn't look forward to what the future held. No, I mourned the end of an era—a precious time of my life when our children were young and their voices rang in the halls of our house. I couldn't hide the tears as we hugged good-bye at Gate 18. Then Shirley and I drove alone to our house, where a beloved son and daughter had grown from babies to young adults. There I lost it again!

The house that we had left three hours earlier in a whirlwind of activity had been transformed in our absence. It had become a monastery—a morgue—a museum. The silence was deafening to us both. Every corner of it held a memory that wafted through the air. I meandered to Ryan's room and sat on the floor by his bed. His crib had once stood on that spot. Though many years had passed, I could almost see him as a toddler—running and jumping to my open arms. What a happy time that was in my life. The ghost of a kindergartner was there, too, with his brand-new cowboy clothes and his Snoopy lunchpail. Those images are vivid in my mind today. Then a seven-year-old boy appeared before me. He was smiling, and I noticed that his front teeth were missing. His room was filled with bugs and toads and a tarantula named Pebber. As I reached out to hug him, he quietly disappeared. Then a gangly teenager strolled through the door and threw his books on his desk. He looked at me as if to say, "Come on, Dad. Pull yourself together!"

My own words now come back to mind. I remember saying in my second film series, *Turn Your Heart Toward Home*, that the day was coming soon when "the bicycle tires would be flat, the skateboard would be warped and standing in the garage, the swing set would be still, and the beds would not be slept in. We will go through Christmas with no stockings hanging by the fireplace, and the halls will be very quiet. I know those times will soon be here, and I realize it has to be so. I accept it. I wouldn't for anything try to hold back our son or daughter when it comes time to go. But that will also be a very sad day because the precious experience of parenting will have ended for me." Alas, the day that I anticipated has just arrived.

If you're thinking that I am hopelessly sentimental about my kids, you're right. The greatest thrill of my life has been the privilege of raising them day by day in the service of the Lord. Still, I did not expect such intense pain at the time of Ryan's departure. I thought I was prepared to handle the moment, but I quickly realized just how vulnerable I am to the people I love.

In a large sense, however, it is not merely the end of formal parenting that has shaken my world today. I grieve for the human condition itself. When Ryan boarded that plane in Los Angeles, I comprehended anew the brevity of life and the temporary nature of all things. As I sat on the floor in his room, I heard not only Ryan's voice, but the voices of my mother and father who laughed and loved in that place. Now they are gone. One day Shirley and I will join them. First one and then the other. We are just "passing through," as the gospel songwriters used to say. All of life boils down to a series of happy "hellos" and sad "good-byes." Nothing is really permanent, not even the relationships that blossom in a healthy home. In time, we must release our grip on everything we hold dear. Yes. I felt the chilly breeze of change blowing through my home this morning, and I understood its meaning.

If we really grasped the brevity of our lives on this earth, we would surely be motivated to invest ourselves in eternal values. Would a fifty-year-old man pursue an adulterous affair if he knew how quickly he would stand before his God? Would a woman make herself sick from in-law conflict or other petty frustrations if she knew how little time was left to her? Would men and women devote their lives to the pursuit of wealth and symbols of status if they realized how soon their possessions would be torn from their trembling hands? It is the illusion of permanence, you see, that distorts our perception and shapes our selfish behavior. When eternal values come in view, our greatest desire is to please the Lord and influence as many of our loved ones for Him as possible.

⟶ Finishing Well ⟵

During my freshman year, I entered the mile run in a field of about twenty men. I was in good shape and finished second to an outstanding senior who rarely lost. He graduated that year and left the vacancy to me. Unfortunately, I discovered girls in my sophomore year, and I let myself get a little soft. I had no idea that my body was going to play dead on that day of the race. I walked onto the track full of expectancy and determination. With the sound of the gun I tore off around the first turn, leaving the pack far behind. I felt marvelous. But by the second turn, my side was splitting and the pack was closing in. By the time I completed the first lap, I was sucking air frantically, and my chest was heaving like a great gray whale. Runners I had beaten the year before were passing me on every side, and I had only one desire—*Get your body off this track before your lungs explode.* I collapsed on the infield grass in a sweating heap of shame and failure. I looked up just in time to see my girlfriend leave the stadium with her head down. What a tough moment for a once-proud sophomore!

Fortunately, I learned a valuable lesson that day on the track. It became clear to me that great beginnings are not as important as the way one finishes. We have all seen men and women quickly dazzle the world and then fade in dishonor and ruin. Most of life, you see, is a marathon and not a sprint. It just goes on and on, and the pressure to give up seems to increase with the passage of time.

That is certainly true in the Christian life. It is what the apostle Paul referred to when he said, "I have fought the good fight, I have finished the race, I have kept the faith" (2 Timothy 4:7). By these words, Paul was expressing satisfaction at having crossed the finish line without yielding to the pressure to cave in.

Alas, married life is a marathon, too. *It is not enough to make a great start toward long-term marriage.* You will need the determination to keep plugging, even when every fiber in your body longs for the infield. Only then will you make it to the end. But hang in there. Shirley and I will be waiting for you at the finish line.

∼ **The Heritage** ∼

During the Christmas season 1969, my father's two surviving brothers and his sister gathered in California for a family reunion. And on that happy occasion, they spent the better part of five days reminiscing about their childhood and early home life. One of the grandchildren had enough initiative to record the discussions on cassette tapes, and I was privileged to obtain a complete set. What a rich heritage this provided, granting insight into my grandparents' home and the early experiences of my dad.

While all the conversations were of interest to me, there was a common thread that was especially significant throughout the week. It focused on the *respect* with which these four siblings addressed the memory of their father (my grandfather). He died in 1935, a year before my birth, yet they spoke of him with an unmistakable awe more than thirty-four years later. He still lived in their minds as a man of enormous character and strength.

I asked them to explain the qualities that they admired so greatly, but received little more than vague generalities.

"He was a tower of strength," said one.

"He had a certain dignity about him," said another, with appropriate gestures.

"We held him in awe," replied the third.

It is difficult to summarize the subtleties and complexities of the human personality, and they were unable to find the right words. Only when we began talking about specific remembrances did the personality of this patriarch become apparent. My dad provided the best evidence by writing his recollection of Grandfather Dobson's death, which I've reproduced below. Flowing throughout this narrative is the impact of a great man on his family, even three decades after his demise.

The Last Days of R. L. Dobson

The attack that took his life occurred when he was sixty-nine years of age, and resulted ultimately in the breakup of the family circle. For many years after his death, I could not pass Tri-State Hospital without noting one particular window. It stood out from the rest, hallowed because it represented the room where he had suffered so much. The details of those tragic days and nights remain in my memory, unchanged by the passage of time.

We had been three days and three nights practically without sleep, listening to him struggle for breath, hearing the sounds of approaching death, smelling the smells of death. Dad lay in a deep coma. His heavy breathing could be heard up and down the corridor. We walked the halls of that old hospital for hours listening to the ceaseless struggle that now was becoming fainter and fainter. Several times the nurse had called us in and we had said the last "good-bye"—had gone through the agony of giving him up, only to have his heart rally, and then the end-less vigil would begin all over again. Finally, we had gone into an adjoining room not prepared for sleep, but some in the chairs and some across the beds, we had fallen into the sleep of utter exhaustion.

At five minutes to four o'clock the nurse came in and awakened one of my twin brothers. Robert roused with a start. "Is he gone?" he asked.

"No, but if you boys want to see your dad one more time while he is alive, you'd better come, now."

The word quickly passed around, and we filed into the room to stand around his bed for the last time. I remember that I stood at his left side: I smoothed back the hair from his forehead, and laid my hand on his big old red hand, so very much like my own. I felt the fever that precedes death: 105. While I was standing there, a change came over me. Instead of being a grown man (I was twenty-four at the time), I became a little boy again. They say this often happens to adults who witness the death of a parent. I thought I was in the Union Train Station in Shreveport, Louisiana, in the late afternoon, and I was watching for his return. The old Kansas City Southern passenger train was backing into the station and I saw it come 'round the curve. My heart swelled with pride.

I turned to the little boy standing next to me and said, "You see that big man standing on the back of the train, one hand on the air brake and the other on the little whistle with which he signals the engineer? That big man is my dad!" He set the air brakes and I heard the wheels grind to a stop. I saw him step off that last coach. I ran and jumped into his arms. I gave him a tight hug, and I smelled the train smoke on his clothes. "Daddy, I love you," I said.

It all comes back. I patted that big hand and said, "Good-bye, Dad," as he was sinking fast now. "We haven't forgotten how hard you worked to send five boys and one girl through college, how you wore those old conductor uniforms until they were slick—doing without— that we might have things that we didn't really need. . . ."

At three minutes to four o'clock, like a stately ship moving slowly out of time's harbor into eternity's sea, he breathed his last. The nurse motioned us to leave and pulled the sheet over his head, a gesture that struck terror to my heart, and we turned with silent weeping to leave the room. Then an incident occurred that I will never forget. Just as we got to the door, I put my arm around my little mother and said, "Mama, this is awful."

Dabbing at her eyes with her handkerchief, she said, "Yes, Jimmy, but there is one thing Mother wants you to remember now. We have said 'good night' down here, but one of these days we are going to say 'good morning' up there."

I believe she did say "good morning," too, eleven years later, and I know he met her "just inside the Eastern Gate."

His death was marked by quietness and dignity, just like the life he had lived. Thus came to an end the affairs of R. L. Dobson, and thus ended, too, the solidarity of the family. The old home place was never the same again. The old spirit that we had known as children was gone forever!

Though this illustration reveals few of the specific characteristics that made R. L. Dobson such a powerful influence in his family, it does tell us how his son felt about him. I happen to know some of the other details. He was a man of absolute integrity and honesty. Though not a Christian until shortly before his death, he lived by an internal standard that was singularly uncompromising. As a young man, for example, he invested heavily in a business venture with a partner whom he later discovered to be dishonest. When he learned of the chicanery, he virtually gave the company to the other man. That former partner built the corporation into one of the most successful operations in the South and became a multimillionaire. But my grandfather never looked back. He took a clean conscience with him to his grave.

CHAPTER SEVEN

Dealing with Emotions

In our world today, emotional experience has become the primary motivation of values and actions and, in some cases, spiritual beliefs. Furthermore, we are living in a day when people are being encouraged to release their emotions, to grant them even greater power in ruling their destinies. We are told, "If it feels good, do it!"

We live and breathe by the vicissitudes of our feelings. Reason is now dominated by feelings, rather than the reverse as God intended.

Every river of emotion running deep within the human spirit has the capacity of overflowing its banks and flooding the mind with its rampaging waters. So we must fortify the banks of those rivers with scriptural truth and psychological understanding. Nothing could be more dangerous than to permit our emotions to rule our destinies. To do so is to be cast adrift in the path of life's storms.

∼ The Thrill of the Moment ∼

My mother attended a small-town high school in Oklahoma during the 1930s that had produced a series of terrible football teams. They usually lost the big games and were invariably clobbered by their archrivals from a nearby community. Understandably, the students and their parents began to get depressed and dispirited by the drubbing their troops were given every Friday night. It must have been awful.

Finally, a local automobile dealer decided to take matters into his own hands. He asked to speak to the team in the locker room after yet another devastating defeat. What followed was one of the most dramatic football speeches of all times. This businessman proceeded to offer a brand-new Ford to every boy on the team and to each coach if they would simply defeat their bitter rivals in the next game.

The team went crazy with anticipation. They howled and cheered and slapped each other on their padded shoulders. For seven days, the boys ate, drank, and breathed football. At night they dreamed about touchdowns and rumble seats. The entire school caught the spirit of ecstasy, and a holiday fever pervaded the campus. Each player could visualize himself behind the wheel of a sleek roadster with eight or ten gorgeous girls hanging all over his body.

Finally, the big night arrived, and the team assembled in the locker room. Excitement was at an unprecedented high. The coach offered several last-minute instructions, and the boys hurried out to face the enemy. They assembled on the sidelines, put their hands together, and shouted a simultaneous "Rah!" Then they ran onto the field—and were demolished, 38–0.

All their exuberance didn't translate into a single point on the scoreboard. Seven days of hoorah and whoop-de-do simply couldn't compensate for the players' lack of discipline, conditioning, practice, study, coaching, drill, experience, and character. Such is the nature of emotion. It has a definite place in human affairs. But it must always be ruled by the higher mental faculties of will and intellect. When left to stand alone, feelings usually reveal themselves to be unreliable and even a bit foolish.

So enjoy the exhilaration when it comes. Take the ride to the heights when you get the opportunity. But don't get hooked on the thrill of the moment. Take charge of your emotions. And when it comes time to do the right thing, don't let your feelings lead you to compromise. That is the way to live a happier, more successful life and one that is more pleasing to God.

⁓ Highs and Lows ⁓

It is important to understand that anything that takes you up will also bring you down, and vice versa. For example, mild depression is likely to appear following a busy holiday, the birth of a baby, a job promotion, or even after a restful vacation. The cause for it is physical in nature. Elation and excitement are driven by adrenaline, which results in a greater consumption of energy. After a few days in that hyper-state, there has to be a come-down. If you understand that mechanism, you can brace yourself for the low end of the cycle.

That is what happened to Shirley and me when we bought a new house some years ago. We had waited for years to find a home we could afford, and we became very excited when escrow closed and it was finally ours. The elation lasted for several days, during which I thought about this cyclical principle. I remember telling Shirley we could not remain elated much longer. We needed to prepare ourselves for the lower end of the curve.

Sure enough, we both became mildly depressed in a couple of days. It wasn't a severe reaction, just a case of what some people call "the blahs." The house didn't seem so wonderful, and we worried about the price we had paid for it. We lived there for nineteen years and grew to love the place, but we thought we had made a mistake during our brief moment in the pits.

Your own occasional depression will be more tolerable if you understand it as a relatively predictable occurrence. Highs must be followed by lows. It is governed by a physical law; you can depend on it. But in the healthy individual, lows eventually give way to highs, too. It cuts both ways.

⟶ The Prowler ⟵

In the fall of 1969, a wild man named Charles Manson and his young followers, known as "the family," went on a bloody rampage in the city of Los Angeles. They killed actress Sharon Tate, who was nine months' pregnant, and four or five other innocent people. A few nights later, they broke into the home of Leno and Rosemary LaBianca and butchered them in cold blood. Millions of people in that area read about these murders and were paralyzed with fear. Neighbors wondered who would be next. My mother was convinced she was the prime candidate.

Sure enough, Mom and Dad were confronted by the intruder as they lay in bed one night. They heard a loud *thump!* coming from the other side of the house.

"Did you hear that?" whispered my mother.

"Yes, be quiet," said my father.

They lay staring at the darkened ceiling, breathing shallowly and listening for confirmation that someone was indeed there. A second *thump* brought them to their feet. They felt their way to the bedroom door, which was closed. At this point, we see a striking difference in the way my mother and father faced a crisis. Her inclination was to hold the door shut to keep the intruder from entering their bedroom. Thus, she propped her foot at the bottom of the door and braced herself against the top. My father's approach was to confront the attacker head-on. He reached through the darkness and grasped the doorknob, but his pull met the resistance from my mother.

My father assumed someone was holding the door from the other side while my mother could feel the killer trying to force it open. My parents stood there in the blackness of midnight, struggling against one another and imagining themselves to be in a tug of war with a murderer. Mom then panicked. She ran to the window to scream for help. As she took in a great breath of air with which to summon the entire city of Los Angeles, she realized a light was on behind her. Turning around, she saw that my dad had gone into the other part of the house in search of their attacker. Obviously, he was able to open the door when she released it. As they discovered, there was no prowler in their house. The thumps were never identified, and Charles Manson was soon apprehended in Los Angeles and sent to prison for life.

Impressions

I remember the exciting day I completed my formal education at the University of Southern California and was awarded a doctoral degree. My professors shook my hand and offered their congratulations, and I walked from the campus with the prize I had sought so diligently. On the way home in the car that day, I expressed my appreciation to God for His obvious blessing on my life, and I asked Him to use me in any way He chose. The presence of the Lord seemed very near as I communed with Him in that little red Volkswagen.

Then, as I turned a corner (I remember the precise spot), I was seized by a strong impression that conveyed this unmistakable message: "You are going to lose someone very close to you within the next twelve months. A member of your immediate family will die, but when it happens, don't be dismayed. Just continue trusting and depending on Me."

Since I had not been thinking about death or anything that would have explained the sudden appearance of this premonition, I was alarmed by the threatening thought. My heart thumped a little harder as I contemplated who might die and in what manner the end would come. Nevertheless, I told no one about the experience when I reached my home that night.

One month passed without tragedy or human loss. Two and three months sped by, and still the hand of death failed to visit my family. Finally, the anniversary of my morbid impression came and went without consequence. It has now been more than a decade since that frightening day in the Volkswagen, and there have been no catastrophic events in either my family or among my wife's closest relatives. The impression proved invalid.

Through my subsequent counseling experience and professional responsibilities, I have learned that my phony impression was not unique. Similar experiences are common, particularly among those who have not adjusted well to the challenge of living.

For example, a thirty-year-old wife and mother came to me for treatment of persistent anxiety and depression. In relating her history she described an episode that occurred in a church service when she was sixteen years old. Toward the end of the sermon, she "heard" this alarming message from God: "Jeanie, I want you to die so that others will come to Me."

Jeanie was absolutely terrified. She felt as though she stood on the gallows with the hangman's noose dangling above her head. In her panic, she jumped from her seat and fled through the doors of the building, sobbing as she ran. Jeanie felt she would commit a sin if she revealed her impression to anyone, so she kept it to herself. For nearly twenty years she had awaited the execution of this divine sentence, still wondering when the final moment would arrive. Nevertheless, she appeared to be in excellent health many years later.

Not only do death messages sometimes prove to be unreliable, but other apparent statements of God's will can be equally misunderstood. A college student once was awakened from a dream in the middle of the night with a strong impression that he should marry a certain young lady. They had only dated once or twice and hardly knew each other. Yet "God" assured him "this is the one!" The next morning, he called the coed and told her of his midnight encounter. The girl felt no such impulse but didn't want to oppose so definite a message from the Lord. The young man and woman were married shortly thereafter, and have suffered through the agony of an unsuccessful and stormy marriage.

The interpretation of impressions is risky business, at best.

A Troubled Seminarian

I once lectured before faculty and students at a seminary on the subject of inferiority, since they would deal with many such problems in their congregations. I relayed the story of "Danny," a distressed high-school student whose grief over his inadequacy became intolerable and eventually turned to anger. After I spoke, I received the following anonymous letter:

Dear Dr. Dobson:

I am one of the "Dannys" you spoke of in chapel today. Believe me, for I have experienced this for as long as I can remember. It is a miserable way to live.

Yes, I'm a student at the seminary, but that doesn't make the problem any less acute. Through the years, particularly the last five, I have periodically gained a revived hope that somehow (?) this problem can be overcome—go away or something. Then to my great disappointment, I find it is still very much a part of me. That's when I lose hope of ever conquering it. I want to be a minister of the gospel and feel that this is God's will. At the same time I am aware of the paralyzing effect this deep problem has upon me. I want so badly to be adequate so that I could better serve God and others.

I wish I could talk with you, even for a short time. However, I realize your busy schedule. At any rate, thank you for coming to the seminary.

Sincerely,

A troubled seminarian

Since this broken young man had not identified himself publicly, I read and discussed his letter with the student body the following morning. Many of the three hundred seminarians seemed moved by his words; for some, it undoubtedly reflected their own predicament as well. Following my lecture that morning, the "troubled seminarian" introduced himself to me. He stood with tears streaming down his cheeks as he spoke of the great sense of inadequacy he had experienced since early childhood. Later, an administrator of the seminary told me that this young man was the last member of the student body he would have expected to feel this way. As I have observed so many times, this sense of inferiority is the best-kept secret of the year. It is harbored deep inside, where it can gnaw on the soul.

⁓ Flower Power ⁓

As an impetuous young student in college, I had perfected the art of verbal combat to a high level of proficiency. I took pride in my ability to "put down" an opponent, particularly those whom I perceived as being unfair or disrespectful to me or my friends. It is a skill that I recall with some embarrassment today, although the exchange of insults and verbal abuse is not uncharacteristic of young people between eighteen and twenty-two years of age.

After graduating from college and getting married, however, I began to be aware that God disapproved of the way I handled human conflict. "A soft answer turneth away wrath," I read in Proverbs, and the same theme was inescapable throughout the teachings of Jesus. This was plainly an area wherein the Lord expected me to bring my behavior into harmony with His Word. Yet, the bad habits of childhood are not easily broken.

It seems as though divine providence allowed a series of offensive people to cross my path during that period, each one teaching me a little more about self-control and tolerance. Every time I failed to represent the Christian love I professed, the Holy Spirit seemed to rebuke me in the days that followed. There were many "tests" involved in this learning experience, but the final examination occurred about three years later.

I had decided to surprise my wife with a corsage on Easter Sunday morning, being a firm believer in marital "flower power." The local florist took my order and promised that an orchid would be ready after 5:00 Saturday afternoon. All week long I harbored this noble deed in my generous heart, smiling to myself and anticipating the moment of truth after breakfast the following Sunday.

When Saturday afternoon rolled around, I found a phony excuse to leave the house in the car for a few minutes and drove to the florist to retrieve the secret package. The shop was crowded with customers, and the lady behind the counter was obviously overworked and stressed. My first mistake, I suppose, was in not perceiving her tension soon enough, or the beads of sweat which ringed her upper lip. I patiently waited my turn and watched each patron carry his order past me and out the door. When I finally reached the counter and gave my name, the saleslady shuffled through a stack of tickets, and then said matter-of-factly, "We're not going to be able to fill your order. You'll just have to get your flowers somewhere else."

She did not offer a reason or apologize for the error. Her voice had a definite take-it-or-leave-it sound that I found irritating. She stood, hands on hips, glaring at me as though I had somehow caused the mistake.

At first I was puzzled, and then I asked, "Why did you accept my order if you were unable to prepare it? I could have gone somewhere else, but now it is too late to buy a corsage at another shop."

I remember distinctly that my response was very controlled under the circumstances, although my displeasure was no doubt apparent. My brief question had no sooner been uttered than a curtain swung open at the rear of the building and a red-faced man burst into the shop. He stormed toward me and pressed his chest against mine. I have no idea how big he was; I only know that I'm six-foot-two and weigh 190 pounds, yet my eyes focused somewhere between his pulsating Adam's apple and his quivering chin. It was immediately apparent that Goliath was not merely upset—he was livid with rage! He curled his lip upward and shook his clenched fist in the vicinity of my jaw.

For the next two minutes or so, he unloaded the most violent verbal attack I had ever sustained. He used every curse word I knew and then taught me a few I hadn't even heard in the army. Then, after questioning my heritage, he announced his intention of throwing a certain portion of my anatomy out the front door.

It is difficult to describe the emotional shock of that moment. It was a conflict I neither sought nor anticipated. Suddenly, without warning, I had tripped a spring that must have been winding tighter and tighter throughout that hectic day (or year). The next move was clearly mine. Silence fell on the shop as a half-dozen customers gasped and awaited my response.

The toughest part of the encounter involved the instantaneous conflict between what my impulses dictated and what God had been trying to teach me. In a matter of two or three seconds, it seemed as though the Lord said to me, *Are you going to obey Me, or not?*

I muttered some kind of defensive reply and then did the most difficult thing I had ever been required to do: I turned on my heels and walked from the shop. To the customers, I probably appeared cowardly—especially in view of the size of my adversary. Or, perhaps they assumed I could not think of an appropriate reply. All of these agitating thoughts reverberated through my head as I walked to my car.

Did I go home in triumph at having done what God wanted of me? Certainly not immediately. Hot blood pulsed through my veins. My immediate response was to do something primitive—like heave a brick through the window where a bouquet of roses sat. Gradually, however, my physiological state returned to normal, and I looked back on my restraint with some satisfaction.

The kind of frustration I experienced in the floral shop, whether it be called anger or some related emotion, is of importance to others trying to live the Christian life. I'm not the only one who has had to learn how to control his tongue and the tumultuous undercurrents that often propel it.

My Taxes Are Too Low!

Several years ago, my wife and I bought our first home, which was small but adequate for the two of us. When our daughter was born the following year, however, we felt it necessary to construct a family room. Fortunately, the man who had owned the house before us had entertained the same idea and had built the roof and poured a concrete floor before abandoning the project. I hired a carpenter to enclose the walls and finish the interior of the room.

When the construction began, I was advised by my weekend builder (who was employed full-time in another line of work) to avoid getting a building permit. He said that it would only make my taxes go up and was probably unnecessary. He was telling me just what I wanted to hear. I convinced myself that it was probably not mandatory to inform the city about my project primarily because I was not changing the square footage under the roofline. It was, as they say, a bloody rationalization.

I had my way, and the new room was completed on schedule. The city was none the wiser, and I settled the moral issue and laid it to rest. But it wouldn't stay down. When the property tax bill arrived the following spring, I could think only of the additional assessment I should have been paying for having improved my home. I argued down the guilt once again, but with greater effort than before. Then when the county assessor came by that summer, I watched him reevaluate my property from the street. He didn't look at the back of the house because he had no way of knowing anything new had been constructed there. That did it! For the first time, I faced the guilt squarely and subjected it to the tests of the intellect and will.

Failing to comply with city and county ordinances couldn't be right or honest. In a sense, I was stealing the difference between my lower tax bill and the amount it should have been. The Bible was abundantly clear on the issue of thievery. My guilt stood firm against all intellectual criteria.

The clincher occurred in the test of my will. I had to admit to myself that from the beginning I had known of the legal requirement to get a building permit. Despite my careful rationalization, I had willfully disobeyed the law. My guilt emerged intact.

The following day I sat down and wrote a letter to the county assessor. Explaining the whole story in detail, I provided the date of the construction and invited a representative to reevaluate the worth of my house. The sense of condemnation and blame seemed to flow from the end of my pen and was gone by the time I finished the letter. I asked God to forgive me and the issue was laid to rest—forever.

Incidentally, the county assessor receives a million letters a year from people who are complaining about their taxes being too high. I doubt if he has ever gotten a letter from someone asserting that his taxes were too low! He must have been completely unequipped to handle my note because he sent me a form letter telling me how I could appeal my exorbitant taxes if I was convinced I had been cheated. That was not exactly what I had in mind.

The Difficult Diagnosis

In October 1959, my mother began to deteriorate physically and emotionally. She became extremely nervous and irritable, and she experienced unrelenting depression for weeks at a time. Her face was drawn, and the area around her eyes was black and hollow. She made an appointment with a physician who examined her and diagnosed her symptoms as emotional in origin. He prescribed a tranquilizer to "calm her nerves," although the medication had precisely the opposite effect. It made her feel like climbing the walls. She visited a second doctor who made the same diagnosis and prescribed a different tranquilizer. It had the same consequence. She continued to search for an answer to the distressing disorder that had beset her, but no one seemed to know what to do. Six physicians were consulted, each diagnosing her problem as psychological in nature, prescribing medications that only aggravated her difficulties further.

My mother began to lose weight, and she found it more difficult to cope with the responsibilities of everyday living. She became preoccupied with her own death, and on one occasion called me on the telephone to tell me the clothes in which she wished to be buried. My father and I knew this was not characteristic of her, and we agreed that she was deteriorating rapidly. The next day I called a physician who had been a friend of our family for several decades. "Paul," I said with concern, "you are going to have to help me with my mother, because we are rapidly losing her." He asked me to describe her symptoms, which I did. He listened to the details for a few moments and then interrupted to say, "Send your mother to see me. I can help her."

The next morning, my mother went to see the physician with whom I had consulted. He determined that she was in a state of extreme estrogen deprival as a consequence of menopause, and he prescribed an immediate injection of this essential hormone. She returned a week later for a second injection and continued every seven days for years to come. Though her "cure" did not occur instantaneously, the effect of the medication was like turning from darkness to light. Her depression vanished; her dark eyes returned to normal; she became interested in life again and the woman we had known and loved through the years was with us once more.

My mother's emotional and physical health remained stable for ten years, until she and my father moved fifteen hundred miles away from the physician who had provided the essential estrogen. Once again, the search for an understanding doctor began. The man to whom she turned said he disagreed with the diagnosis, but he would prescribe estrogen simply because she seemed to be doing so well at the time. "Why change a winning combination?" he commented. However, one day when she arrived for her weekly injection, he informed her that she was to receive no more. She began the desperate search for another physician, and finally found one approximately fifteen miles from her home.

The treatment continued to be successful for another year, at which time I began to receive the same kind of distressing telephone calls that had characterized her earlier trauma. She lost an incredible forty pounds in a few weeks and cried for hours at a time. Her heart raced and palpitated, and she was beset by great weakness and trembling. One desperate call to her physician brought the comment, "It sounds like nerves to me." He prescribed tranquilizers, which made her wildly nervous, as before. Another physician spent a half-hour explaining the dangers of estrogen. Finally, she was admitted to a hospital where she underwent scores of diagnostic tests. Her physicians put her through the customary upper and lower gastrointestinal series, glucose tolerance tests and many other diagnostic procedures. But no certain disorder could be identified. Other physicians administered different tests, though nothing definitive was found.

It was clear to me that my mother's primary problem was physical in origin. She and my father had visited our home in California immediately before the onset of these symptoms, and she had been happy and relaxed. Then suddenly, without undue environmental stress, she had begun to decline. I made a long-distance call to another physician-friend in Kansas City. I asked him if he felt her problem could again be hormonal, since the symptoms were so similar to the experience thirteen years earlier. He denied the possibility. "Frankly," he said, "I believe estrogen shots are a kind of placebo: They work simply because a woman *thinks* they're going to help. I don't believe they really do very much of anything."

Still, the calls for help came, sometimes two or three tomes a week. My mother was often crying when she phoned, saying she had neither slept nor eaten in twenty-four hours. Finally, I picked up the telephone and called the Chief of Obstetrics and Gynecology at USC School of Medicine, where I also serve on the faculty. I described her recurrence of symptoms to him and asked if it sounded hormonal, once more. He answered in the affirmative and gave me the name of a knowledgeable gynecologist at the University of Kansas. I immediately relayed the information to my mother.

To make a long story shorter, the mystery was solved two days later. Through the course of twelve years of injections every week, my mother had accumulated scar tissue in the hip where she received the additional estrogen. Though she continued to get a shot every seven days, she was absorbing practically none of the hormone itself. Her physicians had ruled out the need for estrogen because of the weekly injections, but in reality, she was in a state of severe deprival once more. We are indebted to the man who recognized her plight and rectified the problem with a regular dosage of oral estrogen.

At the time of my mother's initial difficulties in 1959–1960, I was a young graduate student at USC. Though unintentionally, she was giving me a valuable lesson in problems associated with the female climacteric (hormonal readjustment during menopause). I was to need that introduction. Since that time I have kept abreast of the professional literature on this subject and have seen many women who were suffering from the same undetected disorder. They are referred to my office for treatment of emotional distress, yet within minutes the same pattern of hormonal symptoms begins to unfold. Several times I have guessed the disorder correctly even before the woman has said a word, simply by the characteristic look on her face.

Lonely Summers Looking for Love

When I was in college, my parents traveled throughout the year. Therefore, I had no place to go when school was not in session. During the summer months especially, I had to stay in the school dormitory while other students went home to visit their parents. I usually got a job nearby and would return from work each evening to my quiet, boring room. A couple of other guys also stayed in the dormitory, but I didn't know either of them very well. Consequently, I usually spent a very lonely summer during those college days.

As you can imagine, I would begin to get excited near the end of August each year, anticipating the return of my friends in September. Finally they would arrive, and the old dormitory would again rock with laughter and noise and fun. Those were great days. But I was even more anxious for the *girls* to return to school. I hadn't had a date since May, and I couldn't wait for the "crop" of young ladies to show up for classes. Therefore, I was ripe for love every autumn. I would fall hopelessly in love with someone . . . anyone . . . on September 12 of each year. There was no question about it happening—

the same thing occurred four years in a row. Each September, my world would suddenly turn upside down: I couldn't sleep, I couldn't eat, and I couldn't study. (In fact, studying was one of the first things to go!) It was a truly thrilling event, as predictable as Thanksgiving or Christmas.

Don't you see how self-centered my "love" was each September? I would tell my friends, "I can't believe how fantastic this is. I never felt this way before. This is the greatest thing that ever happened to me." There can be little doubt about it—I had not fallen in love with a girl, but I had fallen in love with love! The young lady for whom I had "gone bananas" was merely a prize to be won . . . an object to be captured. She was usually forgotten and replaced the following January.

~ Puppy Love ~

It began at 11:00 one morning when I was in the seventh grade. I was sitting in my school classroom when a boy near me motioned toward the door. I looked in that direction and saw my father beckoning me to come outside. He said we were going home and that I would not be returning to school that day. He didn't explain why.

As we walked to the car, I knew that my dad must have something awful to tell me. I could see the tension in his eyes, but I was afraid to ask him what happened. Finally he turned to me and said, "Jim, I have some bad news for you, and I want you to take it like a man."

I said, "Is it my mom?"

He replied, "No."

I said, "Then it's my dog, isn't it?"

My father nodded and then began to tell me the details. He said my mother had been driving home in our car a few minutes earlier. My little dog (whose name was Pippy) saw her coming and ran into the street to greet her. He jumped on the side of the car as it passed, but apparently lost his footing and fell under the rear wheel. Mother then felt the sickening thud as the dog was struck and run over. Pippy screamed in pain, eventually lying motionless at the edge of the road.

Mother stopped the car immediately and ran back to where my dog lay. She bent over him and talked softly to the pup. He could not respond because his back was broken, but he could roll his little brown eyes to see who she was. When he recognized her, Pippy wagged his stubby tail in appreciation. He was still wagging that little tail when his eyes grew glassy in death.

Now it may not seem too terrible to lose a dog, but Pippy's death was like the end of the world for me. I simply cannot describe how important he was to me when I was thirteen years old. He was my very special friend whom I loved more than anyone can imagine. I could talk to him about things that no one else seemed to understand. He met me on the edge of the sidewalk after school each day and wagged his tail to greet me (which no one else ever did for me). I would take him out in the backyard and we would play and run together. He was always in a good mood, even when I was not. Yes, Pippy and I had something going between us that only dog lovers can comprehend.

When my father told me this story of Pippy's death, I thought I was going to die. I couldn't swallow, and I found it very hard to breathe. I wanted to run away . . . to scream . . . to cry. Instead, I sat quietly in the car with a great lump in my throat and a pounding sensation in my head.

I don't remember exactly how I spent that afternoon at home, although I do recall crying most of the day. I soon composed a poem in honor of my dog, titled "To Pippy." It was not the greatest literary masterpiece of all time, but it expressed my feeling pretty well. The last four lines of the poem read:

My mother, she hit him, and oh how I cried
And softly and gently, a puppy dog dies
And if there's a dog heaven, I know he'll be there
He's my poor little Pippy, with hair white and fair.

Later in the afternoon our family conducted a funeral service for the dearly departed dog. I dug a small hole behind the grapevine at the back part of our property, and as the sun was going down we put his still little body in the grave. Just before we covered him over, I reached in my pocket and retrieved a copper penny. I placed it on the bloody fur of his chest. Today I'm not sure why I did that. I guess it was merely my childish way of telling my pup that I loved him. And my father, who had told me to take the loss like a man, bawled like a baby on that day behind the grapevine. It was without question the saddest day of my childhood.

It is important to understand that there have been many more significant moments in my life since that day of Pippy's death. There have been more meaningful days, and certainly there have been greater losses than the one I experienced on that cloudy morning. However, there have been few sadder days even to this moment. Why? Because I was thirteen years old when Pippy died. That made it all seem so much worse.

~ Will You Forgive Me? ~

Corrie ten Boom and her family were sent by the Nazis to an extermination camp at Ravensbruck, Germany, during the latter years of World War II. They suffered horrible cruelty and deprivation at the hands of S.S. guards and, ultimately, only Corrie survived. After the war, she became a celebrated author and spoke often on the love of God and His intervention in her life. But inside, she was still bitter at the Nazis for what they had done to herself and her family. Two years after the war, Corrie was speaking in Munich, Germany, on the subject of God's forgiveness. After the service, she saw a man making his way toward her. This is what she would later write about that encounter:

And that's when I saw him, working his way forward against the others. One moment I saw the overcoat and the brown hat; the next, a blue uniform and a visored cap with its skull and crossbones. It came back with a rush; the huge room with its harsh overhead lights; the pathetic pile of dresses and shoes in the center of the floor; the shame of walking naked past this man. I could see my sister's frail form ahead of me, ribs sharp beneath the parchment skin. Betsie, how thin you were!

The place was Ravensbruck, and the man who was making his way forward had been a guard—one of the most cruel guards.

Now he was in front of me, hand thrust out.

"A fine message, Fräulein! How good it is to know that, as you say, all our sins are at the bottom of the sea!"

And I, who had spoken so glibly of forgiveness, fumbled in my pocketbook rather than take that hand. He would not remember me, of course—how could he remember one prisoner among those thousands of women?

But I remembered him and the leather crop swinging from his belt. I was face-to-face with one of my captors, and my blood seemed to freeze.

"You mentioned Ravensbruck in your talk," he was saying. "I was a guard there." No, he did not remember me.

"But since that time," he went on, "I have become a Christian. I know that God has forgiven me for the cruel things I did there, but I would like to hear from your lips as well. Fräulein,"—again the hand came out—"will you forgive me?"

And I stood there—I whose sins had again and again to be forgiven—and could not forgive. Betsie had died in that place—could he erase her slow terrible death simply for the asking?

It could not have been many seconds that he stood there—hand held out—but to me it seemed hours as I wrestled with the most difficult thing I had ever had to do.

For I had to do it—I knew that. The message that God forgives has a prior condition: that we forgive those who have injured us. "If you do not forgive men their trespasses," Jesus says, "neither will your Father in heaven forgive your trespasses."

I knew it not only as a commandment of God, but as a daily experience. Since the end of the war I had had a home in Holland for victims of Nazi brutality. Those who were able to forgive their former enemies were able also to return to the outside world and rebuild their lives, no matter what the physical scars. Those who nursed their bitterness remained invalids. It was as simple and horrible as that.

And still I stood there with the coldness clutching my heart. But forgiveness is not an emotion—I knew that too. Forgiveness is an act of the will, and the will can function regardless of the temperatures of the heart. "Jesus, help me!" I prayed silently. "I can lift my hand. I can do that much. You supply the feeling."

And so woodenly, mechanically, I thrust my hand into the one stretched out to me. And as I did, an incredible thing took place. The current started in my shoulder, raced down my arm, sprang into our joined hands. And then this healing warmth seemed to flood my whole being, bringing tears to my eyes.

"I forgive you, brother," I cried. "With all my heart."

For a long moment we grasped each other's hand, the former guard and the former prisoner. I had never known God's love so intensely, as I did then. But even so, I realized it was not my love. I had tried, and did not have the power. It was the power of the Holy Spirit as recorded in Romans 5:5, ". . . because the love of God is shed abroad in our hearts by the Holy Ghost which is given unto us."[1]

Corrie's words have great relevance for us. Bitterness of all varieties, including that which is seemingly "justified," will destroy a person spiritually and emotionally. It is a sickness of the soul. Corrie forgave an S.S. guard who shared responsibility for the deaths of her family members; surely, we can forgive with God's help.

⟶ The Power of Forgiveness ⟵

My friend Paul Powers was one of the most pathetic victims of child abuse I've ever known. Both his mother and father were alcoholics who produced or adopted twelve children, despite their inability to care for them. When Paul was seven years old, his mother came home from a party in a drunken stupor and collapsed before she reached the front door. The children found her the next morning lying in the snow. She contracted pneumonia and grew gravely ill. Two weeks later when Paul came home from school, his mother called him to her bedside and reached out to take his hand, but she died before she could convey her thoughts. Seeing that she was gone, the child ran sobbing to his drunken father who pushed him away and began beating him with his fists. The man screamed, "Shut up! Boys don't cry like babies!" Paul's nose and two ribs were broken, and his teeth were knocked out. Even today, he bears a two-inch scar on the inside of his lower lip from the beating his father gave him that day. Paul didn't cry again until he was twenty-two years old.

That was typical of Paul's developmental years. Especially after the death of his mother, he and his siblings were subjected to cruel and vicious beatings on a regular basis. The father's abuse was reported to local authorities on numerous occasions, and each time a social worker visited the home. As soon as she had left, Paul and several of his brothers were taken to the basement, stripped, and beaten until they could not get up from the floor.

It is not surprising that Paul and every one of his eleven siblings have spent time in prison. At twelve years of age, Paul committed his first murder in a robbery attempt. He shot a female carnival worker who refused to give him her money. The judge asked Paul's father what he wanted done with the boy, and he said, "Send him to hell!" Paul was confined in prison for this and related crimes and was filled with hatred and bitterness. But there in prison five years later, the most significant event in Paul's life occurred. He was seventeen years of age when he saw a Billy Graham film and began to be acquainted with the Lord Jesus Christ! Sometime later he repented of his sins and was marvelously converted. Can you imagine what it must have been like for this young man who had never known love, who had experienced nothing but pain and suffering and sorrow, to be made clean and to know he was loved by the Creator Himself? His entire life was changed on that incredible day.

Paul was eventually released from prison, married a Christian woman, and became the father of a little girl. He felt God wanted him to distribute Christian films, since he had found the Lord through this medium. But times were rough. Paul and his wife were struggling to survive financially in their little ministry. It was Christmastime, and they lacked money even for groceries.

By contacting churches that had shown his films, Paul managed to collect a few dollars that were owed to him. His wife took $8.00 to the grocery store to buy food, and when she returned, he was furious to learn that she had foolishly spent $1.00 for wrapping paper and tape. While Paul and his wife argued with one another, their three-year-old daughter was quietly rummaging through the sack of groceries. When she found the wrapping paper, she took it into the living room and used it to cover a shoebox.

Paul finally realized the child was gone and went looking for her. He found her sitting on the floor with the box covered by crooked paper and half a roll of tape. When Paul saw that the child had wasted the valuable materials, his temper blew again. He resorted to the behavior he had seen as a child, grabbing the toddler by one arm and flailing her violently. Then he sent her sobbing to her room, literally terrorized. He cannot talk about the event today without crying.

The next day when gifts were exchanged, the little girl ran behind the tree and retrieved her gold box. She handed it to Paul and said, "Daddy, this is for you!" He was embarrassed that he had spanked her unmercifully for something she perceived as a gift. He slowly began unwrapping the paper and lifted the lid to find the box completely empty.

Paul's anger flared once more and he said, "What have you done? There's nothing in this box. Why did you give me an empty box? When you give someone a present you're supposed to put a gift inside it!"

The three-year-old looked up at her father innocently and said, "Oh, no, Daddy. The box is not empty! It is full of love and kisses for you. I stood there and blew kisses in there for my daddy, and I put love in there, too. And it is for you!"

Paul was broken. He wrapped his arms around his little girl and begged her to forgive him. Then he got on his knees before the Lord, repenting and pleading for God to purge the violent temper he had learned as a child. Never again did this remarkable man abuse any of his sons or daughters. He kept that gold box beside his bed for years, and whenever he would be hurt or discouraged, he would reach into the box and lift out an imaginary kiss from his child. Then he would place it on his cheek and say, "Thank You, Lord."

I must share a more recent chapter in Paul's story that also moved me to tears. Paul and his father had gone their separate ways in 1956 and rarely saw each other in the two decades that followed. All of Paul's attempts to make contact had been rejected. Then one day, Paul received a call from his father, who was at the Union Train Station in their town, asking if Paul could come see him. He said he would be there for only one hour. Paul and his wife jumped into the car and drove through rush-hour traffic to get to the station on time. They arrived just three minutes before the train was to leave. Paul climbed aboard the train, wondering what he would say to the old man. They had been mortal enemies when they last parted company. Paul searched frantically for his father, and when they saw each other, they paused and then embraced affectionately. For the first time in his life, this seventy-nine-year-old man told his boy that he loved him. The conductor then shouted, "All aboard!" and Paul had to hurry from the train. They had only time enough to agree that they would meet soon in a nearby city.

Paul got off the train in a state of shock. His father had never hugged him in his life and, in fact, had seemed totally incapable of love. "But more than that," Paul told his wife, "there was a different look about him! I saw it in his eyes. He was not the same man! I can't explain it, but that man is different!" He anticipated the time when they could talk leisurely and heal the wounds they had inflicted on one another in earlier years.

Unfortunately, the rendezvous was never held because the old man suffered a heart attack and died the following Monday. As with his mother so many years before, Paul was deprived of his father's last words. But a local pastor filled in the details at the funeral. Paul's father had indeed experienced an encounter with Jesus Christ and had become a born-again Christian in the closing months of his life. In fact, his train journey had been a last desperate attempt to reach out to several of his children and reestablish relationships that had been ruptured for years.

CHAPTER EIGHT

Facing Adversity

Most believers are permitted to go through emotional and spiritual valleys that are designed to test their faith in the crucible of fire. Why? Because faith ranks at the top of God's system of priorities. Without it, He said, it is impossible to please Him (Hebrews 11:6). And what is faith? It is "the substance of things hoped for, the evidence of things not seen" (Hebrews 11:1 KJV). This determination to believe when the proof is not provided and when the questions are not answered is central to our relationship with the Lord. He will never do anything to destroy the need for faith. God guides us through times of testing to specifically cultivate belief and dependence on Him. We discover a deeper and richer faith that only comes through facing adversity.

Expecting the Unexpected

Our family took a trip to Kenya and Tanzania a few years ago. The highlight of our tour was a visit to the Serengeti, a magnificent national park where legendary African animals roam wild and free. It had rained all day before we arrived, and the unpaved roads were extremely muddy. Before we had driven fifteen miles into the park, our car slid into a ditch and bogged down to the axles in thick, African mud. We would have certainly spent the night out there on the savanna if it had not been for a native in a double-wheeled truck who gave us a hand.

Later that afternoon we came to a stretch of road that was even more torn up and muddy. There it divided and ran parallel for several hundred yards before coming back together. It was obvious that drivers earlier that day had forged the new trail to get around a mudhole, but we had no way of knowing on which side it lay. We sat there for a moment trying to decide which road to take. If we made a mistake, we would probably get stuck again and have to sleep in the car—without dinner, toothbrushes, bathroom facilities, or even water to drink.

Our seventeen-year-old son, Ryan, then volunteered to help.

"I'll run ahead and look at the road," he said. "Then I'll wave to let you know which way to go."

The missionary who was with us said, "Um, Ryan, I don't think that is a very good idea. You just don't know what might be out there in the tall grass."

Eventually we chose what looked like the best road and were indeed able to get through. But when we reached the place where the two trails came back together, a surprise was waiting for us. A huge male lion was crouched in the grass off to one side. He rolled his big yellow eyes toward us and dared us to take him on. Large cats like that one consider humans to be just another easy dinner. They can cover one hundred yards in less than three seconds and wouldn't hesitate to devour any city dweller who was foolish enough to tempt them.

Ryan looked at the lion and agreed that he probably ought to stay in the car!

In a manner of speaking, our experience on the Serengeti illustrates the passage from late adolescence to young adulthood. The journey goes smoothly and uneventfully for some individuals. They drive right through without a hitch. But a surprisingly large number of us encounter unexpected "mudholes" that trap and hold us at an immature stage of development. Still others are plagued by predators lurking in the tall grass. Among them are an addiction to alcohol or drugs, marriage to the wrong person, failure to achieve a coveted dream, suicide, homicide, or various criminal offenses. It is very easy to get off the trail and into the ditch in the morning of our lives.

Why Did He Have to Die?

Chuck Frye was a bright young man of seventeen, academically gifted and highly motivated. After graduating near the top of his class in high school, he went on to college, where he continued to excel in his studies. Upon completion of his bachelor's of science degree, he applied for admittance to several medical schools.

The competition for acceptance in medical school was, and is, fierce. At the time, I was a professor at the University of Southern California School of Medicine, where only 106 students were admitted each year out of six thousand applicants. That was typical of accredited medical programs in that era. Despite these long odds, Chuck was accepted at the University of Arizona School of Medicine and began his formal training.

During that first term, Chuck was thinking about the call of God on his life. He began to feel that he should forgo high-tech medicine in some lucrative setting in favor of service on a foreign field. This eventually became his definite plan for the future. Toward the end of that first year of training, however, Chuck was not feeling well. He began experiencing a strange and persistent fatigue. He made an appointment for an examination in May and was soon diagnosed with acute leukemia. By November, Chuck Frye was dead.

How could Chuck's heartsick parents then, and how can we now, make sense of this incomprehensible act of God? This young man loved Jesus Christ with all his heart and sought only to do His will. Why was he taken in his prime despite many agonized prayers for his healing by godly family members and faithful friends? The Lord clearly said no to them all. But why?

Thousands of young doctors complete their education every year and enter the medical profession, some for less-than-admirable reasons. A tiny minority plan to spend their professional lives with the down-and-outers of the world. But here was a marvelous exception. If permitted to live, Chuck could have treated thousands of poor and needy people who otherwise would have suffered and died in utter hopelessness. Not only could he have ministered to their physical needs, but his ultimate desire was to share the gospel with those who had never heard this greatest of stories. Thus, his death simply made no sense.

Visualize with me the many desperately ill people Dr. Chuck Frye might have touched in his lifetime, some with cancer, some with tuberculosis, some with congenital disorders, and some being children too young to even understand their pain. Why would divine Providence deny them his dedicated service?

There is another dimension to the Frye story that completes the picture. Chuck became engaged to be married in March of that first year in medical school. His fianceé was named Karen Ernst, who was also a committed believer in Jesus Christ. She learned of Chuck's terminal illness six weeks after their engagement, but she chose to go through with their wedding plans. They became husband and wife less than four months before his tragic death. Karen then enrolled in medical school at the University of Arizona, and after graduation, became a medical missionary in Swaziland, South Africa. Dr. Karen Frye served there in a church-sponsored hospital until 1992. I'm sure she wonders—amid so much suffering—why her brilliant young husband was not allowed to fulfill his mission as her medical colleague. And yes, I wonder, too.

The great theologians of the world can contemplate the dilemma posed by Chuck Frye's death for the next fifty years, but they are not likely to produce a satisfying explanation. God's purpose in this young man's demise is a mystery, and there it must remain. Why, after much prayer, was Chuck granted admittance to medical school if he could not live to complete his training? From whence came the missions call to which he responded? Why was so much talent invested in a young man who would not be able to use it? And why was life abbreviated in such a mature and promising student, while many drug addicts, winos, and evildoers survive into old age as burdens on society? These troubling questions are much easier to pose than to answer. And . . . there are many others.

⟍ A Father's Love ⟋

Not only is the Lord "mindful" of each one of us, but He describes Himself throughout Scripture as our Father. In Luke 11:13, we read, "If you then, though you are evil, know how to give good gifts to your children, how much more will your Father in heaven give the Holy Spirit to those who ask him!" Psalm 103:13 says, "As a father has compassion on his children, so the LORD has compassion on those who fear him." But on the other hand, He is likened to a mother in Isaiah 66:13: "As a mother comforts her child, so will I comfort you."

Being a parent of two children, both now grown, I can identify with these parental analogies. They help me begin to comprehend how God feels about us. Shirley and I would give our lives for Danae and Ryan in a heartbeat if necessary. We pray for them every day, and they are never very far from our thoughts. And how vulnerable we are to their pain! Can it be that God actually loves His human family infinitely more than we, "being evil," can express to our own flesh and blood? That's what the Word teaches.

An incident occurred during our son's early childhood that illustrated for me this profound love of the heavenly Father. Ryan had a terrible ear infection when he was three years old that kept him (and us) awake most of the night. Shirley bundled up the toddler the next morning and took him to see the pediatrician. This doctor was an older man with very little patience for squirming kids. He wasn't overly fond of parents, either.

After examining Ryan, the doctor told Shirley that the infection had adhered itself to the eardrum and could only be treated by pulling the scab loose with a wicked little instrument. He warned that the procedure would hurt and instructed Shirley to hold her son tightly on the table. Not only did this news alarm her, but enough of it was understood by Ryan to send him into orbit. It didn't take much to do that in those days.

Shirley did the best she could. She put Ryan on the examining table and attempted to hold him down. But he would have none of it. When the doctor inserted the pick-like instrument in his ear, the child broke loose and screamed to high heaven. The pediatrician then became angry at Shirley and told her if she couldn't follow instructions she'd have to get her husband. I was in the neighborhood and quickly came to the examining room. After hearing what was needed, I swallowed hard and wrapped my six-foot-two, 190-pound frame around the toddler. It was one of the toughest moments in my career as a parent.

What made it so emotional was the horizontal mirror that Ryan was facing on the backside of the examining table. This made it possible for him to look directly at me as he screamed for mercy. I really believe I was in greater agony in that moment than my terrified little boy. It was too much. I turned him loose—and got a beefed-up version of the same bawling-out that Shirley had received a few minutes earlier. Finally, however, the grouchy pediatrician and I finished the task.

I reflected later on what I was feeling when Ryan was going through so much suffering. What hurt me was the look on his face. Though he was screaming and couldn't speak, he was "talking" to me with those big blue eyes. He was saying, "Daddy, why are you doing this to me? I thought you loved me. I never thought you would do anything like this! How could you? Please, please! Stop hurting me!"

It was impossible to explain to Ryan that his suffering was necessary for his own good, that I was trying to help him, that it was love that required me to hold him on the table. How could I tell him of my compassion in that moment? I would gladly have taken his place on the table, if possible. But in his immature mind, I was a traitor who had callously abandoned him.

Then I realized that there must be times when God also feels our intense pain and suffers along with us. Wouldn't that be characteristic of a Father whose love was infinite? How He must hurt when we say in confusion, "How could You do this terrible thing, Lord? Why me? I thought I could trust You! I thought You were my friend!" How can He explain within our human limitations that our agony is necessary, that it does have a purpose, that there are answers to the tragedies of life? I wonder if He anticipates the day when He can make us understand what was occurring in our time of trial. I wonder if He broods over our sorrows.

⤙ Heroes Hall of Fame ⤚

In my first film series, *Focus on the Family*, I shared a story about a five-year-old African-American boy who will never be forgotten by those who knew him. A nurse with whom I worked, Gracie Schaeffler, had taken care of this lad during the latter days of his life. He was dying of lung cancer, which is a terrifying disease in its final stages. The lungs fill with fluid, and the patient is unable to breathe. It is terribly claustrophobic, especially for a small child.

This little boy had a Christian mother who loved him and stayed by his side through the long ordeal. She cradled him on her lap and talked softly about the Lord. Instinctively, the woman was preparing her son for the final hours to come. Gracie told me that she entered his room one day as death approached, and she heard this lad talking about hearing bells ring.

"The bells are ringing, Mommie," he said. "I can hear them."

Gracie thought he was hallucinating because he was already slipping away. She left and returned a few minutes later and again heard him talking about hearing bells ring.

The nurse said to his mother, "I'm sure you know your baby is hearing things that aren't there. He is hallucinating because of the sickness."

The mother pulled her son closer to her chest, smiled, and said, "No, Miss Schaeffler. He is not hallucinating. I told him when he is frightened—when he couldn't breathe—if he would listen carefully, he could hear the bells of heaven ringing for him. That is what he's been talking about all day."

That precious child died on his mother's lap later that evening, and he was still talking about the bells of heaven when the angels came to take him. What a brave little trooper he was. His courage was not reported in the newspapers the next day. Neither Tom Brokaw nor Dan Rather told his story on the evening news. Yet he and his mother belong forever in our "heroes hall of fame."

My next candidate of faithful immortality is a man I never met, although he touched my life while he was losing his. I learned about him from a docudrama on television that I saw many years ago. The producer had obtained permission from a cancer specialist to place cameras in his clinic. Then with approval from three patients, two men and a woman, he captured on film the moment each of them learned they were afflicted with a malignancy in its later stages. Their initial shock, disbelief, fear, and anger were recorded in graphic detail. Afterward, the documentary team followed these three families through the treatment process with its ups and downs, hopes and disappointments, pain and terror. I sat riveted as the drama of life and death unfolded on the screen. Eventually, all three patients died, and the program ended without comment or editorial.

There was so much that should have been said. What struck me were the different ways these people dealt with their frightening circumstances. The two who apparently had no faith reacted with anger and bitterness. They not only fought their disease, but they seemed to be at war with everyone else. Their personal relationships and even their marriages were shaken, especially as the end drew near. I'm not being critical, mind you. Most of us would respond in much the same manner if faced with imminent death. But that's what made the third individual so inspiring to me.

He was a humble black pastor of a small, inner-city Baptist church. He was in his late sixties and had been a minister throughout his adult life. His love for the Lord was so profound that it was reflected in everything he said. When he and his wife were told he had only a few months to live, they revealed no panic. They quietly asked the doctor what it all meant. When he had explained the treatment program and what they could anticipate, they politely thanked him for his concern and departed. The cameras followed this little couple to their old car and eavesdropped as they bowed their heads and recommitted themselves to the Lord.

In the months that followed, the pastor never lost his poise. Nor was he glib about his illness. He was not in denial. He simply had come to terms with the cancer and its probable outcome. He knew the Lord was in control, and he refused to be shaken in his faith.

The cameras were present on his final Sunday in his church. He actually preached the sermon that morning and talked openly about his impending death. To the best of my recollection, this is what he said:

"Some of you have asked me if I'm mad at God for this disease that has taken over my body. I'll tell you honestly that I have nothing but love in my heart for my Lord. He didn't do this to me. We live in a sinful world where sickness and death are the curse man has brought on himself. And I'm going to a better place where there will be no more tears, no suffering, and no heartache. So don't feel bad for me.

"Besides," he continued, "our Lord suffered and died for our sins. Why should I not share in His suffering?" Then he began to sing, without accompaniment, in an old, broken voice:

> Must Jesus bear the cross alone,
> And all the world go free?
> No, there's a cross for everyone,
> And there's a cross for me.
>
> How happy are the saints above,
> Who once went sorr'wing here;
> But now they taste unmingled love,
> And joy without a tear.
>
> The consecrated cross I'll bear,
> Till death shall set me free,
> And then go home my crown to wear,
> For there's a crown for me.[1]

I wept as this gentle man sang of his love for Jesus. He sounded very weak, and his face was drawn from the ravages of the disease. But his comments were as powerful as any I've ever heard. His words that morning were his last from the pulpit, as far as I know. He slipped into eternity a few days later, where he met the Lord he had served for a lifetime. This unnamed pastor and his wife have a prominent place among my spiritual heroes.

I will tell you about one more inductee into my hall of fame. She is a woman named Marian Benedict Manwell, who is still living. I was first introduced to her in a letter she wrote to me in 1979, and I never forgot what she said. I have kept that letter all these years, and in fact, I called her this week. I found this delightful lady still holding tightly to her faith in Jesus Christ. But let me share what she wrote me in the original correspondence so many years ago.

Dear Dr. Dobson:

I'm going to tell you my experience as an "ugly duckling." I was the first child of a young minister and his school-marm wife. They were about 30 years old when I was born. (Now brace yourself for this.) When I was 8 months of age, the heavy spring of the jumper in which I was bouncing suddenly snapped. Being taut, it came straight down and tore through the first thing it hit—the soft spot on my head.

There was nothing to be done. My parents and my uncle and aunt (with whom we were vacationing) believed me to be dead. They finally found a doctor who took me to the hospital eight miles away, but there was nothing they could do but cleanse and bandage the wound. They gave my parents no hope at all that I would live.

They were godly people and they believed in prayer, as did all our relatives and friends. Their faith is responsible for my life. By the mercy of God I lived, even though the doctors told my family I would be a hopeless cripple and mentally incompetent. That did not happen, but there were many problems.

To begin with, I was not a beautiful child. I was very homely, and gimpy too. Oh yes, I walked. The Lord saw to that when He healed me of total paralysis. I was also blessed with a quick mind. Still, as you have written, people look for beauty in children. My younger brother had the beauty of the family. He looked like our dad, auburn hair, brown eyes, and he was a charmer. I could not run, or jump rope, or play ball, or catch anything thrown to me. I was crippled on my left side. I guess that's why I became a loner. I developed an imagination that allowed me to live a wonderful life through the hundreds of books that I read and the daydreams I invented.

When I told my mother, who died of cancer when I was 10 years old, that I wanted to be a nurse and a missionary, she said, "That's wonderful." She knew that I could never be either because of my infirmity. Then we moved to another small town when our father remarried two years after my mother's death. Thing's became even more difficult. I was not popular through high school. I was a P.K. (preacher's kid). And long before this time I had given my heart to the Lord. That, added to my introverted personality, did not draw me into the cliques of our little town school.

One day as I trudged along the walk to the school, a teenage boy came up behind me and asked loudly, "What's wrong with you? What's ya limping for? Nobody wants to go with a girl that acts like that."

I had a very difficult time learning that Christ could give me the strength to be calm and composed in such a situation.

Let me interrupt Mrs. Manwell's letter briefly to summarize the circumstance she shared. This child was neurologically handicapped from infancy and unable to play like other boys and girls. The rejection of her peers forced her to meet her social needs through her fantasies. She almost casually mentioned the death of a very sensitive and caring mother when she was ten, and the arrival of a stepmother at the beginning of adolescence. Add to that the ridicule of the opposite sex as a teenager and further rejection because she was a preacher's kid. Here are the ingredients for lifelong psychological damage in most children. But this was no ordinary young lady.

Later, I married a boy I went to school with, and the Lord has blessed me with six sons and two daughters! All of them are married to wonderful Christian mates. For almost 40 years now, [my husband] Clinton has protected me, sometimes when I would foolishly have bitten off more than I could chew. He has given me the confidence I needed to use the imagination that I developed as a child (to write poetry and short stories).

It is so rewarding to see our children leading lives as respected and honored members of their communities and as caring members of their mate's families. My older daughter came home from a visit with a former school friend two or three years ago and was shocked to learn that many of her former classmates were dropouts from life—they were on drugs or were drinking heavily. They were divorced or were unwed parents. Some were in prison.

Beth said, "When I see our big family that often did not have any of the nice things of life and yet everyone is a solid, law-abiding citizen, I have so much to be thankful for. I think you must have prayed a lot for us."

And I cried. That's the most rewarding aspect of parenthood for me. Thank you for letting me use so much of your time, Dr. Dobson, and God bless you.

Marian Benedict Manwell

Thank you, Marian, for revealing your faithfulness to us. You could easily have blamed God for making life so difficult. Even as a child, I'm sure you understood that He could have prevented that spring from breaking or redirected it away from your head. He didn't have to take your mother when you needed her so badly. He should have made you pretty, or popular, or athletic. It would have been reasonable, given these limitations, for you to have been bitter at the Lord. The deck did seem stacked against you. But nowhere in your letter was there a hint of anger or disillusionment. Nor do we sense any self-pity as you described your plight. Instead, as you told us, "Long before this time, I had given my heart to the Lord."

I admire you greatly, Marian Benedict Manwell. The Lord must feel the same. Although He seemed not to care in those days, He was quietly working behind the scenes to send a Christian husband to love and protect you. Then He blessed you with eight children, each of them growing up to serve Him. What a capstone to a life of faith! If you had yielded to bitterness because of your handicap, your sons and daughters would certainly have observed it. Some probably would have adopted the same attitude. Thank you for holding tightly to your faith even when God made no sense in the affairs of your life! You are also a cherished member of my all-time hall of fame.

⤳ I Had to Have a Hamburger ⤳

I was going through a period of challenge several years ago when frustrations were coming by the boatloads. I felt like Job when the bearers of bad news were standing in line to tell their stories. It had been that kind of month. Then one night when Shirley had gone out of town to attend a conference, I decided to visit my favorite restaurant—a local drive-through hamburger stand. (This was before my cardiologist and my wife got together and destroyed one of the finer joys of living.)

I jumped into our son's Honda, not remembering that I had canceled the insurance on his car when he went back to college. I had gone about three blocks when it dawned on me that I was driving without liability coverage. *One stupid mistake and we could lose our house*, I thought. I was only two blocks from the drive-in, so I slowed the car to a crawl. At each corner I virtually stopped, looking both ways before inching on down the road. I'm sure people thought I was either senile or weird—or both.

I arrived safe and sound at the beloved In 'N' Out Hamburger and heaved a sigh of relief. "May I have your order, please?" said a muffled adolescent voice from the little black box. I told the guy what I wanted and then drove forward to the take-out window. Soon a sack of great-smelling stuff was handed to me and I reached for it. There I was, hanging out the window nice and loose—when an elderly lady lost control of the Mercedes behind me. Her foot slipped off the brake and crammed the accelerator. It was like a Sherman tank hitting a baby buggy! Suddenly, Ryan's Honda and I went flying down the driveway for parts unknown. I never did find the hamburger.

When the car finally came to a halt, I was too stunned to move. Then this sweet, eighty-one-year-old lady came hurrying up to my window to see if I was all right and begged me not to call the police. "I'm so sorry," she said. "I did this to someone else two weeks ago. Please don't report me! I'll fix your car."

I should have made a record of the accident, but I just didn't have the heart. The lady in the tank and I were having approximately the same kind of month.

⤳ Their Finest Hour ⤳

All wars are horrible. Word War II claimed fifty million lives and virtually destroyed a continent before it was over. Still, those who survived the ordeal were forced to adapt in order to endure their season in hell. Look at the effect of that adaptation.

The Germans were subjected to terrible devastation near the end of the war, just as they had inflicted it on others. Some of their larger cities were bombed around the clock—by the Americans throughout the day and by the British at night. Death and destruction were everywhere. Food was extremely scarce, as were all the essentials to life. By the end of the war, 80 percent of the men born in 1922 were dead, spreading grief and heartache throughout the land. These tragedies resulted from Nazi aggression, of course, but the suffering by individual German families was no less real. What is remarkable from today's perspective is the degree to which they hung tough. They did not crack! Even in the winter of 1945, when factories had been bombed, trains were destroyed, and bridges shattered, the productivity of the nation was still nearly 80 percent of prewar capacity. Morale remained high. They continued to exhibit a national resolve—even when Allied armies were tightening the noose around Berlin.

No less impressive was Britain's record during the war. Churchill rallied the people to personal heroism. He began by addressing their expectations, offering them nothing "but blood, toil, sweat, and tears." That helped steel them against hardship. In the darkest days of the blitz when their beloved homeland was in imminent danger of invasion, the Brits dug in. No one was certain whether or not Hitler and his minions could be stopped. Yet England's most popular song in the ominous hour expressed hope—not fear. It was called "The White Cliffs of Dover," referring to a coastal area that bristled with guns, planes, and radar equipment. These are the lyrics that I remember from childhood:

> There'll be Bluebirds over
> The white cliffs of Dover
> Tomorrow, just you wait and see
> There'll be love and laughter
> And peace ever after
> Tomorrow, when the world is free
>
> The Shepherd will tend His sheep
> The valley will bloom again
> And Jimmy will go to sleep

In his own little room again
There'll be bluebirds over
The white cliffs of Dover
Tomorrow, just you wait and see.

This song came to symbolize the courage of a people looking past death and sacrifice to a better day ahead. Churchill called that era "their finest hour."

This same indomitable spirit was evident in many of the other war-torn countries during that time. It reached a culmination in the city of Leningrad (now called St. Petersburg), where the Russian people endured horrible deprivation during an 872-day siege by German and Finnish armies. More than 650,000 Leningraders died in 1942 alone, mostly from starvation, disease, and shelling by distant guns. But the survivors refused to surrender to tyranny. Their response to unimaginable horror stands as one of the world's most striking examples of raw human courage. St. Petersburg is called the "Hero City" today.

~ A Purpose in Pain ~

A few months ago, we received a phone call here at Focus on the Family from a Mr. Greg Krebs. He wanted to get a message through to me, and this is what he told our telephone representative. Mr. Krebs and his wife have a twenty-one-year-old son named Chris, whom they had been advised to abort when still in the womb. They chose to give him life, and he was born with cerebral palsy. He is also profoundly retarded. His parents do not regret their decision to bring him into the world, because they believe that all life is precious. They are thankful for this son, who has touched their lives in warm and wonderful ways.

"God has used him as he is," Mr. Krebs said.

Then he described something that happened when Chris was just seven years old. He said, "My wife worked in a hospital at the time, and I had taken Chris with me to pick her up. She was late getting off, so Chris and I waited for her in one of the family rooms. There was another man there who was not well dressed and, in fact, was a little smelly. I went to the nurses' station to ask how much longer my wife would be, and when I returned, I saw Chris sitting by the man. The man was sobbing, and I wondered what Chris had done to offend him. I began to apologize.

"'I'm sorry if my son offended you,' I said.

"The man replied, 'Offended me? Offended me? Your son is the only person who has hugged me in the last twenty years!'

"I realized at that moment Chris had a more Christlike love for this man than I did."

Thank you, Mr. and Mrs. Krebs, for loving and valuing your son despite his limitations. I agree wholeheartedly that there is no "junk" in God's value system. He loves every one of us the same, and He uses each person—even the profoundly retarded—to accomplish some part of His purpose. He will also use your pain, although it is not always immediately possible to interpret it.

⟶ No Coincidence ⟵

I recall today that tragic time in 1987 when my four friends were killed in a private plane crash. We had been together the night before, and I had prayed for their safety on the journey home. They took off early the next morning on their way to Dallas but never made it. I can never forget that telephone call indicating the wreckage had been found in a remote canyon—but there were no survivors! I loved those men like brothers, and I was staggered by the loss.

I was asked by four families to speak briefly at their funeral. The untimely deaths of such vibrant and deeply loved men seemed to scream for an explanation. Where was God in their passing? Why did He let this happen? Why would He take such godly men from their families and leave them reeling in grief and pain? There were no answers to these agonizing questions, and I did not try to produce them. But I did say that God had not lost control of their lives, and that He wanted us to trust Him when nothing made sense. His presence was very near.

As we exited the sanctuary that day, I stood talking with loved ones and friends who had gathered to say good-bye. Suddenly, someone pointed to the sky and exclaimed, "Look at that!" Suspended directly above the steeple was a small rainbow in the shape of a smile. There had been no precipitation that day and no more than a few fleecy clouds. Yet this beautiful little rainbow appeared above the church. We learned later that it had been hovering there through most of the funeral service. It was as though the Lord was saying to the grieving wives and children, *Be at peace. Your men are with Me, and all is well. I know you don't understand, but I want you to trust Me. I'm going to take care of you, and this rainbow is a sign to remember.*

A gentleman residing near the church, Mr. William Mueller, had the presence of mind to photograph it at that moment. When it was developed, we saw what no one recognized at the time. There is a small private plane cradled near the center of the rainbow.

Cynics and nonbelievers will say the rainbow and the plane are coincidences that have no spiritual significance. They are entitled to their opinion. But for every member of four wounded families, and certainly for me, the Lord used that phenomenon to convey His peace to us all. He has fulfilled His promise to take care of those four courageous widows and their children.

~ God's Messenger ~

On August 15, 1990, I was playing an early morning round of basketball, as was my custom. At fifty-four years of age, I thought I was in great physical condition. I had recently undergone a medical examination and was pronounced to be in excellent health. I could play basketball all day with men twenty-five years my junior. But there were unpleasant surprises in store for me on that particular morning. I was just a few feet from where NBA legend Pete Maravich had died in my arms two years earlier. (The gym floor is hallowed for me now, as you can understand.)

Suddenly, I was stricken by a moderate pain in the center of my chest. I excused myself, telling my friends I didn't feel well. Then I foolishly drove alone to a nearby emergency clinic and booked a room. This was the same hospital, by the way, where my father was taken after his heart attack twenty-one years earlier. So began ten days that would change my life.

It is a great shock for a man who still thinks of himself as "Joe College" to acknowledge that he is looking death in the face. It took a while for that thought to sink in. My first afternoon in the cardiac care unit was spent working on a new book I was writing with Gary Bauer entitled *Children at Risk*. I had the nurses tape five possible cover designs on the wall, and votes were taken as hospital staff came through. I wrote throughout the afternoon. But when the enzyme report came back about midnight and confirmed that I had suffered some damage to the heart muscle, I knew I was in serious trouble. It was later confirmed that my left anterior descending artery, the one cardiologists call "widow maker," was entirely blocked.

Hospital staff came at me from every direction. Tubes and IVs were strung all over me. An automatic blood pressure machine pumped frantically on my arm every five minutes throughout the night, and a nurse delicately suggested that I not move unless absolutely necessary. That does tend to get your attention. As I lay there in the darkness, listening to the *beep-beep-beep* of the oscilloscope, I began to think very clearly about the people I loved and what things did and did not really matter.

Fortunately, the damage sustained to my heart proved to be minor, and I have fully recovered. I exercise an hour each morning, seven days a week, and I'm eating some of the finest birdseed money can buy. I used to be a junk-food junkie, and I'm still not thrilled about cauliflower, alfalfa, squash, and other things that would have made me gag a few years ago. Nor am I yet convinced that God intended for full-grown men to eat like rabbits and gophers. Surely there is a place in His scheme of things for enchiladas, pizza, donuts, ice cream, and cherry pie. Nevertheless, I'm playing by the rules these days. My diet is designed by some very petite nutritionists who look like they've never eaten a real meal in their lives. It's a sad story, I tell you, but I sure feel wonderful. Pass the yogurt, please.

During those last nine days in the cardiac care unit, I was keenly aware of the implications of my illness. I had watched my father and four of his brothers die of the same disease. I understood full well that my time on this earth could be drawing to an end. Still, I felt the kind of inexplicable peace I described earlier. There were thousands of people praying for me around the country, and I seemed to be cradled in the presence of the Lord. I had lived my life in such a way as to be ready for that moment, and I knew that my sins had been forgiven. That is a priceless awareness when everything is on the line.

There was one brief period, however, when my confidence began to crumble. The day before I was discharged, I underwent an angiogram to determine the nature of my arterial network and the extent of my heart damage. The initial report from that procedure was much more threatening than would later be confirmed, and those ominous findings did not escape my notice. I saw the concern on the faces of technicians. I heard a young Japanese medical resident read the report and mutter in broken English, "Oh, dat not good." She might as well have said, "Dis is gonna kill you."

I was taken back to my room and left to ponder what was going on. For the first time in the long ordeal, anxiety swept over me. Modern medicine can terrorize those it seeks to serve, as laboratory reports and tentative diagnoses trickle in. You can adjust to anything if given time. It's the uncertainty that rattles the nerves. I was going through that drill while waiting for my cardiologist to come by. That's when I uttered a brief and ineloquent prayer from the depths of my soul. I said, "Lord, You know where I am right now. And You know that I am upset and very lonely. Would You send someone who can help me?"

A short time later, my good friend Dr. Jack Hayford, pastor of The Church on the Way in Los Angeles, unexpectedly walked through the door. Many of you know him from his writings and television ministry. We greeted each other warmly, and then I said, "Jack, your church is on the other side of town. Why did you take the time to come see me today?" I didn't tell him about my prayer.

I'll never forget his reply. He said, "Because the Lord told me you were lonely."

That's the kind of God we serve. He lovingly sent that good man to see me even before I had asked for help. Now admittedly, the Lord doesn't always solve our problems instantaneously, and He sometimes permits us to walk through the valley of the shadow of death. Eventually we'll all take that journey. But He is there with us even in the darkest hours, and we can never escape His encompassing love. I was warmly embraced by it throughout my hospitalization, even in the darkest hour.

Psalm 73:23–26 meant so much to me during my convalescence. I think you will understand why. It reads:

Yet I am always with you; you hold me by my right hand. You guide me with your counsel, and afterward you will take me into glory. Whom have I in heaven but you? And earth has nothing I desire besides you. My flesh and my heart may fail, but God is the strength of my heart and my portion forever.

⤙ This Is My Will for You ⤚

When my friend Von Letherer was just one year old, his parents noticed that he bruised badly whenever he bumped into furniture or even tumbled in his crib. They took him to their doctor, who diagnosed Von with hemophilia—the heredity "bleeder's disease." His blood lacked the substance necessary to coagulate, actually threatening his life each time he suffered a minor injury. There was very little treatment for hemophilia in those days, and Von was not expected to live beyond childhood. Indeed, he survived because of prayer, and because of nearly four hundred pints of blood transfused by the time he reached the end of adolescence.

During those teen years when Von's life repeatedly hung in the balance, there was a young lady standing by his side. Her name was Joann, and she was his childhood sweetheart. Joann understood very well that Von's future was uncertain, but she loved him dearly. Hemophilia, they decided, was not going to determine the course of their lives. The couple was married when he was twenty-two and she was nineteen years old.

A new crisis occurred several years later when Joann was carrying their second child. She became seriously ill and was diagnosed with Hodgkin's disease, a type of cancer that attacks the lymph glands. It was usually fatal in that day. Although a treatment program had been developed, Joann's pregnancy prevented the doctors from prescribing it for her. She and Von could have aborted their baby, of course, but they chose instead to place themselves in the hands of the Lord.

They began asking for a miracle—and promptly received one. Several weeks after the initial diagnosis, the hospital repeated the laboratory and clinical tests. Doctors concluded that there was no sign of Hodgkin's disease in Joann. She has been cancer-free from that day to this.

Now, notice what occurred in this instance. As we have seen, Von was born with a painful, debilitating illness about which his father, a minister, and his mother prayed diligently. They asked repeatedly for God to heal their son. When Von got older, he began praying on his own behalf. Then Joann came along and joined the chorus. Despite these and many other petitions, the Lord chose not to heal Von's hemophilia. At fifty-six years of age, he is still afflicted with this disorder and suffers daily from immobile joints and related physical difficulties. Von has taken medication every day for many years, just to cope with the pain. Yet his indomitable spirit has been a witness to me and to thousands of others through the years.

Why has the Lord been unwilling to heal this good man? I don't know. Some might say that his prayer team lacked faith, except for the fact that Joann was healed in response to their petitions. The same people who asked for intervention in her life were also praying for Von. In one instance the answer was yes, and in the other it was no. And life goes on. The Lord has offered no explanation or interpretation of His response, except by inference, *This is My will for you.*

～ Answered Prayer ～

The year was 1957, and I was a senior in college. An ominous telephone call came one afternoon from my parents, who sounded anxious and upset. Mom quickly told me that my dad had developed an angry-looking sore on his right hand. They had watched it for some time and realized it was not healing. Finally they went to see a dermatologist and had just returned from his office. My father, age forty-six, was diagnosed as having squamous cell carcinoma—a type of skin cancer that is curable in the early stages but dangerous if not treated. The doctor seemed concerned. He told them that a microscopic examination of tissue revealed a "very mature" cell. He couldn't tell whether or not it had metastasized (spread to other parts of the body), but he could not rule out that possibility.

It was decided to treat the cancer with radiation over a period of six weeks. At the end of that time, the healing process should begin. If the lesion were controllable locally, it would disappear entirely in about five more weeks. But if it did not heal, more serious problems were ahead. The specter of amputation was raised. My father was an artist, and the thought of losing his right arm (or his life) alarmed the entire family. We began praying for him.

Four weeks after completing the radiation treatments, the sore was still much the same. No sign of healing had occurred. Tension mounted as we continued to get discouraging medical reports. (I'm not sure the disease would be less challenging today than in the 1950s, but the episode was extremely distressing at that time.) My father's physician began contemplating the next step.

It was time to do some more intensive praying. Dad went to our denominational leaders and requested that they anoint him with oil and specifically ask the Lord to heal the cancer. That brief service occurred two days before the end of the fifth week, at which point the dermatologist had indicated a further decision would have to be made. Exactly two days later, the sore healed over. It never returned.

Faith under Fire

My friend Robert Vernon is a former assistant chief of police, Los Angeles Police Department, where he served with distinction for years. Toward the end of his tenure, however, he was unjustly and illegally pressured to resign because of his conservative Christian beliefs. After many unsuccessful attempts by the media to discredit him in the police department, Chief Vernon's critics began looking at his private life for something with which to embarrass him. They soon found it. Someone dug up a cassette recording of a speech Bob had delivered at his church fourteen years earlier. On the basis of comments he made about family life, taken out of context and wildly distorted, they forced an investigation of Vernon's work at the police department. It was a clear violation of his First Amendment rights. Since when can a person be persecuted for expressing his religious views in his own church? That question is being considered now by the courts, but there is clear evidence of bias there, too.

Please understand, there was never any accusation of professional malfeasance against Chief Vernon in any official capacity. Nevertheless, a full-scale investigation was conducted to see if his religious views might have affected his work. He was eventually cleared of all wrongdoing, although his leadership was so damaged by the inquisition that he felt it necessary to resign. I know Chief Vernon personally, and I can say with certainty that he was hounded out of office simply because of his faith, despite his thirty-seven years of unblemished service.

Chief Vernon's experience offers us an opportunity to examine a classic case of "faith under fire." His situation bears all the typical components: a very troubling event, an element of injustice or unfairness (*Why me?*), a silent God who could have intervened but didn't, and a million unanswered questions. Have you ever been there?

Bob was asked to speak at a recent chapel service for employees of Focus on the Family, and he elected to discuss his own difficulties. I think you'll find his remarks helpful, especially if you're enduring your own private trial at this time. This is what the veteran policeman said to our staff:

When it became apparent that Daryl Gates would soon resign as Chief of Police, an article appeared in a Los Angeles magazine. It said, "Those who are anxious to get rid of Gates ought to see who's standing in the wings to take his place. It's one Robert L. Vernon, who has very strange religious beliefs." Then they listed three things that I had reportedly said in a speech recorded fourteen years earlier. I stand by what I actually said, and I'm not apologizing for it. Those concepts came from the Word of God. But the magazine perverted my actual comments and said, "First, he believes homosexuality is a sin." That's true. Second, they said, "He believes that women should submit to men." That's not true. I referred to what the Bible says about mutual submission in husband-wife relationships. Third, my critics twisted what I had said about child discipline. I was talking about a father who had not kept his promise to his son and provoked the boy to wrath. When the child became rebellious, the father said, "If you have a rebel on your hands, you have to break him—and to break him you have to beat him." I was quoting the father, not speaking for myself. I went on to say, "Who was wrong in this scenario? The father was at fault, not the son."

The magazine, however, ascribed the father's words to me, and then concluded, "Here's what Chief Vernon thinks about raising children." They edited the tape in such a way that the listener heard only my voice recommending that we beat children until they break. That edited tape was given to the news media, which released it widely. It was a very clever maneuver.

As a result, my reputation was severely damaged. I eventually had to leave the Los Angeles Police Department and have not been able to get a job in police work elsewhere. I recently applied for a position north of Denver, but they didn't even interview me. I am, you see, a religious kook. I believe weird things.

I now know what Solomon meant when he said, "A good name is better than gold and silver, yea, precious stones."

I even have Christian friends who have heard my recording on the radio and said, "We know you denied it, Bob, but we heard you say that children should be beaten until they break." I try to explain, but sometimes it's hard to make them understand. I have to confess something to you. I not only got depressed about this situation, but I also became angry at God. And that wasn't right.

About that time I had an experience that helped clarify some things for me. My son and I decided to float down the Colorado River on a raft. It was a dramatic ride. I can assure you. We left with eighteen friends from a place called Lee's Ferry. As we floated out for the eight-day journey, someone said, "Well, we're committed." We sure were. By the third day, there were some who had had enough. But that was too bad. There was no way out of the canyon except down the river. That's the way the Lord works when we're faced with a time of difficulty. Don't think about ways to squirm out of trouble. Just stay committed and you'll come through in due course.

There were some extremely turbulent places along the path of the river. At Lava Falls, for example, the raft dropped thirty-seven vertical feet in a distance of seventy-five feet. Our raft-master, named Robin, would say as we approached such a place, "This is gonna be a good one." By that he meant, "We're all gonna die!" Finally, we came to Kermit Falls, which for us was the most violent spot in the river.

Suddenly, Robin seemed to lose control of the raft just as we started down the rapids. It spun sideways at the worst possible moment. For an instant, I was tempted to jump overboard. I really thought we were going to die. Then I heard the big Evinrude engine roaring at peak performance behind the raft. I realized that Robin had turned sideways on purpose. Then I saw a huge, jagged rock that had tumbled down from the walls of that great canyon. It was sticking up menacingly in the center of the river. That's why Robin spun the craft. He did it so the full power of the motor could push us around the dangerous rock. If I had jumped from the raft, I'd have drowned or would have been crushed on the jagged rock.

To those of you who are plunging over the falls today, resist the temptation to jump overboard! God knows what He is doing. He has your raft sideways for a reason. Even though your reputation may have been ruined, you're depressed, and you're wondering what to do next. If you'll listen carefully, you'll hear the One who said to David, "Trust in Me!"

From my experience on the river, and from reading Psalm 37, I've learned not to fret. I've confessed my anger to Him and said, "You know what You're doing even though my raft seems out of control. I will trust You. I delight in You. I've committed my way unto You. Now, I'm resting in my circumstances." But then, I had to learn the most difficult lesson of all. As my wife and I read the other Psalms, one word kept jumping out at us. It was the word *wait*.

"No, Lord! I don't want to wait. I want relief today. Please take revenge on those who have hurt me." But He says, "Be still, and know that I am God." Then He led me to the final four verses in Psalm 37, which tell us: "Consider the blameless, observe the upright; there is a future for the man of peace. But all sinners will be destroyed; the future of the wicked will be cut off. The salvation of the righteous comes from the Lord; he is their stronghold in time of trouble. The Lord helps them and delivers them; he delivers them from the wicked and saves them, because they take refuge in him" (vv. 37–40).

Those words from Chief Vernon reflect great maturity and faith, considering the injustice and pain he and his wife, Esther, have suffered. I have shared his message here because so many of my readers have experienced similar difficulties. Are you one of them? Is your raft skidding sideways in the river today? Is it plunging down the rapids toward the rocks below, terrifying everyone on board? Have you considered jumping into the river and trying to swim to safety on your own? That is precisely what Satan would have you do. He wants you to give up on God, who seems to have lost control of your circumstances. But I urge you not to leave the safety of His protection. The Captain knows what He is doing. There are purposes that you cannot perceive or comprehend. You may never understand—at least not in this life—but you must not let go of your faith. It is, after all, "the evidence of things not seen" (Hebrews 11:1 KJV).

⟶ It's Either Despair or It's God ⟵

I'll let Dr. Conway tell his own story, as heard on the Focus on the Family radio broadcast:

When our daughter was fifteen years of age, she began having trouble with one of her knees. For a year and one-half, she saw doctors, had laboratory tests and scans, and two extensive biopsies on the tumor they found. We waited for weeks for word from the many pathology labs around the United States who were studying her mysterious lump.

Finally one evening our physician came to our house and gave some very distressing news. He said that Becki had a malignancy and that it was necessary to amputate her leg. You can imagine how that devastated Sally and me. I refused to believe it. I determined to prevent this surgery by praying until God promised to heal her.

"You're not going to have your leg amputated," I told Becki. "I believe God is going to do a miracle. He said we could come to Him in times of trouble. I'm absolutely convinced you are going to be spared this surgery." Our church then began a twenty-four-hour vigil of fasting and prayer. Thousands of people around the United States and overseas were praying for Becki's healing.

On the morning when the surgery was scheduled, I said to our physician, "Scott, as you go into the operating room, please verify that the cancer has been healed. God is going to come through, I'm sure." He left and did not immediately return. Forty-five minutes went by, and still, Sally, my other two daughters, and I sat in the waiting room. An hour passed, and then two. I began to realize that a lengthy medical procedure must be in progress.

Then the doctor came out and told me that they had amputated Becki's leg. I was absolutely shattered. I was crushed. I lost God! In anger, I was beating on the walls of the hospital and saying, "Where are You, God? Where are You?" I was in a state of shock and wandered down to the morgue in the basement of the hospital. That's where I felt I belonged, surrounded by death. I was dealing with more than Becki's surgery, as terrible as that was. I struggled to handle the theological implications of what had happened. I could not understand why God permitted this to happen. You see, if I had been a plumber instead of a pastor, I could have gone out to fix pipes the next day, and my spiritual confusion would not have affected my work. But my job required me to stand before people and teach them the principles of the Bible. What could I tell them now? If I had been a liberal pastor who didn't believe the Bible to be literally true, I could have survived by doing book reviews and talking about irrelevant stuff. But I pastored a Bible church. My style of teaching was exposition of the Word, reviewing it verse by verse and drawing out its meaning. How could I go back and tell my people that God had let my daughter lose her leg? It was a terrible moment in my life.

As I sat outside the morgue that day, a friend found me in the bowels of the hospital and came to my rescue. He was a godsend to me! I'm not part of the charismatic movement, but it was Dick Foth, an Assembly of God pastor, who stood by my side and cried with me and prayed for me. He said, "I'm not worried about Becki. I'm worried about you. There are a couple of thousand people in your church and thousands more elsewhere who are hanging on for you. You're going to get through this."

Then he and two other guys took turns working with me. One would go for a coffee break and the others would take over. They just kept me talking—letting me spill out the frustration and the anger. They didn't condemn me even though I was so angry at God. At one point I said, "I think He was so busy finding a parking spot for a little old lady that He didn't have time to save Becki's leg." Dick would listen and then say, "Is there anything else you need to say?" I didn't have to worry that if I said something disturbing, maybe these guys would doubt God. I didn't worry about them giving up on me. I didn't have to hold anything in and say, "I've got to keep up the professional front because I'm a preacher. I've got to be good." They let me deal with the pain.

When a person is going through this kind of terrible depression, some believers don't know how to respond. They say, "I'll pray for you," which may mean, "I'm no longer really listening to you." That can be a way of ending one's responsibility to shoulder the load. In fact, when it comes to bearing one another's burdens, the secular world sometimes does that job better than we do. They know the importance of letting resentment and anger spill out, whereas Christians may feel they have to hold it inside. The Scripture tells us, "The righteous cry out, and the LORD hears them; he delivers them from all their troubles" (Psalm 34:17).

It also bothered me later when people began offering simplistic explanations and flippant comments to "cheer me up." It was irritating when they quoted Romans 8:28, "all things work together for good," when they had not earned the right to brush off my pain. I wanted to say, "Tell me about it, Charlie. Tell me about it when your sixteen-year-old daughter's leg is amputated. Come back when you've gone through something like this, and then we'll talk again." Sometimes we get so used to the "cheer-up" mode in Christianity that we become unreal. I almost heard people saying to me in those days, "Shhhhh! Don't say those things. What if God hears them?" As if God didn't know what I was thinking and struggling with! God knew what I was going through, and He understood my passion. My love for Becki originated with Him in the first place. So who would I be trying to fool by covering up the agony of my soul?

I remember a guy I saw in a restaurant a few days after Becki underwent surgery. He was sitting at a table, and as I walked by he reached out and grabbed my coat. He said, "Jim, I think God has allowed this to happen because it has brought about a revival in our church." I said, "So what is God going to do to bring another revival when this one passes, chop off Becki's other leg? Then her arm and her other arm? There isn't enough of Becki to keep any church spiritually alive, if that is what it takes." When you start reaching for puny answers like that, it dehumanizes those who suffer and insults our magnificent God who loves and cares for the oppressed.

I couldn't explain why Becki had to lose her leg, but I knew the answers being given were not right. Probably the most important thing I learned in this entire process is this: I became deeply aware that there were only two choices that I could make. One was to continue in my anger at God and follow the path of despair I was on. The other choice was to let God be God, and somehow say, "I don't know how all this fits together. I don't understand the reasons for it. I'm not even going to ask for the explanation. I've chosen to accept the fact that You are God and I'm the servant, instead of the other way around." And there I left it. It was in that choice that I came to cope with my situation.

I frankly admit that after all these years, I still struggle with some things. I still get sick to my stomach when I see my daughter hopping on one leg. But I have come to recognize that God has a higher purpose and I just don't understand that purpose. I am prepared to wait until eternity to receive answers to my questions, if necessary. Like Job, I am now able to say, "Though he slay me, yet will I trust in him" (Job 13:15 KJV). It's either despair, or it's the acceptance of His sovereignty. Those are the alternatives. Let me say it again. It's either despair, or it's God. There's nothing in between. Our family has chosen to hold on to God.

Thank you, Dr. Jim Conway and your wife, Sally, and daughter, Becki, for letting us share your deepest pain. Seldom in the Christian community have we witnessed such honesty and vulnerability. I trust that God will continue to use your experience to strengthen the faith of those who sit alone today, symbolically, in the morgue. All they have believed and hoped for has been assaulted by the forces of hell. The philosophical and theological foundation on which everything rests has just given way. So what do they do now?

There is only one answer, and it is the conclusion drawn by Dr. Jim

Conway in his hour of crisis: Don't demand explanations. Don't lean on your ability to understand. Don't turn loose of your faith. But do choose to trust Him, by the exercise of the will He has placed within you. The only other alternative is despair.

~ Trusting God's Timing ~

In 1985, I was asked by the United States Attorney General, Edwin Meese, to serve on his Commission on Pornography. It was without doubt the most difficult and unpleasant assignment of my life. For eighteen months, the ten other members and I handled a thankless and nauseating responsibility. We traveled extensively and examined the most wretched magazines, books, films, and videotapes in existence anywhere in the world. Since the United States is the fountainhead for obscenity worldwide, we were immersed in this filth for what seemed like an eternity. Furthermore, the pornographers and smut peddlers tracked our commission like a pack of wolves following a herd of caribou. They did everything they could to intimidate and humiliate us.

I remember sitting in the public hearings day after day with various types of cameras, including videos, aimed at my face. I could see my reverse image reflected in their lenses for hours, which tends to make one self-conscious. The photographers were waiting for me to do something embarrassing, such as make a weird face or put my finger near my nose. One day when I stood up to leave for a lunch break, I turned around and was confronted by a photographer and his clicking camera just inches from my face. Always, there were microphones taped beside my place at the table to record every whispered word or remark. My comments were then parodied the following month in various pornographic publications. *Hustler* magazine superimposed my picture on the backside of a donkey, awarding me the title Ass ___ of the Month. The attorney general never said it would be easy.

These efforts at harassment were momentary irritants. Bigger guns would be rolled out later, and they were fired soon enough. A $30 million lawsuit was filed by three organizations, Playboy, Penthouse, and the American Magazine Association, shortly before we issued our final report. It named as defendants every member of the commission, its executive director (Alan Sears), and Attorney General Edwin Meese. The complaint was a trumped-up bit of legalese that our lawyers said was totally without merit. Attorneys at the Department of Justice told us not to worry—the case should be thrown out of court in short order. They were wrong.

The matter was assigned to Judge John Garrett Penn, one of the most liberal judges in the Northeast. Incredibly, he held the ridiculous case on his desk for more than two years before ruling on a relatively simple motion for summary judgment. Eventually, he decided in our favor. The litigants immediately appealed, and we spent another year in limbo. We won the next round, which was followed by yet another appeal. For six years this threatening suit hung over our heads as it worked its way through the legal system. It finally reached the Supreme Court in early 1992, which thankfully ended the ordeal. This is the way eleven citizens were rewarded for serving without compensation at the request of their country!

Getting back to our theme, Shirley and I prayed about the lawsuit when it was filed back in 1986. I was carrying heavy responsibilities at Focus on the Family and certainly didn't need this distraction. We asked that the "cup" be removed from us, but there was no immediate reply from the Lord. Thus, the process was allowed to run its course with its inevitable drain on my physical and emotional resources. Six years later, Jesus "showed up," and the issue was resolved. But why, I wondered, did He come "four days late"? Was there anything gained by dragging out the case in the courts? I'm sure there was, knowing that every prayer is answered either positively or negatively. I also believe literally that "in all things God works for the good of those who love him, who have been called according to his purpose" (Romans 8:28). Nevertheless, I am unable to explain or understand why I had to go through six years of wasted time and energy to settle this irritant. But then, it really doesn't matter, does it? It is unnecessary for me to be told why the Lord permitted the suit to continue. As long as I know He loves me and He never makes a mistake, why should I not be content to rest in His protection?

∼ The Lost Marble ∼

When I was a boy, I heard a mystery program on the radio that captured my imagination. It told the story of a man who was condemned to solitary confinement in a pitch-black cell. The only thing he had to occupy his mind was a marble, which he threw repeatedly against the walls. He spent his hours listening to the marble as it bounced and rolled around the room. Then he would grope in the darkness until he found his precious toy.

One day, the prisoner threw his marble upward—but it failed to come down. Only silence echoed through the darkness. He was deeply disturbed by the "evaporation" of the marble and his inability to explain its disappearance. Finally he went berserk, pulled out all his hair, and died.

When the prison officials came to remove his body, a guard noticed something caught in a huge spider's web in the upper corner of the room.

That's strange, he thought. *I wonder how a marble got up there.*

As the story of the frantic prisoner illustrates, human perception sometimes poses questions the mind is incapable of answering. But valid answers always exist. For those of us who are followers of Jesus Christ, it just makes good sense not to depend too heavily on our ability to make the pieces fit—especially when we're trying to figure out the Almighty!

∼ Invasion of the Killer Vine ∼

James 1:8 refers to an individual as a "double minded man [who] is unstable in all his ways" (KJV). He, of all people, is most miserable and confused!

Such a person reminds me of a vine that grew behind the house Shirley and I owned in southern California. It was an ambitious plant that had a secret plan to conquer the world! In its path was a gorgeous, 150-year-old oak tree that I was most anxious to protect. Every few months, I would look out the back window and notice that the vine had again attacked the tree. There it was, winding its way up the trunk and around the upper branches. If allowed to continue, the oak tree would eventually succumb to the invasion of the killer vine!

The solution was really quite simple. Instead of jerking the plant off the tree, which would have damaged the bark, I made one quick cut near the bottom of the vine. Then I walked away. Though nothing appeared to have changed, the green monster had suffered a mortal blow. The next day, its leaves looked a little dull. Two or three days later they were slightly discolored around the edges. Soon they began turning brown with cancerous-looking black spots near the center. Then they started falling off, eventually leaving just a dry stick extending up the trunk. Finally, the stick fell away and the tree stood alone. So much for blind ambition.

Is the analogy clear? Christians who lose God during a period of spiritual confusion are like the vine that has been cut off from its source. They are deprived of nurture and strength. They seem to cope at first, but the concealed wound is mortal. They begin to wither in the heat of the sun. They usually drop out of the church and quit reading the Bible and praying. Some go off the deep end and begin doing things they would never have contemplated before. But there is no peace within. Indeed, some of the most bitter, unhappy people on earth are those who have become estranged from the God they no longer understand or trust.

⌒ No Room for Self-Pity ⌒

In my reading about astronomy some years ago, I came across the work of a man named Dr. Stephen Hawking. He is an astrophysicist at Cambridge University and perhaps the most intelligent man on earth. The mantle of Einstein has fallen on his shoulders, and he has worn it with dignity. He has advanced the general theory of relativity farther than any person since the old man died. Dr. Hawking is also credited with mathematical calculations suggesting the existence of black holes in space and other widely acclaimed theories.

Unfortunately, Dr. Hawking is afflicted with a rare degenerative neuro-muscular disorder called amyotrophic lateral sclerosis (ALS syndrome), or Lou Gehrig's disease. It will eventually take his life. He has been confined to a wheelchair for years, where he can do little more than sit and think. He cannot even write down the mathematical formulae that govern the progression of his thoughts. *Omni* magazine said of Hawking back in 1979, "His mind is a blackboard. He memorizes the long strings of equations that give life to his ideas, then dictates the results to his colleagues or secretary—a feat that has been compared to Beethoven's writing an entire symphony in his head or Milton's dictating *Paradise Lost* to his daughter."

In more recent years, Hawking has lost the ability even to speak, and now he communicates by means of a computer that is operated from the tiniest movement of his fingertips. Quoting *Omni* again: "He is too weak to write, feed himself, comb his hair, fix his glasses—all this must be done for him. Yet this most dependent of all men has escaped invalid status. His personality shines through the messy details of his existence."

That acceptance of catastrophic illness is what makes Stephen Hawking of interest in the present discussion, even though he does not believe in the God of the Bible. He might be a deist, although he wrote a book in 1988 entitled A Brief History of Time, in which he labored to explain away the need for a Creator. Nevertheless, what Hawking learned from his disability is remarkable and can be enlightening to those of us who live by faith.

He said that before he became ill, he had very little interest in life. He called it a "pointless existence" resulting from sheer boredom. He drank too much and did very little work. Then he learned he had ALS syndrome and was not expected to live more than two years. The ultimate effect of that diagnosis, beyond its initial shock, was extremely positive. He claimed to have been happier after he was afflicted than before. How can that be understood? Hawking provided the answer.

He said, "When one's expectations are reduced to zero, one really appreciates everything that one does have." Stated another way, contentment in life is determined, in part, by what a person anticipates from it. To a man like Hawking who thought he would soon die quickly, everything takes on meaning—a sunrise or a walk in a park or the laughter of children. Suddenly, each small pleasure becomes precious. By contrast, those who believe life owes them a free ride are often discontent with its finest gifts.

Hawking also said this about his physical limitations: "If you're disabled, you should pour your energies into those areas where you are not handicapped. You should concentrate on what you can do well, and not mourn over what you cannot do. And it is very important not to give in to self-pity. If you're disabled and you feel sorry for yourself, then no one is going to have much to do with you. A physically handicapped person certainly cannot afford to be psychologically handicapped as well."

Another way of expressing Hawking's point is that a person faced with extreme hardship must press himself to get tougher. Whining and self-pity, as logical as they seem, are deadly indulgences. An individual in crisis will either grow stronger or become demoralized. Within certain limits, of course, adversity can have a positive effect on people by helping to build character. For Christians, Scripture says to develop and enhance that precious characteristic called faith (James 1:2–4).

⟿ Disappointment with Dad ⟿

A very close and respected friend of mine, whom I'll call Martha, has a father who has never revealed any depth of love for her. Though she is now grown and has two children of her own, she continues to hope that he will suddenly become what he has never been. This expectation causes Martha repeated disappointment and frustration. When her infant son failed to survive his first week of life, her insensitive father didn't even come to the funeral—a fact that has caused deep wounds and scars through the years.

After receiving a letter from Martha in which she again mentioned her father's latest insult (he refused to come to her son's wedding), I sent her a few reactions and suggestions. She said she obtained so much help from what I had written that she shared it with three other women experiencing similar frustrations from people who have "failed" them. Finally, she returned a copy of my letter and asked me to include it in a future book of this nature. It appears below.

Martha, I am more convinced every day that a great portion of our adult effort is invested in the quest for that which was *unreachable* in childhood. The more painful the early void, the more we are motivated to fill it later in life. Your dad never met the needs that a father should satisfy in his little girl, and I think you are still hoping he will miraculously become what he has never been. Therefore, he constantly disappoints you—hurts you—rejects you. I think you will be less vulnerable to pain when you accept the fact that he cannot, nor will he ever, provide the love and empathy and interest that he should. It is not easy to insulate yourself in this way. I'm still working to plug a few vacuums from my own tender years. *But it hurts less to expect nothing than to hope in vain.*

I would guess that your dad's own childhood experiences account for his emotional peculiarities, and can perhaps be viewed as his own unique handicap. If he were blind, you would love him despite his lack of vision. In a sense, he is emotionally "blind." He is unable to see your needs. He is unaware of the hurt behind the unpleasant incidents and disagreements—the funeral of your baby, the disinterest of your life, and now Bob's wedding. His handicap makes it *impossible* for him to perceive your feelings and anticipation. If you can accept your father as a man with a permanent handicap—one that was probably caused when *he* was vulnerable—you will shield yourself from the ice pick of rejection.

You didn't ask for this diatribe, and it may not hit your particular target at all. Nevertheless these are the thoughts that occurred to me as I read your letter.

At least *we* are looking forward to the wedding, Martha. Best wishes to John and Bob and the entire Williams enterprise.

Sincerely,
Jim

This letter was of help to Martha, but not because it improved her distressing circumstances. Her father is no more thoughtful and demonstrative today than he was in years past. It is Martha's *perspective* of him that has been changed. She now sees him as a victim of cruel forces in his own childhood that nicked and scarred his young psyche and caused him to insulate his emotions against the outside world. Since receiving this letter, Martha has learned that her father was subjected to some extremely traumatic circumstances during his childhood. (Among other things, his aunt told him unsympathetically that his father had died suddenly and then she reprimanded him severely for crying.) Martha's father is, as I suspected, a man with a handicap.

∽ A Matter of Perspective ∽

When I first began driving to my hospital office in 1966, I noticed a nice-looking man who invariably stood at the window of an old apartment house, which is located across the street from the doctors' parking lot. Morning after morning this man, whom I would judge to have been in his middle forties, appeared at that same open window as I drove past. He was always there when I went home at the end of the day, as well. I began to wave or smile to the man in the window, and he would return my greeting with a similar gesture. Though it seems unlikely, we developed a friendship in the absence of any personal knowledge of one another, or without a single conversation between us.

My curiosity finally compelled me to get better acquainted with the man behind the smile. One noontime I walked from my office to the building where my congenial friend lived and climbed a dark stairway to the second floor. I knocked on the door, and it was opened by "the man in the window." He introduced himself as Tommy and invited me to come into his two-room apartment. During the next hour he told me his story. He had been a successful executive until devastated by a massive coronary thrombosis about six years earlier. His heart ailments were compounded by emphysema and other physical disorders, which prevented his engaging in any form of work. I also noticed that his right arm was deformed, being much smaller than his left. Tommy, I learned, was rarely able to leave his tiny apartment. He was not married and seemed to have no relatives or close friends. His situation was not unlike being sentenced to virtual solitary confinement in a two-room cell.

The beautiful part of Tommy's story is how he chose to cope with his personal tragedy. He had every reason in the world to be depressed and despondent, but he exuded confidence and optimism. He had decided that he would make friends with as many people as possible among those driving to and from their work, and that comprised his entire social life.

I said, "Tommy, what can I do for you? Do you need anything? Can I help in any way?"

He said, "Thank you, sir, and I appreciate your offer. But I'm doing all right. I really don't need anything."

There was not one ounce of self-pity apparent anywhere in our conversation, and he steadfastly refused to let me treat him as an invalid. His only acknowledgment that life was difficult came in response to my question, "Do you ever become discouraged with your situation here?"

Tommy replied, "Well, in the morning when everyone is coming to work, I enjoy greeting the people at the start of a new day. But when they are heading for their homes at night and I'm saying good-bye, I sometimes feel a little blue." That was the only negative statement I ever heard him utter. Tommy had obviously made up his mind to accept life as it was.

For something more than fifteen years, Tommy stood his watch above the noise and traffic of the street, and we remained good friends. I stopped my car beneath his window on January 3 of this year, to greet him after I had been gone for a brief Christmas vacation. Without thinking, I asked him the traditional question which friends exchange following the New Year's Eve: "Did you have a good holiday?"

Tommy replied, "It was great."

I later learned that he had spent the entire Christmas season in the solitude of his room, watching the harassed shoppers and commuters below him.

A few weeks later, Tommy failed to appear at his usual place at the window. The second morning he was absent again, and both his shades were drawn. I learned from the parking lot attendant that Tommy had died during the previous weekend. My friend was gone. His funeral had already been held, though I doubt if anyone attended it. Now as I drive past the apartment building each morning, I can hear Tommy saying the last words he ever spoke to me, "It was great."

My point in telling you about Tommy is to illustrate the fact that depression is usually a matter of perspective. Everything depends on how you look at a given situation. I saw a couple win $3,000 cash on the television program *Let's Make a Deal*, but they went home literally sick because they barely missed winning a $12,000 automobile. If Monty Hall had met them on the street and handed them $3,000, they would have been overjoyed. But they were dismayed by the knowledge that they could have won more. It was all a matter of perspective.

A small advertisement appeared in *McCall's* magazine for a product that offers to rid women of that dreaded disorder, *stretch marks*. The ad quoted the sad testimony of a young mother who spoke right from her heart: "I've had two children, but I am so unhappy with the stretch marks on my legs, body, and bust. They make me feel ashamed to be seen in a bathing suit or low-cut clothes." It is entirely possible that this young woman is the mother of two healthy children; she may have a good husband who loves her, and judging from her picture, she is still in the bloom of her youth and physical vitality. Everything important may be going right for her, yet she is "so unhappy" and feels "ashamed" because she is not perfect. Her problem is one of perspective. She has allowed one tiny flaw to establish her dominant mood. And don't you know it is pleasant for her husband and children to come home to her each evening!

I know life can bite and cut, and I don't mean to sound unsympathetic regarding the circumstances that adversely affect one's mood. But it will help some readers to recognize that we often *permit* routine things to depress us. Let's consider the example of in-law conflict (which ranked as the ninth most common source of depression in the women surveyed). A wife can decide how she will react to an overpossessive or irritating mother-in-law; she can cry and gnash her teeth and let the conflict drill little holes in the lining of her stomach—or she can view it from a less agitated perspective. Though it sounds a bit silly, my point will be made by imagining that such a woman had loving, respectful, supportive in-laws, but she also had a child in the leukemia ward of our hospital. Let's suppose that by some stroke of magic I could offer her a healthy child if she would accept a hostile mother-in-law. She would grab the exchange and be forever thankful for the miracle. It is, as I said, simply a matter of perspective—determined entirely by how one looks at a problem.

⌒ Crisis Will Come ⌒

I was invited a few years ago to take a three-day whitewater rafting trip down the Rogue River in Oregon. A friend and experienced rafter, Dr. Richard Hosley, said to me as we were preparing to launch the gear, "One thing you'll soon learn is that the river is always boss." I didn't know what he meant then, but three days later I understood that principle very clearly.

Rather than floating on the raft for fifty miles in relative serenity and safety, I chose to paddle along behind in a plastic eight-foot canoe. And on the second afternoon, I insisted on rowing this flimsy craft into the most treacherous part of the river. It was a bad decision.

Ahead lay a section of the river known as the "Coffeepot," so named because the narrowing of the rock-walled banks creates an unpredictable, bubbling current that has been known to suck small boats and their passengers below the surface without warning. Several men and women have drowned in that precise spot, one of them only the summer before. But ignorance is bliss, and blissful I was.

I seemed to be handling the task quite well for the first few minutes . . . before everything came unraveled. Then I was caught in the current flowing around a large rock and was capsized in the turbulent water. It seemed like an eternity before I came to the surface, only to find breathing impossible. A bandanna that had been around my neck was now plastered across my mouth and held there by my glasses, which were strapped to my head. Just as I clawed free and gasped for air, churning water hit me in the face and gurgled into my lungs. Again, I came up coughing and sputtering before taking another trip below the surface. By then I was desperate for air and keenly aware that the Coffeepot was only a hundred yards downstream.

A kind of panic gripped me that I had not experienced since childhood! I definitely considered the possibility that I was drowning. You see, I have a nagging little habit of breathing every few minutes and don't cope well when prevented from doing so. I knew that getting sucked under again at that moment might be the end of the line. My family and friends watched helplessly from the raft as I bobbed through the rapids and into the narrowest section of the river. They were unable to reach me because the current had carried them farther downstream.

By using his incredible rafting skill, however, Dr. Hosley managed to "hold" the raft by maneuvering it to an eddy at the side of the river. There it spun until I caught up and grabbed the rope that rims the upper exterior structure. I could not pull myself into the craft because of the rapids, my soaked clothing, and the distance of the rope above my head. That's why I expected Dr. Hosley to help me aboard. Instead, I noticed that he was struggling with the oars and looking very concerned. I learned later what was worrying him. He feared that the large raft would be thrown against the vertical rock walls bordering the Coffeepot and that I would be crushed by its massive force.

Indeed, the raft was thrown against the wall, but I saw it coming. Using all of the strength left within me, I pulled my feet up and sprang off the rock, propelling myself high enough on the raft to scramble on board. I then collapsed in the bottom of the craft and stayed there sucking air for about thirty minutes.

The only casualty from the experience is a matter of collegiate pride. Dr. Hosley was wearing a shirt with his beloved Stanford University named across the front. It survived the trip. But somewhere on the bottom of the Rogue River in dishonor lies a watersoaked hat bearing the logo of the University of Southern California. It was a sad moment in the historic rivalry of the two schools. At least I didn't wind up lying on the rocky bottom clutching my USC banner!

You can probably see how this story relates to our theme. Life is like the beautiful Rogue River in some ways. There are long stretches when the water is calm and serene. You can see your reflection as you lean out of the raft. The scenery is gorgeous, and the river carries you peacefully downstream. Then without warning you are propelled into the white water. Suddenly, you're gasping for air and struggling to keep your head above water. At the moment when you think you might be drowning, you float right into the turmoil of the Coffeepot.

Please understand that this WILL happen to you sooner or later. No one travels down the river of life without encountering turbulence. You might as well brace yourself for it. There will be moments of serenity and beauty when you lean back and take in the wonder. But there will also be times of sheer terror when you'll be tossed out of the boat and at the mercy of the good Lord. It's all part of the ride. That's why it is necessary before those crises arrive to get yourself stabilized—to figure out who you are and what you will do when the pressure is on.

CHAPTER NINE

Living with Purpose

Until we know who we are and why we are here, no amount of success, fame, money, or pleasure will provide much satisfaction. Until we get a fix on the "big picture," nothing will make much sense.

Achievements and the promise of posthumous acclaim will bring some satisfaction, no doubt. But your highest priorities will be drawn from another source. When all is said and done and the books are closing on your life, I believe your treasures will lie much closer to home. Your most precious memories will focus on those you loved, those who loved you, and what you did together in the service of the Lord. Those are the basics. Nothing else will survive the scrutiny of time.

Is This All It Comes Down To?

One of my professional colleagues died toward the end of my final year on the staff of Children's Hospital of Los Angeles. He had served on our university medical faculty for more than twenty-five years. During his tenure as a professor, he had earned the respect and admiration of both professionals and patients, especially for his research findings and contribution to medical knowledge. This doctor had reached the pinnacle of success in his chosen field and enjoyed the status and financial rewards that accompany such accomplishment. He had tasted every good thing, at least by the standards of the world.

At the next staff meeting following his death, a five-minute eulogy was read by a member of his department. Then the chairman invited the entire staff to stand, as is our custom in situations of this nature, for one minute of silence in memory of the fallen colleague. I have no idea what the other members of the staff thought about during that sixty-second pause, but I can tell you what was going through my mind.

I was thinking, *Lord, is this what it all comes down to? We sweat and worry and labor to achieve a place in life, to impress our fellowmen with our competence. We take ourselves so seriously, overreacting to the insignificant events of each passing day. Then finally, even for the brightest among us, all these successes fade into history and our lives are summarized with a five-minute eulogy and sixty seconds of silence. It hardly seems worth the effort, Lord.*

But I was also struck by the collective inadequacy of that faculty to deal with the questions raised by our friend's death. Where had he gone? Would he live again? Will we see him on the other side? Why was he born? Were his deeds observed and recorded by a loving God? Is that God interested in me? Is there a purpose to life beyond investigative research and professorships and expensive automobiles? The silent response by 250 learned men and women seemed to symbolize our inability to cope with those issues.

⟶ Life in the Fast Lane ⟵

I sat recently in the international airport in Atlanta, Georgia, eating a fat-free yogurt and watching all the busy people rushing to and fro. Fascinating little dramas were played out before me. A mother scurried past on her way to Gate 92. Trailing far behind her was a toddler who couldn't care less about catching their plane. He was singing little songs and dawdling happily through the terminal. Mom finally turned around and tried to speed him up. No chance! As they disappeared into the crowd, he was ten feet behind his mama and still losing ground.

Then came a maintenance man en route to a broken pipe or a blown circuit. He wore a yellow rubber apron on which he had written the name "Whippie." I wondered how he got that nickname and why he wanted the world to know about it. If you're out there, Whippie—I noticed!

A teenage girl and her mother then walked by. They looked like they had been in a big fight earlier that morning. Maybe it was the girl's weird hairdo that had set them on edge. Whatever started the battle, the kid apparently won it. Mom was pretty haggard for so early in the day. The adolescent had obviously spent hours that morning trying to make herself look sexy and older than her years. She had succeeded. Hang in there, Mom!

Hundreds of other people hurried past my observation post before I finished the yogurt. All of them were deep in thought—intent on getting somewhere quick and doing whatever they came to do. I couldn't help wondering who these human beings were and what concerns they carried on this day. Back in the 1960s, the Beatles rock group sang about, "All the lonely people, where do they all come from." Yes, I saw a few folks who looked like they desperately needed a friend. But mostly, I saw busy, exhausted men and women who appeared to be hours behind schedule. Would it really have created an international crisis if they had pulled up a chair beside me and watched the people go by for a few minutes? I know! I know! Planes don't wait.

What I witnessed in the Atlanta airport is characteristic of the modern way of doing things. You may not yet be caught up in it, having so recently enjoyed the carefree days of adolescence. But life in the fast lane is coming your way. I guarantee it. The frantic pace of living that almost deprives us of meaning is very contagious, and most people find themselves on its treadmill sooner or later.

⁓ Game-Show Greed ⁓

When it comes to purposes and goals, most people appear motivated primarily by the pursuit of money and the things it can buy. If you doubt that, turn on daytime television and watch the contestants as they compete for prizes and cash. Observe the cuckoo birds as they leap in the air, frothing at the mouth and tearing at the clothes of the host. Notice that their eyes are dilated and their ears are bright pink. It's a condition known as game-show greed, and it renders its victims incapable of rational judgment.

Yes, BETTY MOLINO, YOU have won a NEW WASHING MACHINE, a year's supply of CHEWY CANDY BARS, and this marvelous new doll, WANDA WEE-WEE, that actually soaks your daughter's lap!

CONGRATULATIONS, BETTY, and thanks for playing "GRAB BAG" (frantic applause).

How do I know so much about game-show greed? Because I've been there! Back in 1967, my lovely wife managed to drag me to the *Let's Make a Deal* show, which was the rage at that time. Shirley put toy birds all over her head and blouse, and I carried a dumb sign that said, "My wife is for the birds." Really funny, huh? It was good enough to get the host, Monty Hall, to choose us as lucky contestants. The producers placed us in the two front seats near the cameras but began the program by "dealing" with other suckers.

I kept thinking as I sat there in contestants' row, *What in the world am I doing here holding this stupid sign?* I couldn't have been more skeptical about the proposition. Finally, Monty called our names, and the cameras zoomed in.

"Here behind door number one is . . . (a curtain opens) . . . A NEEEEW CAAR!!" (The audience goes crazy with excitement.)

Suddenly, I was gripped by a spasm in the pit of my stomach. My mouth watered profusely, and my heart began knocking on the sides of my chest. There on that stage was the car of my dreams—a brand-new Camaro. Desire came charging up my throat and stuck in the region of my Adam's apple. My breathing became irregular and shallow, which was another unmistakable clue that I had been struck by game-show greed.

To understand this reaction, you would have to know that I have owned several of the worst cars in automotive history. Throughout my college years I drove a 1949 Mercury convertible (I called it Ol' Red) that had power seats, power windows, power top, power everything—but no power to run them. I put the windows up in the winter and down in the summer. There they remained, despite fluctuating temperatures. Shirley, who was then my girlfriend, must have loved me tremendously to have put up with that car. She hated it! The front seat had a spring with a bad temper that tore her clothes and punctured her skin. Nor did Ol' Red always choose to run. Every few days, Shirley and I would take this junk heap out for a push.

The crowning blow occurred shortly after our graduation from college. We were invited to appear for important job interviews, and we put on our Sunday best for the occasion. There we were, suit and tie, heels and hose, going sixty miles an hour down the road in Ol' Red, when the convertible top suddenly blew off. Strings and dust flapped us in the face as the canvas waved behind the car like Superman's cape. The ribs of the top protruded above our heads, reminiscent of undersized roll-over bars. It was very embarrassing. And can you believe that Shirley got mad at me for letting that happen? She crouched on the floorboard, blaming me for driving such a beat-up car. It is a miracle that our relationship survived that emotional afternoon.

Although Ol' Red had been put to sleep long before our appearance on *Let's Make a Deal*, I still had never owned a new car. Every available dollar had been allocated for tuition in graduate school. I had finished my Ph.D. just two months earlier.

This explains my reaction to the beautiful automobile behind door number one.

"All you have to do to win the car," said Monty, "is tell us the prices of four items."

Shirley and I guessed the first three but blew it on number four. "Sorry," said Monty. "You've been zonked. But here, take a vacuum cleaner and three dollars. And thanks for playing *Let's Make a Deal!*"

Shirley and I were just sick. On the way home we talked about how our emotions had been manipulated in that situation. We both experienced incredible greed, and the feeling was not comfortable. I have since learned a very valuable lesson about lust and how it operates in a spiritual context. It has been my observation that whatever a person hungers for, Satan will appear to offer in exchange for a spiritual compromise. In my case, a new automobile was the perfect enticement to unleash my greed. If illicit sex is your desire, it will eventually be made available. Don't be surprised when you are beckoned by a willing partner.

If your passion is for fame or power, that object of lust will be promised (even if never delivered).

Remember that Jesus was offered bread following His forty-day fast in the wilderness. He was promised power and glory after He had been contemplating His upcoming road to the cross. My point is that Satan uses our keenest appetites to tempt us.

Likewise, if you hunger and thirst for great wealth—beware! You are in a very precarious position. If you doubt it, look at 1 Timothy 6:9, which says, "People who want to get rich fall into temptation and a trap and into many foolish and harmful desires that plunge men into ruin and destruction."

What incredible insight into the nature of mankind. If you watch people who care passionately about money, you'll observe that many of them are suckers for wild-eyed schemes and shady deals. They are always on the verge of a bonanza that seems to slip through their fingers. Instead of getting rich, they just get taken.

Billionaire John D. Rockefeller had some cogent advice for those who wanted to be rich. "It's easy," he said. "All you have to do is get up early, work hard—and strike oil." Easy for him to say.

⌒ Something for Nothing ⌒

My son and I took a deer-hunting trip when he was a teenager. We got into the stand very early in the morning before the sun came up. About twenty yards away from us was a feeder that operated on a timer. At 7:00 A.M. it automatically dropped kernels of corn into a pan below.

Ryan and I huddled together in this stand, talking softly about whatever came to mind. Then, through the fog, we saw a beautiful doe emerge silently into the clearing. She took nearly thirty minutes to get to the feeder near where we were hiding. We had no intention of shooting her, but it was fun to watch this beautiful animal from close range. She was extremely wary, sniffing the air and listening for the sounds of danger. Finally, she inched her way to the feeder, still looking around skittishly as though sensing our presence. Then she ate a quick breakfast and fled.

I whispered to Ryan, "There is something valuable to be learned from what we have just seen. Whenever you come upon a free supply of high-quality corn, provided unexpectedly right there in the middle of the forest, be careful! The people who put it there are probably sitting nearby in a stand, just waiting to take a shot at you. Keep your eyes and ears open!"

Ryan may not always remember that advice, but I will. It isn't often that a father says something to his teenage son that he considers to be profound. The greedier you become, the more vulnerable you are to the con men of our time. They will bait the trap with high-quality "corn," whether it be money, sex, an attractive job offer, or flattery. You'll hardly be able to believe your eyes. What a deal! But take care! Your pretty head may already be in the scope of someone's rifle.

⟿ A Higher Call ⟬

My father had his life laid out, and he needed no help from God or anyone else in fulfilling it. From his earliest childhood, Dad knew he wanted to be a great artist. Even before kindergarten, he told his family he intended to draw and paint when he grew up. This passion was not simply a choice he had made. It was in his blood. All through childhood and his teen years, he never wavered from this desire to become another Rembrandt or Michelangelo. While his five brothers were uncertain about what they wanted to be, this youngest among them was chasing a lofty dream.

Then one day as he walked along a street during his sixteenth year, he seemed to hear the Lord speaking to him. It was not an audible voice, of course. But deep within his being he knew he had been addressed by the Almighty. It was a simple message that conveyed this thought: *I want you to set aside your great ambition to be an artist and prepare for a life of service in the ministry.*

My father was terrified by the experience. He replied, "No! No, Lord. You know I have my plans all made, and art is my consuming interest." He quickly argued down the impression and convinced himself that his mind had deceived him. But when he got it all resolved and laid to rest, it would reappear. Month after month, the nagging thought reverberated in his mind that God was asking—no, demanding—that he abandon his dream and become a preacher. It proved to be one of the greatest struggles of his life, but he shared it with no one.

For two years this inner battle went on. Then toward the end of his senior year in high school, the time came for him to select a college to attend in the fall. His father told him to pick out any school in the country, and he would send him there. But what was he to do? If he yielded to the voice within, he would have to attend a college that would begin preparing him for the ministry. But if he followed his dream, he would go to art school. Would he obey God, or would he have his own way? It was a terrible dilemma.

One morning a few weeks before graduation, he got out of bed to prepare for school. But the minute his feet touched the floor, my father heard the voice again. It was as if the Lord said, *Today you will have to make up your mind.* He wrestled with that issue all day at school but still shared his turmoil with no one. After his last class in midafternoon, he came home to an empty house. He paced back and forth in the living room, praying and struggling with this unrelenting demand of God. Finally, in an act of defiance, he suddenly turned his face upward and said, "It's too great a price, and I won't pay it!"

My father later described that moment as the most terrible experience of his life. He said the Spirit of the Lord seemed to leave him as one person would walk away from another. He was still shaken and pale when his mother came home a few minutes later. She could see his distress, and she asked him what was wrong.

"You won't understand this, Mom," he said, "but God has been asking me to give up my plans to be an artist. He wants me to become a minister. I don't want to do it. And I won't do it. I've just said no to Him, and He's gone."

My grandmother was a very righteous woman who could always touch the heart of God in her prayers. She said, "Oh, honey, you're just emotional. Let's pray about it."

They got down on their knees, and my grandmother began talking to the Lord about her son. Then she stopped in midsentence. "I don't understand it," she said. "Something is wrong."

"You don't understand it," said my father, "but I do. I've just refused to obey God, and He's gone."

It would be seven long years before my father would hear the voice of the Lord again. You see, his love of art had become his god. It mattered more to him than anything on earth and even outranked his relationship with the Father. That's what was going on in his heart. There was nothing sinful or immoral in his love of art. The problem was that God had no place in it.

In the next few days, my father chose the Art Institute of Pittsburgh (AIP), one of the best art schools in the country. He enrolled there in the fall, and his professors immediately recognized his unusual talent. Indeed, when he graduated, he was honored as the most gifted student in his class. But as he was walking down the aisle to the platform where a big NUMBER ONE banner had been draped on his paintings, the scripture again came into his mind: *Except the Lord build the house, they labour in vain that build it.*

My father graduated and went out to begin his great career in the field of art. Unfortunately, the Great Depression was under way in the United States and in most countries around the world. That was a scary time in American history when huge numbers of people were out of work. Businesses failed, banks closed, and opportunities were few and far between. My dad was one of the millions who couldn't find a job of any type—much less one in his chosen profession. He was finally hired at a Texaco service station to pump gas and wipe the windshields of cars. It was pretty humbling for a man who wanted to be another Leonardo da Vinci.

Here is the most incredible part of the story. Right at that moment when my dad was desperate for a career break, the president of the Art Institute of Pittsburgh wrote him a letter and offered him a job as an instructor at the unbelievable salary of three hundred dollars per month! It was precisely what he had dreamed about since childhood. But somehow that letter became lost on the president's desk. The man later found and mailed it with another note saying he had wondered why my dad hadn't even done him the courtesy of responding to his offer. But by the time the second letter came, my father had grown sick of himself and his lofty plans. He had found a place of prayer and yielded himself completely to the call of God on his life. So by the time the job offer came, he wrote back to say, "Thanks, but I'm no longer interested."

My dad's future, and undoubtedly mine, hung in the balance at that critical juncture. If he had received the original offer from the president of AIP, he would have been launched on a career that was obviously out of the will of God. Who knows how his life would have changed if he had "labored in vain" in the wrong vineyard? What prevented him from making the mistake of his life? Well, my grandmother was out there praying for him every day, asking the Lord to draw her youngest son back to Himself. I believe God answered her prayers by interfering with the delivery of the letter on which everything seemed to depend.

Does it seem cruel of the Lord to deprive this young man of the one thing he most wanted? Good question! Why would God give him remarkable ability and then prevent him from using it? Well, as is always the case in His dealings with us, the Lord had my father's best interests at heart. And He took nothing away from him.

As soon as my dad yielded to the will of the Lord, his art was given back to him. He then used his talent in ministerial work all his life, and when he died he was chairman of the art department at a Christian college. He left beautiful paintings and sculptures all over the United States. More important, thousands of people came to know Jesus Christ through the preaching ministry of my father. They will be in heaven because of the calling that was on his life.

⌒ A Father's Final Prayer ⌒

In August 1977, my wife and children joined me on a trip to Kansas City, Missouri, for a short visit with my parents. We enjoyed several days of family togetherness before it was time to leave. As we drove to the airport where we said good-bye, I asked my father to pray for us. I will never forget his words. He closed with this thought:

> And Lord, we want to thank You for the fellowship and love that we feel for each other today. This has been such a special time for us with Jim and Shirley and their children. But heavenly Father, we are keenly aware that the joy that is ours today is a temporal pleasure. Our lives will not always be this stable and secure. Change is inevitable and it will come to us, too. We will accept it when it comes, of course, but we give You praise for the happiness and warmth that has been ours these past few days. We have had more than our share of the good things, and we thank You for Your love. Amen.

Shortly thereafter, we hugged and said good-bye, and my family boarded the plane. A week later, my father suddenly grabbed his chest and told my mother to call the paramedics. He left us on December 4 of that year. Shortly after, my mother joined him in heaven. How quickly life changes!

Even today, so many years later, my dad's final prayer echoes in my mind. An entire philosophy is contained in that simple idea. "Thank You, God, for what we have . . . which we know we cannot keep." I wish every newlywed couple could capture that incredible concept. If we only realized how brief is our time on this earth, then most of the irritants and frustrations which drive us apart would seem terribly insignificant and petty. We have but one short life to live, yet we contaminate it with bickering and insults and angry words. If we fully comprehended the brevity of life, our greatest desire would be to please God and to serve one another. Instead, the illusion of permanence leads us to scrap and claw for power and demand the best of ourselves.

⤙ When All Is Said and Done, ⤚
What Really Matters?

When all is said and done and the books are closing on your life, I believe your treasures will lie close to home. Your most precious memories will focus on those you loved, those who loved you, and what you did together in the service of the Lord. Those are the basics. Nothing else will survive the scrutiny of time.

To elaborate on that concept, let me take you back to that gymnasium where my heart attack occurred. Two years earlier, another highly significant event had occurred just a few feet from where I was stricken. My friends and I played basketball three times a week on that court, and on that particular morning, we had invited Pete Maravich to join us.

It was an audacious thing to do. "Pistol Pete," as he was dubbed by the media, had been one of the greatest basketball players of all times. He was the Michael Jordan or the Magic Johnson of his day. He set more than forty NCAA college records at Louisiana State University, many of which still stand. He had averaged forty-four points per game during his three years at LSU. After graduation, Pete was drafted by the National Basketball Association and became the first player ever to receive a million-dollar contract. When he retired because of knee problems, he was elected to the NBA Hall of Fame the first year he was eligible. There is very little that can be done with a basketball that Pete Maravich didn't accomplish.

So for a bunch of "duffers" to invite a superstar like Pete to play with us took some gall, even though he was forty years old at the time. To our delight, he agreed to come and showed up at 7:00 A.M. I quickly learned that he had been suffering from an unidentified pain in his right shoulder for many months. Aside from playing in the NBA "Legends Game," which was televised nationally, Pete had not been on a basketball court in more than a year. Nevertheless, we had a good time that morning. Pete moved at about one-third his normal speed, and the rest of us huffed and puffed to keep up. We played for about forty-five minutes and then took a break to get a drink. Pete and I stayed on the court and talked while waiting for the other players to come back.

"You can't give up this game, Pete," I said. "It has meant too much to you through the years."

"You know, I've loved playing this morning," he replied. "I really do want to get back to this kind of recreational basketball. But it wouldn't have been possible in the last few months. The pain in my shoulder has been so intense that I couldn't have lifted a two-pound ball over my head."

"How are you feeling today?" I asked.

"I feel great," he said.

Those were Pete's last words. I turned to walk away, and for some reason looked back in time to see him go down. His face and body hit the boards hard. Still, I thought he was teasing. Pete had a great sense of humor, and I assumed that he was playing off his final comment about feeling good.

I hurried over to where Pete lay and still expected him to get up laughing. But then I saw that he was having a seizure. I held his tongue to keep his air passage open and called for the other guys to come help me. The seizure lasted about twenty seconds, and then Pete stopped breathing. We started CPR immediately, but were never able to get another heartbeat or another breath. Pistol Pete Maravich, one of the world's greatest athletes, died there in my arms at forty years of age.

Several of us accompanied the ambulance to the hospital, where we prayerfully watched the emergency room staff try to revive Pete for about forty-five minutes. But it was no use. He had left this earth, and there was nothing anyone could do to bring him back.

An autopsy revealed a few days later that Pete had a congenital malformation of the heart and never knew it. That was why his shoulder had been hurting. Whereas most of us have two coronary arterial systems that wrap around the heart, Pete only had one. How he was able to do such incredible exploits on the basketball court for so many years is a medical mystery. He was destined to drop dead at a fairly young age, and only God knows why it happened during the brief moment when his path crossed mine.

The shock of Pete's untimely death is impossible to describe. None of the men who witnessed the tragedy will ever forget it. My heart goes out to his lovely wife, Jackie, and their two sons, Jason and Joshua. I spoke at his funeral three days later and still feel a bond of friendship with his little family.

It is important to know something about Pete's background to understand who he was. Quite frankly, he had been a troublemaker when he was younger. He was a heavy drinker who broke all the rules. His attitude deteriorated in the NBA, and he finally quit in a huff. This man who had

received every acclaim that can come to an athlete hit the skids emotionally. After retirement, he stayed in his house day after day to avoid autograph-seeking fans and because he had nowhere to go. There he sat,
depressed and angry, for two years.

Something incredible happened at that crucial moment in Pete's life. He
was in bed one night when he heard someone speak his name. He sat
upright, wondering if he had been dreaming. Then he heard the voice again.
Pete realized that God was calling him. He immediately knelt beside his bed
and gave his heart to the Lord. It was a total consecration of his mind, body,
and soul.

For the last five years of his life, all he wanted to talk about was what Jesus
Christ had done for him. He told that story to reporters, to coaches, to fans,
and to anyone who would listen. The day Pete died, he was wearing a T-shirt
that bore the inscription, "Looking unto Jesus."

I was able to share that testimony with the media, which took it around
the world within an hour. "You think Pete's great love was basketball," I told
them, "but that was not his passion. All he really cared about was Jesus
Christ and what He had done in Pete's life." And now I'm relaying that message to you. Perhaps that is why the Lord placed this good man in my arms
as his life ebbed away.

Now I need to tell you something highly personal that happened next. I
went home and sat down with our son, Ryan, who was seventeen years old
at the time. I asked to talk to him about something of extreme importance
to us both.

I said, "Ryan, I want you to understand what has happened here. Pete's
death was not an unusual tragedy that has happened to only one man and
his family. We all must face death sooner or later and in one way or another.
This is the 'human condition.' It comes too early for some people and too
late for others. But no one will escape, ultimately. And, of course, it will also
happen to you and me. So without being morbid about it, I want you to
begin to prepare yourself for that time.

"Sooner or later, you'll get the kind of phone call that Mrs. Maravich
received today. It could occur ten or fifteen years from now, or it could come
tomorrow. But when that time comes, there is one thought I want to leave
with you. I don't know if I'll have an opportunity to give you my 'last words'
then, so let me express them to you right now. Freeze-frame this moment in

your mind, and hold on to it for the rest of your life. My message to you is, Be there! Be there to meet your mother and me in heaven. We will be looking for you on that resurrection morning. Don't let anything deter you from keeping that appointment.

"Because I am fifty-one years old and you are only seventeen, as many as fifty years could pass from the time of my death to yours. That's a long time to remember. But you can be sure that I will be searching for you just inside the Eastern Gate. This is the only thing of real significance in your life. I care what you accomplish in the years to come, and I hope you make good use of the great potential the Lord has given to you. But above every other purpose and goal, the only thing that really matters is that you determine now to be there!"

⌒ The Rest of the Story ⌒

It occurred in 1945, shortly after the end of the Second World War. A young associate pastor named Cliff and his fiancée, Billie, were anxious to get married, even though they had very little money. They managed to scrape together enough funds for a simple wedding and two train tickets to a city where he had been asked to hold a revival with a friend. By combining this responsibility with their honeymoon, they thought they could make it. They planned to stay at a nearby resort hotel.

The couple got off the train and took a bus to the hotel, only to learn that it had been taken over by the military for use as a rehabilitation center. It was no longer open for guests. There they were, stranded in an unfamiliar city with only a few dollars between them. There was little to do but attempt to hitch a ride on the nearby highway. Soon a car pulled over, and the driver asked them where they wanted to go.

"We don't know," they said and explained their predicament. The man was sympathetic and said perhaps he could offer a suggestion. A few miles down the road was a grocery store that was owned by a woman he knew. She had a couple of empty rooms upstairs and might be willing to let them stay there inexpensively. They were in no position to be choosy.

The lady rented them a room for five dollars, and they moved in. During their first day in residence, the new bride spent the afternoon practicing the piano, and Cliff played the trombone he had brought with him. The proprietor of the store sat rocking in a chair listening to the music. When she realized they were Christians, she referred them to a friend, who invited them to spend the rest of their honeymoon in his home. Several days later, the host mentioned that a young evangelist was speaking at a youth rally at a nearby Christian conference center. They were invited to attend.

That night, it so happened that the regular song leader was sick, and Cliff was asked to take charge of the music for the service. What a historic occasion it was! The evangelist turned out to be a very young Rev. Billy Graham. The groom was Cliff Barrows. They met that evening for the first time, and a lifetime partnership was formed. As the Christian world knows so well, Cliff and his wife, Billie, have been members of the Billy Graham Evangelistic Association ever since that evening and have been used by the Lord in thousands of crusades all around the world. I suppose Paul Harvey would say, "And now you know . . . the rest of the story."

Isn't it amazing the lengths to which the Lord went to bring these now inseparable team members together? Some would call their meeting a coincidence, but I disagree. I recognize the hand of God when I see it.

⌐ **In the Hands of God** ⌐

Ultimately, the comprehension of God's will requires a careful balance between rational deliberation on one hand, and emotional responses on the other. Each Christian must find that balance in his own relationship with God, yielding to the teachings of the Holy Spirit. One man's search for this understanding was expressed beautifully by the Reverend Everett Howard, a veteran missionary to the Cape Verde Islands. Here is his personal account of how he learned to put himself completely in the hands of God:

> I've spent thirty-six years in missionary service—a lifetime that has passed so quickly. About fifty years ago when I was just a young boy I knew that God was calling me, but I was confused. I didn't know just where or when or what He wanted me to do. Years passed and I went on through school and college and into Lincoln and Lee Dental University in Kansas City, Missouri. I was still fighting and battling away, unsure of God's direction for my life.

One day I came to the point of a definite decision. My dad was a Christian and his prayers were inspirational. But that was secondhand, and I wanted something that could be mine—something I could take through life with me. So I went into the little church where my dad was pastoring and locked the doors so I could be alone. I guess I was ashamed for anyone to hear me pray, but that's the way it was. I knelt down at the little altar and took a piece of paper and a pencil and said, "Now this is going to be for life!"

I listed everything on that page. I filled it with promises of what I would do for God, including my willingness to be a missionary, and every possible alternative I could think of. I promised to sing in the choir and give my tithes and read the Bible and do all the things I thought God might want of me. I had a long list of promises and I really meant them.

Then when I had finished the well-written page I signed my name at the bottom and laid it on the altar. There alone in the church I looked up and waited for "thunder and lightning" or some act of approval from the Lord. I thought I might experience what Saint Paul did on the road to Damascus, or something equally dramatic. I knew that God must be terribly proud of me— a young fellow who would make a consecration like that. But nothing happened. It was quiet, still, and I was so disappointed.

I couldn't understand it, so I thought I must have forgotten something. I took out my pencil again and tried to think about what I'd left out. But I couldn't remember anything else. I prayed again and told the Lord that I had put everything possible on the paper. Still nothing happened, though I waited and waited.

Then it came. I felt the voice of God speaking to my heart. He didn't shout or hit me over the head. I just felt in my own soul a voice speak so clearly. It said, "Son, you're going about it wrong. I don't want a consecration like this. Just tear up the paper you've written."

I said, "All right, Lord." And I took the paper I had written so carefully and wadded it up.

Then the voice of God seemed to whisper again, "Son, I want you to take a blank piece of paper and sign your name on the bottom of it and let Me fill it in."

"Oh! Oh! That's different Lord," I cried. But I did what He said there at the altar in the little church.

It was just a secret between God and me, as I signed the paper. And God has been filling it in for the last thirty-six years.

Maybe I'm glad that I didn't know what was going to be written on the page. Things like . . . lying sick in the lonely mountains of the Cape Verde Islands, burning up with fever, with no medicine and no doctor, and the closest hospital more than three thousand miles away. And the famine, when almost a third of the population in our part of the country had starved to death . . . money wasn't coming through . . . nine months without one single check or penny . . . everything we owned had to be sold in order to live . . . that wasn't written on the page until the time came. But, you know, there was no depression. Those were the most blessed days, because God was there! And if I could turn around and do it again, I'd go every step of the way that we've traveled for the last thirty-six years.

To those who are listening to me tonight, I hope you will also put your name at the bottom of a blank sheet of paper and let God fill it in. Especially if you're worried about who you should marry or where to go to school or what training you should get, and all those questions which cause young people to struggle. You don't know the answers to such questions and neither do I. If I tried to tell you what to do it would probably be wrong. But God knows. Let Him fill in the page, regardless of where He leads or the difficulties you will experience. And of this I am absolutely confident: The Lord will make His purposes and plans known in plenty of time for you to heed them.

Reverend Howard retired after thirty-six years in the service of his Master. He affirmed that God was still writing on the page he signed as a youth. For me, volumes of theological analysis cannot equal the wisdom in his words. I hope his story encourages you (as it has me) to sign a blank page and let God determine the direction your life will take.

⌒ A Man of Honor ⌒

There is, perhaps, no better illustration of this commitment to principle and honor than is seen in a letter written by Major Sullivan Ballou of the Union army. He penned it to his wife, Sarah, on July 14, 1861, one week before the Battle of Bull Run. They had been married only six years. These powerful words still touch my soul:

My Very Dear Sarah:

The indications are very strong that we shall move in a few days—perhaps tomorrow. Lest I should not be able to write again, I feel impelled to write a few lines that may fall under your eye when I shall be no more. . . .

I have no misgivings about or lack of confidence in the cause in which I am engaged, and my courage does not halt or falter. I know how strongly American civilization now leans on the triumph of the Government, and how great a debt we owe to those who went before us through the blood and suffering of the Revolution. And I am willing, perfectly to lay down all my joys in this life to help maintain this Government and to pay that debt. . . .

Sarah, my love for you is deathless: It seems to bind me with mighty cables that nothing but Omnipotence could break, and yet my love of country comes over me like a strong wind, and bears me irresistibly on, with all these chains, to the battlefield.

The memories of all the blissful moments I have spent with you come creeping over me, and I feel most deeply grateful to God, and you, that I have enjoyed them so long. And how hard it is for me to give them up, and burn to ashes the hope of future years, when, God willing, we might still have lived and loved together and seen our sons grown up to honorable manhood around us.

If I do not [return], my dear Sarah, never forget how much I love you, and when my last breath escapes me on the battlefield, it will whisper your name. Forgive my many faults and the many pains I have caused you. How thoughtless, how foolish I have oftentimes been. . . .

O Sarah, if the dead can come back to this earth, and flit unseen around those they loved, I shall always be near you in the gladdest day, and in the darkest night, amidst your happiest scenes and gloomiest hours—always, always: and if there be a soft breeze upon your cheek, it shall be my breath: or the cool air cools your throbbing temple, it shall be my spirit passing by.

Sarah, do not mourn me dead: think I am gone, and wait for me, for we shall meet again. . . .

Sullivan

Major Ballou was killed one week later at the first Battle of Bull Run. I wonder, don't you, if he did indeed utter Sarah's name as he lay dying on the battlefield. She undoubtedly suffered the greater pain in the aftermath of that terrible war.

⟶ Will You Pray for Me? ⟵

My paternal grandmother, Juanita Dobson, understood what it meant to "pray without ceasing," even when there was little evidence to encourage her. She was a deeply committed Christian who was married to an independent, non-believing husband. Because he was a moral and decent man, he saw no need for a personal relationship with Jesus Christ. The fact nearly damned him.

He didn't mind his wife going to church and doing her religious thing, but he would have no part in it. He especially resented any effort to drag him into it. That door was slammed shut. Instead of trying to goad her husband into a Christian commitment, therefore, Juanita began a campaign of prayer on his behalf that continued for decades. She fasted for his salvation regularly for years, despite the lack of evidence that her petitions were even being heard!

Still, my grandfather's heart remained hard and cold. But when he was sixty-nine years old, he suffered a series of strokes that left him partially paralyzed. He had been a powerful man, a six-foot-four railroad conductor, who had never been sick a day in his life. It devastated him to be permanently incapacitated. One afternoon his daughter was attending to his needs and preparing his medication. As she leaned toward him to straighten his bed, she saw that he was crying. No one ever remembered seeing this proud, self-made man shed a tear. It shocked her and she said, "Daddy, what's wrong?"

He replied, "Honey, go get your mother."

My little grandmother came running up the stairs and knelt beside her husband's bed. He took her by the hand and said, "I know I am going to die, and I'm not afraid of death. But it is so dark. Will you pray for me?"

My grandmother said, "Will I pray?" She had been waiting for him to ask her that question for more than forty years! She began to call to heaven on behalf of her husband, and he accepted a personal relationship with Jesus Christ there on his sickbed. My grandmother said it was like a host of heavenly angels beginning to sing in her heart. Grandfather Dobson died two weeks later with a testimony on his lips. I'm certain that he and my little grandmother are in heaven today because of the perseverance of her faith.

∾ The Whole World's Singing Now ∾

My parents were married for forty-three years, and their commitment to one another stayed steady for over four decades. Following are the words of my dad—words that he wrote to my mother on the occasion of her fiftieth birthday. The springtime of that year had set him thinking about the brevity of life and the certainty of old age ahead. The poem that follows is entitled, "Your Birthday," and it made my mother cry:

> The whole world's singing now that spring has come
> I saw a robin in the morning sun
> Among the pale-green leaves and bursting buds I heard his talk
> But it is autumn where we walk.
>
> 'Tis true for us the summer too is gone
> Now whiplashed winds arise and further on
> The ice and sleet and cold in grim assault to pierce us through
> Does fall in springtime frighten you?
>
> Impotent shines the April sun so fair
> To melt the wisps of frost within your hair
> My dear, I know you feel the threatening gloom
> But I'm with you
> And hand in hand we'll face the winter, too.

Isn't that a beautiful expression of love in its richest meaning? My dad had promised to stand shoulder to shoulder with my mother, even when assaulted by whiplashed winds and threatening gloom. His commitment is not based on ephemeral emotions or selfish desires. It is supported by an uncompromising will.

⤳ **Our Last Conversation** ⤳

Two years before my father's death, he shared an experience that occurred while he had been praying and reading the Bible. He seemed almost embarrassed to reveal the details, but I coaxed him to tell me the story. It involved an overwhelming impression, almost a divine decree, that he and I were going to cooperate on a very important project. He hastened to say that he didn't want me to think he was trying to "ride on my coattail." In fact, his first impulse was to tell no one about the revelation for fear that his motives would be misunderstood.

His apprehension was unfounded. I learned very early in life that when God "speaks" to Dad, I had better pay attention. This man and his Lord had a very unusual relationship. It often involved sessions of prayer and communion, lasting from four to six hours, focusing especially on his ministry and on those whom he loved. He was known in the small town where I spent my preschool years as "the man with no leather on his shoes." He spent so much time on his knees that he wore out the toes of his shoes before the soles. Thus, James Dobson Sr. and the Lord had a very unique relationship. When God revealed His purpose to His faithful servant, the outcome was an absolute certainty.

But what task would we accomplish together? Neither of us knew the answer to that question, nor did we pursue it further. We did join forces to work on a conference book entitled *Family under Fire*, but that didn't seem to be related to the revelation. The months rolled by, and the matter was filed under the broad heading "Things I don't understand about the Lord."

Then came my father's initial heart attack while I was in San Antonio. That devastating telephone conversation reverberated in my head. "Your dad is dying. He has developed both arrhythmia and congestion, which is usually a fatal combination following a myocardial infarction. We don't expect him to live through the night. Come as quickly as you can get here!"

Two friends rushed me to the airport, where Shirley was already waiting. But as we drove through the San Antonio traffic, the Lord spoke to me. His voice was not audible, nor was it accompanied by smoke and fire. I can't even tell you how the message was conveyed. All I know is that God reminded me of His revelation to my dad, and then He said, "You are going to write a book for husbands and fathers, based on the life of your dad. The inspiration will be derived from his values, his dedication, his walk with Me. This is the joint venture of which I spoke two years ago."

As we made that long plane ride from San Antonio to Kansas City, Shirley and I knew that my dad's condition would be obvious instantly as we stepped into the terminal. If my mother was there to meet us, that would mean he was gone. But if she was not present, then she would still be with him at the hospital. Upon disembarking from the plane, we scanned the crowd breathlessly and to our great relief, Mother was not there. Instead, we were greeted by the wife of the president of the college where my father served as a professor. And she was smiling.

"Your dad is remarkably better," she said. "In fact, he's waiting to see you at the hospital."

I will always be thankful for having the priceless opportunity to see him alive, again—to express those words of appreciation and love that we seldom convey before it is too late. I stood by his bed in that intensive care unit. There amid beeping oscilloscopes and bottles of glucose, I patted those delicate artistic hands that I have loved since my earliest awareness. He was entirely calm and coherent, revealing no hint of his brush with death.

Then I told him about the Lord's message to me on the way to the airport. I explained that his part of the project was already completed: It involved sixty-six years of integrity and devotion and love. I had watched him at home throughout my childhood, where it was impossible to hide his true nature. But not one time did I see him compromise with evil or abandon the faith by which he had lived. His character had been like a beacon for me, illuminating my way and steering me past the snares that entrapped so many of my friends.

"Thank you, Dad," I said, with deep emotion.

He smiled knowingly, and I quietly slipped out of his room.

⟶ How a Good Man Dies ⟵

The last chapter in the life of my dad began at Eastertime 1977, when my parents came to visit Shirley and me in California. I took several days off work and spent that time in pleasant conversation with our loved ones. At one point, I turned to my dad and asked spontaneously, "What do you want for an epitaph at the close of your life?"

He thought briefly and then replied, "Only two words: 'He prayed.'" I can think of no phrase that better summarized his devotion to God and the daily communion he maintained with Him. It is fitting that his final act on earth was to ask for God's blessing on the meal that had been prepared. Accordingly, those two words, "He prayed," appear on his footstone today.

I then turned to my mother and asked, "What epitaph do you want on your tombstone?" She had a rich sense of humor and immediately responded, "I told you I was sick!"

Her remark reminded me of the eighty-year-old man who said, "If I'd have known I was gonna live so long I'd have taken better care of myself!"

We enjoyed that week of laughter and fellowship with my parents, having no idea, of course, that this was to be the last trip my father would take. The clock was ticking down toward zero, with only eight months remaining.

Later in the year, as death approached, my dad was to experience two concluding revelations from God that moved him deeply. I learned about the first in a telephone conversation in September. We were talking about my upcoming television series and various topics of mutual interest. Then suddenly Dad said, "Well, there's one thing I know. God is going to take care of your mother."

I replied, "Yes, I'm sure He will," but wondered why he had chosen that occasion to make such a statement. Five days later, he suffered his near-fatal heart attack.

As my mother and I sat in the hospital waiting for news of his progress, I remembered his strange comment on the telephone. I shared his words with my mother and asked if she understood why he had chosen to tell me about her secure future.

"I know what he meant," she replied. She then told me that two weeks earlier, my dad had been resting on the bed while she worked around the room. She glanced at him and noticed that there were tears in his eyes.

"What's the matter?" she asked.

He paused for a few seconds and then said, "The Lord just spoke to me."

"Do you want to tell me about it?" she continued.

"It was about you!" replied my dad.

"Then you'd *better* tell me!" she said.

"It was a strange experience," said my dad. "I was just lying here thinking about many things. I wasn't praying or even thinking about you when the Lord spoke to me and said, 'I'm going to take care of Myrtle.'" They looked at each other in awe, wondering what it meant.

Five days later, they experienced the most severe trauma of their lives, and eighty-four days hence, my mother learned the meaning of widowhood.

Although many years have passed since the death of my father on that cold December day, the Lord's promise was not forgotten. I won't impose all the details on you. Let it simply be known that the God of my father comforted, provided for, and sustained the woman he left behind.

Of course, she continued to grieve for the man she loved. There is *no* painless way to lose a constant companion and friend of forty-three years. The early evening hours were especially lonely, and my mother used them to write poetry to the memory of her husband. I especially appreciated the following piece, which she permitted me to share with you:

I Thought I Saw You Today
I thought I saw you today.
Standing with your hands in your pockets.
Laughing, the wind playing mischievously
    with your hair.
My heart lunged toward you as
You disappeared, leaving a total stranger
    standing there.
How could I have imagined the
    man to be my darling . . .
My precious darling.

It is the nature of things that *most* married women will eventually become widows. Thus, I'm sure that millions of women would understand perfectly the heartache my mother was conveying with these brief words.

I learned of my dad's second revelation on October 2, 1977, after he had been hospitalized for two weeks. I flew to Kansas City for a brief visit, which was to be the final time I would see him alive. He was brimming over with effervescence on that Sunday morning. He had so much he wanted to say to me. His medical progress appeared encouraging, and he was anticipating being released from the hospital in a few days. Among weightier subjects, we discussed his little dog, Benji, who anxiously awaited the return of his master.

Then my dad became very serious. "There's something I want to try to describe to you," he said. "I had the most incredible experience the morning after my heart attack." He began weeping as he spoke.

I was concerned that his emotional state would affect his heart, and I asked him to wait and tell me later. He agreed and we let the matter drop. I had to leave the following day, and he died before our planned rendezvous at Christmas.

My dad did reveal the details of his experience to my mother and to a friend, Dr. Dean Baldwin, the week prior to his death. Furthermore, in going through his writings after death, I discovered a partially completed description of the event, in his own handwriting. The narrative that follows was taken from those three sources, describing a dramatic vision that he saw the morning after his heart attack. (Remember that his physicians had predicted he wouldn't live through that night.) These are his approximate words.

"It happened in the early morning hours when I was neither awake nor asleep. I was lying there in my quiet hospital room, when I suddenly saw the most beautiful person I'd ever seen. His identity was not immediately revealed, but I now believe Him to have been Jesus. This was no dream, in the classic sense. I was conscious of my circumstances, and the figure was extremely vivid. It was apparent that I was being permitted to observe a kind of courtroom scene—a divine proceeding—but my being there was as an onlooker. No word was addressed to me directly. The 'person' was seated, and he was writing in a book. It seemed that he was considering an extremely important issue. Then I realized it was my case he was evaluating. The details of my life were being reviewed carefully. He stopped writing and began to plead my case directly to God. I have never heard such eloquent language as he described my circumstances, calling me by name repeatedly. Then he continued to write until he came to the bottom of the page, at which time he completed the last sentence and thrust his hand outward in a sudden gesture. Though no words were spoken, his motion and his countenance revealed his conclusion about my life. It said, 'For time and eternity, he is *acceptable!*'"

Dr. Baldwin reports that my father was weeping openly as he described this dramatic experience. Then he explained, with great feeling, that he was given a concluding message of major significance, but it was too personal to disclose. He could not even reveal it to my mother, with whom he shared everything. We can only guess that his impending death was foreseen in that incredible moment.

The vision then disappeared, leaving my dad in the gray, early morning light of the hospital room. He was so deeply affected by the experience that he made no attempt to tell anyone about it until my visit two weeks later. Even to the time of his death, he couldn't talk of the matter without crying.

Some would claim that my dad experienced a drug-induced dream in that hour. I don't believe it. My father, who was not given to mystical exaggeration, was emphatic that the vision had not been a hallucination or imaginary event. I will leave it for the reader to decide. There is one fact, however, of which I am certain. This man *was* found "acceptable" by his Maker. He had lived by an uncompromising standard of devotion to Jesus Christ. He had fought a good fight and kept the faith until the end.

The Twenty-third Psalm promises the righteous that God will walk with them through the valley of the shadow of death. He certainly fulfilled that covenant on behalf of my father. And the life of this good man came to an end, only to continue in greater glory on the other side.

The passing of my dad has changed my own view of death. I still have an instinctual desire to live—especially since my work at home is incomplete—but I no longer perceive the end of life as the greatest of all tragedies. Now, I know I will be welcomed across the threshold by my old friend. I'm sure he will be so excited to show me the stars and planets and the heavenly city. I also expect him to introduce me, face to face, to the Lord I've tried to serve since I was three years old.

But for now, he is gone, and *I* am the one who is on trial in that divine courtroom. I am left with this prayer:

Heavenly Father, I yearn to be the kind of husband and father that You desire of me. My highest ideal on this earth is to earn those words of approval, "Well done, thou good and faithful servant." Yet I feel so inadequate to discharge my responsibility properly. I know that my children's concept of You will be greatly influenced by how they perceive me, and that thought is terrifying. But I know You only expect me to do the best I can, and that thought is comforting. Thank You for the model You gave me in my father. Help me now to perpetuate that example before the children whom You have loaned to Shirley and me. And though I've said it before, keep the circle unbroken when we stand before Your throne.

Finally, Lord, would You also give my dad a brief message for me? Tell him that I love him. No son ever owed his father more!

∽ My Father ∽

Who could have suspected on such a pleasant afternoon that my father, at sixty-six years of age, was enjoying his final moments on this earth? He held the baby and chatted amiably with members of the family. A Sunday dinner was then placed on the table, and Dad was asked to bless the food. This good man, James Dobson Sr., bowed his head one last time and thanked the Lord for His generosity and love. It was to be his own benediction, for, minutes later, God beckoned his soul across the chilly waters of death. There was no struggle, no pain, no agonizing "good-byes." He simply paused, then leaned toward my mother and was gone.

An hour later, my wife reached me by telephone to break the news. I was speaking twelve hundred miles to the west and had devoted my remarks that day to the importance of Christian fatherhood. In fact, I talked throughout the morning about my dad and the beautiful example he had set before me. Then came Shirley's call. We shared an incredible sense of grief and loss in that moment. Only those who "have been there" will fully comprehend such an experience.

The funeral was held three days later, at which time I delivered a tribute to my father. Somehow I managed to express the following words from my heart on that cold December day.

The Tribute

To our friends and loved ones, I want to express appreciation on behalf of our family for each of you being here today. We appreciate your coming to honor the man whom we loved so dearly—the man whose name I share.

I asked my mother for this privilege of paying tribute to my dad, although quite honestly, this is the most difficult moment of my life. This man whose body lies before me was not only my father and my friend, but he was also the source of great inspiration for me. Few people realize that most of my writings are actually an expression of his views and his teachings. Whenever we were together, he would talk and I usually took notes. That's the kind of relationship we had, and his loss is devastating to me.

So I don't apologize for the grief that overwhelms me in this hour. These are not tears of guilt or remorse or regret. I have no bitter memories . . . there were no harsh words that I wish I could retrieve . . . we had no conflicts or struggles or strife. The emotion that you see reflects only the love of a son who has suddenly lost his father and gentle friend.

Some of you are aware that my dad had a very serious heart attack in September of this year. Shirley and I had traveled to San Antonio, Texas, where I was to speak to the Texas Pediatric Society on Friday. When we arrived at the hotel on Thursday night, we received a message from Dr. Paul Cunningham, indicating that my dad was in intensive care in a Kansas City hospital. On Friday morning, Dr. Cunningham called again to say that my father's condition had worsened and he was not expected to live through the night. He also informed me that my uncle, Dr. James McGraw, had died in the same hospital at 10:30 that morning. It is impossible to describe the sorrow that Shirley and I felt as we flew to Kansas City that afternoon. We never expected to see my dad alive again and went through all the agonies of his loss. But when we arrived at the airport, we learned that my dad had made a remarkable improvement and was anticipating our visit at the hospital. How thankful I will always be that God answered our prayers and granted us seventy-nine more days—beautiful, golden days—before He took my dad to heaven on December 4, 1977.

May I share with you what thoughts went through my troubled mind on that endless plane trip from San Antonio to Kansas City? I journeyed backward in time, experiencing a kaleidoscope of early memories. I thought about the very happiest days of my life, occurring when I was between ten and thirteen years of age. My dad and I would arise very early before the sun came up on a wintry morning. We would put on our hunting clothes and heavy boots, and drive twenty miles from the little town where we lived. After parking the car and climbing over a fence, we entered a wooded area that I called the "big woods" because the trees seemed so large to me. We would slip down to the creek bed and follow that winding stream several miles back into the forest.

Then my dad would hide me under a fallen tree that made a little room with its branches. He would find a similar shelter for himself around a bend in the creek. Then we would await the arrival of the sun and the awakening of the animal world. Little squirrels and birds and chipmunks would scurry back and forth, not knowing they were being observed. My dad and I then watched as the breathtaking panorama of the morning unfolded, which spoke so eloquently of the God who made all things.

But most importantly, there was something dramatic that occurred out there in the forest between my dad and me. An intense love and affection was generated on those mornings that set the tone for a lifetime of fellowship. There was a closeness and a oneness that made me want to be like that man . . . that made me choose his values as my values, his dreams as my dreams, his God as my God.

These were among the memories that surged through my mind on that lonely plane trip in September. Then another flood of emotion came over me, as I thought about my own children. I wondered what memories will predominate in their minds when I lie at the point of death, a moment or two from now. What will they remember to be the happiest experiences of their lives? Will they recall a busy father who was preoccupied with writing books and catching planes and answering mail and talking on the telephone and being a "big man"? Or will they recall a patient dad who took time to love them and teach them and enjoy the beauty of God's world with them? I pray that the Lord will help me keep my little family at the top of my list of priorities during the precious primetime years.

James Dobson was a man of many intense loves. His greatest passion was expressed in his love for Jesus Christ. His every thought and deed were motivated or influenced by his desire to serve his Lord. And I can truthfully say that we were never together without my being drawn closer to God by being in his presence. Not because he warned me or chastised me . . . but because his love for the Lord penetrated and shaped my own attitudes.

The last conversation I ever held with my dad reflected my confidence in his faith. Exactly five days before his death, I telephoned him from Los Angeles at 11:27 A.M.

I said, "Dad, I have an appointment at 11:30 and can only talk for three minutes. I am calling because I face some decisions this afternoon which are very important to me professionally, and I want you to pray for me." His final words were, "I *will* pray about it, Jim." You can be sure that he did!

My dad also loved my mother with great intensity. This fact was beautifully illustrated last year when my parents came to visit us in California. Dad and I took a walk in a nearby park one morning, and as usual, he was talking and I was writing. He then reached into his pocket and retrieved a crumpled sheet of paper that looked very old.

He said, "You might be interested in reading this statement. These are words I expressed to your mother before we were married, forty-two years ago. They were not read to her, but I later wrote down the thoughts I had communicated."

This message was written on the paper.

I want you to understand and be fully aware of my feelings concerning the marriage covenant we are about to enter. I have been taught at my mother's knee, and in harmony with the Word of God, that the marriage vows are inviolable, and by entering into them, I am binding myself absolutely and for life. The idea of estrangement from you through divorce for any reason at all (although God allows one—infidelity) will never at any time be permitted to enter into my thinking. I'm not naive in this. On the contrary, I'm fully aware of the possibility, unlikely as it now appears, that mutual incompatibility or other unforeseen circumstances could result in extreme mental suffering. If such becomes the case, I am resolved for my part to accept it as a consequence of the commitment I am now making, and to bear it, if necessary, to the end of our lives together.

I have loved you dearly as a sweetheart and will continue to love you as my wife. But over and above that, I love you with a Christian love that demands that I never react in any way toward you that would jeopardize our prospects of entering heaven, which is the supreme objective of both our lives. And I pray that God Himself will make our affection for one another perfect and eternal.

Isn't that a beautiful way to say "I love you"? How badly America needs husbands and fathers who are committed to their families—men who are *determined* to succeed in this important responsibility. My father was such a man, and his devotion to my mother grew steadily through their forty-three years of marriage. They were *mutually dependent* in the way God intended. It is fitting, therefore, that in his final moment of consciousness, he fell toward my mother and died peacefully in her arms.

Very few people fully comprehended the depth of my dad's love of learning.

When he died, he left a book beside his big chair, opened to a description of the molecular structure of deoxyribonucleic acid and the process by which hereditary characteristics are transmitted from one generation to the next. Beside it was a list (in his handwriting) of the twenty essential amino acids in humans, and how they are genetically coded. (He called them "God's four-letter words.") My dad had an insatiable desire *to know*, alternating regularly between biology, physics, astronomy, ecology, theology, politics, medicine, and the arts. He left a half-finished painting of a mountain stream in his basement, with a photograph propped to its right. A palette of oils still rests where he placed them on that final Saturday night. Yes, my dad loved *everything* God made, and it is thrilling to contemplate the learning process that must be occurring right now on the other side!

Finally, my dad also loved me. I've known that from my earliest moments of awareness. I'm told that when I was a small child, perhaps three years of age, we lived in a one-bedroom apartment. My little bed was located beside the bed of my parents. Dad said it was not uncommon during that time for him to awaken at night and hear a little voice whispering, "Daddy? Daddy?"

He would answer quietly, "What, Jimmy?"

Then I would reply, "Hold my hand!"

My dad would reach across the darkness and grope for my little hand, finally engulfing it in his. He said the instant he encompassed my hand, my arm would become limp and my breathing deep and regular. I had gone back to sleep. You see, I only wanted to know that he was *there!* I have been reaching for him throughout my forty-one years, and he has always been there. And now for the first time in my life, he's gone.

So where do we go from here? Do we leave this church today in despair and discouragement? Certainly not, although our sorrow is incalculable. But my dad is not in that casket before us. He is *alive*, and we will soon see him again. He has achieved the pearl of eternal life, which is our heritage, too. I now understand that the death of my dad was not an isolated tragedy that happened to one unfortunate man and his family. In a real sense, this is the human condition that affects us all. Life will soon be over for everyone in this sanctuary . . . and for everyone whom we love. Therefore, I have determined to live each day as Christ would dictate, keeping in mind the temporal nature of everything which now seems so permanent. Even in death, you see, my dad has taught me about life.

Thank you for allowing me to share my deepest feelings and emotions today. I must acknowledge, in closing, that James Dobson was not a perfect man. It would be unfortunate to eulogize him in a way that would embarrass him if he were sitting among us. My father had a generous assortment of flaws, even as you and I. But I loved him. Perhaps . . . as much as any son ever loved his dad.

Danae and Ryan [addressed to my children], you had a great man for a grandfather. Not because he was president or because he will be remembered in the history books. He was great because of his uncompromising dedication to the Christian faith. And if I can be half the father to you that he was to me, you will be fortunate children, indeed.

Notes

Chapter 1: Growing Up

1. "Oh! My Pa-Pa" (O Mein Papa). English Words by John Turner. Music and Original Lyric by Paul Burkhard. Copyright © 1948, 1950, Musikverlag und Buhnenvertrieb Zurich A.G., Zurich, Switzerland. Copyright © 1953 Shapiro, Bernstein & Co., Inc., New York. Copyrights Renewed. International Copyright Secured. All Rights Reserved. Used by Permission.

2. "I Saw Your Mommy," written by Mike Muir 1984 American Lesion Music (BMI)/You'll Be Sorry Music. Administered by BUG. All rights reserved. Used by permission.

3. Joan Mills, "Season of the Empty Nest." Reprinted with permission from the January 1981 Reader's Digest. Copyright 1981 by the *Reader's Digest* Assn., Inc.

Chapter 3: Raising Children

1. "Cat's in the Cradle" by Harry Chapin and Sandy Chapin. © 1974 Story Songs, Ltd. All Rights Reserved. Used by Permission. WARNER BROS. PUBLICATIONS U.S. INC., Miami, FL 33014

2. Howard Mann, "Dad Coming Home Was a Real Treat," *Los Angeles Times*, 16 June 1985.

Chapter 5: Lifelong Love

1. "That's the Way I've Heard It Should Be." Words and Music by Carly Simon and Jacob Brackman © Copyright 1970 Universal-PolyGram International Publishing, Inc., a division of Universal Studios, Inc. (ASCAP) International Copyright secured. All Rights Reserved.

2. Ann Landers, "Longtime Faithful in Oregon" and others. Permission granted by Ann Landers and Creators syndicate.

3. John F. Whitaker, M.D., "A Personal Marriage Contract," *Woman's Day*.

4. Vicki Kraushaar, "That's the Way Life Goes Sometimes," *American Girl.*,

5. Kay Ebeling, "My Turn: The Failure of Feminism," *Newsweek*, November 19, 1990.

6. Richard Selzer, M.D., *Mortal Lessons: Notes in the Art of Surgery* (New York: Simon & Schuster, 1976), 45–46.

Chapter 6: Life Lessons

1. Eugene Field, "Little Boy Blue." PD.

2. Sue Kidd, "Don't Let It End This Way," *Focus on the Family Magazine*, January 1985, 6–7, 11.

Chapter 8: Facing Adversity

1. Thomas Shepherd and George N. Allen, "Must Jesus Bear the Cross Alone?" PD.

2. "(There'll Be Bluebirds Over) The White Cliffs Of Dover." Words by Nat Burton. Music by Walter Kent. Copyright © 1941 Shapiro, Bernstein & Co., Inc., New York and Walter Kent Music, California. Copyright Renewed. All Rights outside the United States Controlled by Shapiro, Bernstein & Co., Inc., New York. International Copyright Secured. All Rights Reserved. Used by Permission.

Chapter 7: Dealing with Emotions

1. Corrie ten Boom with Jamie Buckingham, Tramp for the Lord (Grand Rapids, Mich.: F.H. Revell, Inc., 1974).

References

"A Boy Named Jeep Fenders" is taken from *Preparing for Adolescence* (Ventura, Calif.: GL Regal Books, 1978), 55–56.

"A Father's Final Prayer" is taken from *Love for a Lifetime* (Sisters, Oreg.: Multnomah Publishers, Inc., 1987), 113–14.

"A Father's Love" is taken from *When God Doesn't Make Sense* (Wheaton, Ill.: Tyndale House Publishers, 1993), 60–62.

"A Higher Call" is taken from *Life on the Edge* (Nashville: Word Publishing, 1995), 12–16.

"A Kiss That Still Works" is taken from *Straight Talk to Men and Their Wives* (Nashville: Word Publishing, 1991), 137–38.

"A Man and His Animals" is taken from *Straight Talk to Men and Their Wives* (Nashville: Word Publishing, 1991), 213–218.

"A Man of Honor" is taken from *When God Doesn't Make Sense* (Wheaton, Ill.: Tyndale House Publishers, 1993), 167–70.

"A Matter of Perspective" is taken from *What Wives Wish Their Husbands Knew About Women* (Wheaton, Ill.: Tyndale House Publishers, 1975), 177–80.

"A Purpose in Pain" is taken from *When God Doesn't Make Sense* (Wheaton, Ill.: Tyndale House Publishers, 1993), 138–40.

"A Troubled Seminarian" is taken from *Preparing for Adolescence* (Ventura, Calif.: GL Regal Books, 1978), 193–95.

"An Overcomer" is taken from *Life on the Edge* (Nashville: Word Publishing, 1995), 184–86.

"Answered Prayer" is taken from *When God Doesn't Make Sense* (Wheaton, Ill.: Tyndale House Publishers, 1993), 96–97.

"Awful Janet" is taken from *Life on the Edge* (Nashville: Word Publishing, 1995), 28.

"Beauty and the Baby" is taken from *Preparing for Adolescence* (Ventura, Calif.: GL Regal Books, 1978), 28–29.

"Bedtime Battle" is taken from *Parenting Isn't for Cowards* (Nashville: Word Publishing, 1987), 109–11.

"Betrayed" is taken from *Love Must Be Tough* (Nashville: Word Publishing, 1983), 206–8.

"Black Sunday" is taken from *Straight Talk to Men and Their Wives* (Nashville: Word Publishing, 1991), 107–8.

"Calling Robert's Bluff" is taken from *Straight Talk to Men and Their Wives* (Nashville: Word Publishing, 1991), 84–85.

"Cat's in the Cradle" is taken from *Straight Talk to Men and Their Wives* (Nashville: Word Publishing, 1991), 66–72.

"Checkpoints" is taken from *The Strong-Willed Child* (Wheaton, Ill.: Tyndale House Publishers, 1978), 113–15.

"Collision Course for Conflict" is taken from *Straight Talk to Men and Their Wives* (Nashville: Word Publishing, 1991), 156–62.

"Come and Gone" is taken from *When God Doesn't Make Sense* (Wheaton, Ill.: Tyndale House Publishers, 1993), 246–48.

"Couldn't We Just Cuddle?" is taken from *Love for a Lifetime* (Sisters, Oreg.: Multnomah Publishers, Inc., 1987), 86–91.

"Courtroom of the Mind" is taken from *Life on the Edge* (Nashville: Word Publishing, 1995), 32–34.

"Crisis Will Come" is taken from *Life on the Edge* (Nashville: Word Publishing, 1995), 5–7.

"Dad Coming Home Was the Real Treat" is taken from *Parenting Isn't for Cowards* (Nashville: Word Publishing, 1987), 163–65.

"Declaration of Independence" is taken from *Preparing for Adolescence* (Ventura, Calif.: GL Regal Books, 1978), 131–32.

"Disappointment with Dad" is taken from *What Wives Wish Their Husbands Knew About Women* (Wheaton, Ill.: Tyndale House Publishers, 1975), 181–83.

"Discipline Goes in the Toilet" is taken from *The Strong-Willed Child* (Wheaton, Ill.: Tyndale House Publishers, 1978), 29–30.

"Don't Let It End This Way" is taken from *Life on the Edge* (Nashville: Word Publishing, 1995),160–64.

"Dropping the Ball" is taken from *Life on the Edge* (Nashville: Word Publishing, 1995), 29–30.

"Everyone Loves Mr. Lyndon" is taken from *The Strong-Willed Child* (Wheaton, Ill.: Tyndale House Publishers, 1978), 111–12.

"Expecting the Unexpected" is taken from *Life on the Edge* (Nashville: Word Publishing, 1995), 3–5.

"Faith under Fire" is taken from *When God Doesn't Make Sense* (Wheaton, Ill.: Tyndale House Publishers, 1993), 77–83.

"Fatherly Wisdom" is taken from *Parenting Isn't for Cowards* (Nashville: Word Publishing, 1987), 228–30.

"Finishing Well" is taken from *Love for a Lifetime* (Sisters, Oreg.: Multnomah Publishers, Inc., 1987), 115–16.

"Flower Power" is taken from *Emotions: Can You Trust Them?* (Ventura, Calif.: GL Regal Books, 1980), 82–85.

"Forgiving Your Parents" is taken from *Life on the Edge* (Nashville: Word Publishing, 1995), 159–60.

"Game-Show Greed" is taken from *Life on the Edge* (Nashville: Word Publishing, 1995), 41–44.

"God's Messenger" is taken from *When God Doesn't Make Sense* (Wheaton, Ill.: Tyndale House Publishers, 1993), 127–31.

"Heroes Hall of Fame" is taken from *When God Doesn't Make Sense* (Wheaton, Ill.: Tyndale House Publishers, 1993), 222–31.

"Highs and Lows" is taken from *Life on the Edge* (Nashville: Word Publishing, 1995), 179.

"Horrible Hayley" is taken from *The New Hide or Seek"* (Grand Rapids, Mich.: F. H. Revell, 1999), 154–57.

"How a Good Man Dies" is taken from *Straight Talk to Men and Their Wives* (Nashville: Word Publishing, 1991), 232–37.

"I Am Committed to You" is taken from *Emotions: Can You Trust Them?* (Ventura, Calif.: GL Regal Books, 1980), 70–72.

"I Don't Need a Mother Anymore" is taken from *Life on the Edge* (Nashville: Word Publishing, 1995), 155–56.

"I Had to Have a Hamburger" is taken from *When God Doesn't Make Sense* (Wheaton, Ill.: Tyndale House Publishers, 1993), 154–55.

"I Wanted to Know Your God" is taken from *The Strong-Willed Child* (Wheaton, Ill.: Tyndale House Publishers, 1978), 192–95.

"If I Hear a Peep Out of You . . . !" is taken from *Parenting Isn't for Cowards* (Nashville: Word Publishing, 1987), 114–15.

"I'm Not Getting Old!" is taken from *What Wives Wish Their Husbands Knew About Women* (Wheaton, Ill.: Tyndale House Publishers, 1975) 171–72.

"Impressions" is taken from *Emotions: Can You Trust Them?* (Ventura, Calif.: GL Regal Books, 1980), 113–15.

"In the Hands of God" is taken from *Emotions: Can You Trust Them?* (Ventura, Calif.: GL Regal Books, 1980), 135–38.

"Invasion of the Killer Vine" is taken from *When God Doesn't Make Sense* (Wheaton, Ill.: Tyndale House Publishers, 1993), 18–20.

"Is This All It Comes Down To?" is taken from *Life on the Edge* (Nashville: Word Publishing, 1995), 263–64.

"It's Either Despair or It's God" is taken from *When God Doesn't Make Sense* (Wheaton, Ill.: Tyndale House Publishers, 1993), 83–89.

"It's Hard to Let Go" is taken from *Parenting Isn't for Cowards* (Nashville: Word Publishing, 1987), 215–16.

"Killer McKeechern" is taken from *Parenting Isn't for Cowards* (Nashville: Word Publishing, 1987), 144–46.

"Laughter: The Key to Survival" is taken from *Parenting Isn't for Cowards* (Nashville: Word Publishing, 1987), 193–94.

"Lessons of Life" is taken from *Preparing for Adolescence* (Ventura, Calif.: GL Regal Books, 1978), 126–28.

"Letting Him Go" is taken from *Preparing for Adolescence* (Ventura, Calif.: GL Regal Books, 1978), 146–48.

"Life in the Fast Lane" is taken from *Life on the Edge* (Nashville: Word Publishing, 1995), 39–40.

"Life Will Trash Your Trophies" is taken from *Life on the Edge* (Nashville: Word Publishing, 1995), 59–63.

"Listen to the Expert" is taken from *The New Dare to Discipline* (Wheaton, Ill.: Tyndale House Publishers, 1992), 33–34.

"Lonely Assassins" is taken from *Preparing for Adolescence* (Ventura, Calif.: GL Regal Books, 1978), 17-19, 206–8.

"Lonely Summers Looking for Love" is taken from *Preparing for Adolescence* (Ventura, Calif.: GL Regal Books, 1978), 95–97.

"Love Mixed with Discipline" is taken from *The New Dare to Discipline* (Wheaton, Ill.: Tyndale House Publishers, 1992), 21–22.

"Magic Chalk" is taken from *The New Dare to Discipline* (Wheaton, Ill.: Tyndale House Publishers, 1992), 148–50.

"Manhood at Its Best" is taken from *Straight Talk to Men and Their Wives* (Nashville: Word Publishing, 1991), 33–36.

"Miracle at Yellowstone" is taken from *When God Doesn't Make Sense* (Wheaton, Ill.: Tyndale House Publishers, 1993), 132–35.

"Museum of Memories" is taken from *Straight Talk to Men and Their Wives* (Nashville: Word Publishing, 1995), 59–62.

"My Father" is taken *from Straight Talk to Men and Their Wives* (Nashville: Word Publishing, 1995), 39–45.

"My Own Mid-Life Crisis" is taken from *Straight Talk to Men and Their Wives* (Nashville: Word Publishing, 1991), 6–12.

"My Taxes Are Too Low!" is taken from *Emotions: Can You Trust Them?* (Ventura, Calif.: GL Regal Books, 1980), 31–33.

"Newlywed Nonsense" is taken from *Love for a Lifetime* (Sisters, Oreg.: Multnomah Publishers, Inc., 1987), 11–12.

"No Coincidence" is taken from *When God Doesn't Make Sense* (Wheaton, Ill.: Tyndale House Publishers, 1993), 125–27.

"No Peas for Me" is taken from *Straight Talk to Men and Their Wives* (Nashville: Word Publishing, 1991), 94–97.

"No Room for Self Pity" is taken from *When God Doesn't Make Sense* (Wheaton, Ill.: Tyndale House Publishers, 1993), 144–47.

"Nobody Cares" is taken from *Preparing for Adolescence* (Ventura, Calif.: GL Regal Books, 1978), 18–20.

"Nothing Is Forever" is taken from *Straight Talk to Men and Their Wives* (Nashville: Word Publishing, 1991),

"Number-One Tennis Player" is taken from *Preparing for Adolescence* (Ventura, Calif.: GL Regal Books, 1978), 109.

"Oh, My Papa" is taken from *Life on the Edge* (Nashville: Word Publishing, 1995), 145–48.

"Our Last Conversation" is taken from *Straight Talk to Men and Their Wives* (Nashville: Word Publishing, 1991), 46–48.

"Parents Pulling for You" is taken from *The Strong-Willed Child* (Wheaton, Ill.: Tyndale House Publishers, 1978), 206–7.

"Puppy Love" is taken from *Preparing for Adolescence* (Ventura, Calif.: GL Regal Books, 1978), 119–23.

"Rivals for Love" is taken from *Preparing for Adolescence* (Ventura, Calif.: GL Regal Books, 1978), 84.

"Robin Hood II" is taken from *The New Dare to Discipline* (Wheaton, Ill.: Tyndale House Publishers, 1992), 40–41.

"Season of the Empty Nest" is taken from *Parenting Isn't for Cowards* (Nashville: Word Publishing, 1987), 232–36.

"Sleeping in the Dark" is taken from *The New Dare to Discipline* (Wheaton, Ill.: Tyndale House Publishers, 1992), 110–11.

"Something for Nothing" is taken from *Life on the Edge* (Nashville: Word Publishing, 1995), 44–45.

"Sometimes the Best Answer Is 'No'" is taken from *The New Dare to Discipline* (Wheaton, Ill.: Tyndale House Publishers, 1992), 46–48.

"Stay Away from Pink Champagne" is taken from *Love for a Lifetime* (Sisters, Oreg.: Multnomah Publishers, Inc., 1987), 84–86.

"Study While You Sleep" is taken from *The New Dare to Discipline* (Wheaton, Ill.: Tyndale House Publishers, 1992), 125–26.

"Success Where It Matters" is taken from *Straight Talk to Men and Their Wives* (Nashville: Word Publishing, 1991), 75–76, 78, 79–82.

"That's the Way Life Goes Sometimes" is taken from *Life on the Edge* (Nashville: Word Publishing, 1995), 89–91.

"The Brat Who Was Me" is taken from *The New Dare to Discipline* (Wheaton, Ill.: Tyndale House Publishers, 1992), 107–8.

"The Cost of Overcommitment" is taken from *Parenting Isn't for Cowards* (Nashville: Word Publishing, 1987), 188.

"The Difficult Diagnosis" is taken from *What Wives Wish Their Husbands Knew About Women* (Wheaton, Ill.: Tyndale House Publishers, 1975), 143–46.

"The Doctor Doesn't Always Know Best" is taken from *Children at Risk* (Nashville: Word Publishing, 1990), 82–83.

"The Failure of Feminism" is taken from *Straight Talk to Men and Their Wives* (Nashville: Word Publishing, 1991), 186–90.

"The Game of Life" is taken from *Straight Talk to Men and Their Wives* (Nashville: Word Publishing, 1991), 13–21.

"The Heritage" is taken from *Straight Talk to Men and Their Wives* (Nashville: Word Publishing, 1991), 52–55.

"The Late Bloomer" is taken from *The New Dare to Discipline* (Wheaton, Ill.: Tyndale House Publishers, 1992), 162–64.

"The Lost Marble" is taken from *When God Doesn't Make Sense* (Wheaton, Ill.: Tyndale House Publishers, 1993), 45–46.

"The Meaning of Commitment" is taken from *Life on the Edge* (Nashville: Word Publishing, 1995), 104–5.

"The Orientation Blues" is taken from *Preparing for Adolescence* (Ventura, Calif.: GL Regal Books, 1978), 42–45.

"The Pain of Powerlessness" is taken from *Parenting Isn't for Cowards* (Nashville: Word Publishing, 1987), 193–94.

"The Power of a Praying Mother" is taken from *Parenting Isn't for Cowards* (Nashville: Word Publishing, 1987), 72–74.

"The Power of Forgiveness" is taken from *Love Must Be Tough* (Nashville: Word Publishing, 1983), 151–55.

"The Powerbroker" is taken from *Life on the Edge* (Nashville: Word Publishing, 1995), 55–56.

"The Prowler" is taken from *Life on the Edge* (Nashville: Word Publishing, 1995), 171–72.

"The Rest of the Story" is taken from *When God Doesn't Make Sense* (Wheaton, Ill.: Tyndale House Publishers, 1993), 135–36.

"The Terrible Twos" is taken from *The Strong-Willed Child* (Wheaton, Ill.: Tyndale House Publishers, 1978), 50–51.

"The Thrill of the Moment" is taken from *Life on the Edge* (Nashville: Word Publishing, 1995), 182–83.

"The Ups and Downs of Courtship" is taken from *Life on the Edge* (Nashville: Word Publishing, 1995), 110–12.

"The Whole World's Singing Now" is taken from *What Wives Wish Their Husbands Knew About Women* (Wheaton, Ill.: Tyndale House Publishers, 1975), 184–85.

"The Worst Punishment" is taken from *The New Dare to Discipline* (Wheaton, Ill.: Tyndale House Publishers, 1992), 72–74.

"The Wounds of an Adolescent Heart" is taken from *Preparing for Adolescence* (Ventura, Calif.: GL Regal Books, 1978), 115–16.

"Their Finest Hour" is taken from *When God Doesn't Make Sense* (Wheaton, Ill.: Tyndale House Publishers, 1993), 148–50.

"This Is My Will for You" is taken from *When God Doesn't Make Sense* (Wheaton, Ill.: Tyndale House Publishers, 1993), 117–19.

"Trombone Serenades" is taken from *Preparing for Adolescence* (Ventura, Calif.: GL Regal Books, 1978), 106–7.

"Trusting God's Timing" is taken from *When God Doesn't Make Sense* (Wheaton, Ill.: Tyndale House Publishers, 1993), 53–55.

"Trying to Buy Acceptance" is taken from *Life on the Edge* (Nashville: Word Publishing, 1995), 26–27.

"Two Toddlers" is taken from *Parenting Isn't for Cowards* (Nashville: Word Publishing, 1987), 59–62.

"Viva La Difference" is taken from *Love for a Lifetime* (Sisters, Oreg.: Multnomah Publishers, Inc., 1987), 37–38.

"Waiting for Mr. Walker to Explode" is taken from *The Strong-Willed Child* (Wheaton, Ill.: Tyndale House Publishers, 1978), 109–11.

"We Dare Not Try to Make It on Our Own" is taken from *Love for a Lifetime* (Sisters, Oreg.: Multnomah Publishers, Inc., 1987), 48–50.

"We'll Marry" is taken from *Life on the Edge* (Nashville: Word Publishing, 1995), 135–36.

"We've All Been There" is taken from *Life on the Edge* (Nashville: Word Publishing, 1995), 21–22.

"What Makes Them Do It?" is taken from *Parenting Isn't for Cowards* (Nashville: Word Publishing, 1987), 3–4.

"When All Is Said and Done, What Really Matters?" is taken from *Life on the Edge* (Nashville: Word Publishing, 1995), 268–72.

"Who Else but You?" is taken from *Love Must Be Tough* (Nashville: Word Publishing, 1983), 198–3.

"Why Did He Have to Die?" is taken from *Life on the Edge* (Nashville: Word Publishing, 1995), 243–45.

"Why Do They Do It?" is taken from *Children at Risk* (Nashville: Word Publishing, 1990), 42–44.

"Will You Forgive Me?" is taken from *When God Doesn't Make Sense* (Wheaton, Ill.: Tyndale House Publishers, 1993), 238–42.

"Will You Pray for Me?" is taken from *When God Doesn't Make Sense* (Wheaton, Ill.: Tyndale House Publishers, 1993), 205–6.

"You Cannot Outgive God" is taken from *Love for a Lifetime* (Sisters, Oreg.: Multnomah Publishers, Inc., 1987), 76–80.

"You Can't Make Me" is taken from *The Strong-Willed Child* (Wheaton, Ill.: Tyndale House Publishers, 1978), 11–15, 235–37.

Additional Selections by Dr. James Dobson

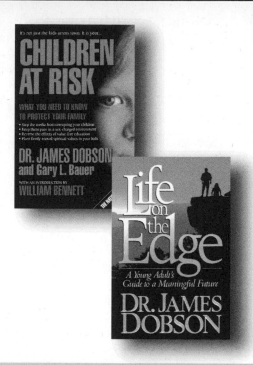

Children At Risk

In this hard-hitting and empowering book, Dr. James Dobson and Gary Bauer expose the cultural forces endangering today's children and show how you can defend your family, faith, and traditional values. A national bestseller revised and expanded for even more knowledge to protect your most precious gift—your children.

Life on the Edge

America's most respected family authority candidly addresses the defining issues that young adults face and the choices—education, marriage, career, vocation—that will impact the rest of their lives. *Life on the Edge* helps young adults make right choices, get control of their lives, and look forward to a meaningful future.

Life on the Edge (Gift Edition)

This gift edition of the bestseller, *Life on the Edge*, combines brief excerpts and select quotes with dramatic art and color photographs. By candidly addressing the defining issues that young adults face in the "critical decade," Dr. James Dobson gives advice and insight on topics such as vocation, lifelong love, money, power, and emotions. An excellent gift for graduates.

Parenting Isn't for Cowards

Speaking both as a therapist and as a parent—and drawing on a landmark study of 35,000 patients—Dr. James Dobson offers time-proven insights on why some children really are harder to raise than others. With over 1 million copies sold, this classic parenting handbook provides sound guidance and "tough love" principles for raising healthy children.

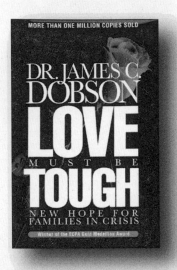

Love Must Be Tough

Love Must Be Tough offers realistic hope for troubled marriages. The principle of "tough love" is discussed in response to the most serious indicator of potential family breakup— a lack of respect. With over 1 million copies sold, this book presents God's plan to restore and maintain love.

Straight Talk To Men

What does it really mean to be a man in today's society? In this modern classic, Dr. James Dobson clears the confusion about men's roles and outlines a workable plan for family leadership. Dr. James Dobson gives special attention to the topics of wives, children, priorities, work, money, masculinity, emotions, sexuality, midlife, God, and morality.

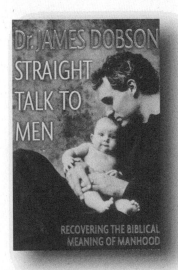